"When the inevitable storms of life hit, it can feel overwhelming, helpless, or even hopeless. *Counseling through the Storm* provides mental health professionals, ministry and lay leaders, and clergy with a compassionate and practical guide to help people navigate through crisis or times of unexpected loss. I am impressed with how Dr. Brooke Osborn and Dr. Karen Roudkovski weave together wisdom, real-life stories, clinical expertise, and biblical truth in such an informative and caring manner."

—**Jeff Cline**, PhD, LPC, NCC, BCC, ACS, BC-TMH, associate professor of counseling, Colorado Christian University

"At some time in everyone's life, the pain of trauma hits. Drs. Osborn and Roudkovski masterfully address a variety of difficult challenges in the lives of children, teenagers, couples, families, and the church itself. Filled with biblically practical strategies and compelling stories, *Counseling through the Storm* will be a valuable resource for those who want to help in time of need."

—**Fernando Garzon**, PsyD, chair, counseling ministries, Regent University

"Brooke and Karen offer invaluable wisdom on the topic of crisis with such grace. This book is a must-read for pastors, church leaders, church members, and mental health professionals to gain a fresh, integrative perspective of different crises that people face and how to handle these crises. Their experience with trauma counseling shines throughout this book."

—**Justin Kelly**, PhD, LPC-S, chair, department of psychology and counseling, and assistant professor of psychology, Belhaven University

"*Counseling through the Storm* by Osborn and Roudkovski masterfully blends theological insights with practical strategies to navigate the human experience of crisis. This work offers a compassionate and integrative approach, making it an essential resource for counselors, church leaders, and fellow Christ-followers. Through its thoughtful exploration of Scripture, psychology, and personal experience, the book provides invaluable instruction for guiding individuals through life's most challenging moments."

—**Jared Thomas**, PhD, LPC-S, vice president, campus ministries and student engagement, North Greenville University

"Life is messy and filled with crises that ride on the waves of various storms. Brooke and Karen have produced a practical guide to help the reader be a life giver to the broken and help them find safety on the shore of grace and forgiveness."

—**Ted Traylor**, pastor, Olive Baptist Church, Pensacola, Florida

"Every pastor in every church faces every kind of counseling imaginable. People hurt in every way and desperately need guidance. Drs. Osborn and Roudkovski's book is an essential reference, packed with biblical mandates and practical wisdom. I could not more highly recommend this well-written book."

—**Don Wilton**, author, ministry-based faculty, New Orleans Baptist Theological Seminary, and pastor emeritus, First Baptist Spartanburg (SC)

COUNSELING
through the
STORM

COUNSELING *through the* STORM

A Guide to Treating Crisis and Trauma

**Brooke Osborn &
Karen Roudkovski**

B&H
ACADEMIC®
BRENTWOOD, TENNESSEE

Counseling through the Storm: A Guide to Treating Crisis and Trauma

Published by B&H Academic®
Brentwood, Tennessee

ISBN: 978-1-0877-8886-9

Dewey Decimal Classification: 361.1
Subject Heading: CRISIS INTERVENTION (MENTAL HEALTH SERVICES) \ SOCIAL PROBLEMS \ COUNSELING

Cover design by Emily Keafer Lambright.

Printed in the United States of America

30 29 28 27 26 25 LB 1 2 3 4 5 6 7 8 9 10

CONTENTS

Part 6: Children and Adolescents

Part 7: Couples and Families

Part 8: The Church

Part 9: Care for the Helpers

FOREWORD

by Dr. Ian F. Jones

We live in a fallen world of brokenness and suffering. From the very first moments when Adam and Eve chose to listen to deceiving, ungodly words, we found ourselves surrounded by the effects of sin, evil, and the curse. Over forty years in counseling ministry have taught me we can never be certain of tomorrow. As James 4:13–15 says, "Now listen, you who say, 'Today or tomorrow we will go to this or that city, spend a year there, carry on business and make money.' Why, you do not even know what will happen tomorrow. What is your life? You are a mist that appears for a little while and then vanishes. Instead, you ought to say, 'If it is the Lord's will, we will live and do this or that'" (NIV). The Bible is replete with stories of crisis and trauma, along with lessons to learn and wise counsel. The book of Job, for example, has taught me not to assume I know the full story of what is going on in a person's life or to always attribute tragedies and problems to sinful behavior. In particular, I have learned that the more you grow in the Christian life, the more difficulties and challenges you are likely to face. Jesus told his disciples a few hours before his death by crucifixion that if they remained faithful to him, they could expect to be pruned or to face trials in life in order to grow and become more fruitful (John 15:1–8).

In 1999, on the night of Wednesday, September 15, I was at Wedgwood Baptist Church in the aftermath of a tragedy where a gunman killed seven people. The counseling needs that followed covered a multitude of areas, from immediate crisis intervention to longer-term trauma counseling addressed to those people who had witnessed the shooting and others who were affected both directly and indirectly by the tragedy. People had different responses requiring diverse counseling interventions, and the process and speed of recovery varied from person to person. At the time, I turned to Scripture and noted the various responses surrounding the crucifixion, including fear (Matt 26:56), denial and guilt (26:69–75), anguish and mourning (Luke 23:27–28), mockery (Matt 27:27–30), intense discussion (Luke 24:13–35), practical responses to immediate needs (Matt 27:57-60; John 19:38-42), secondary traumas (John 20:11–14), struggles with faith (20:21–29), and callous indifference (19:23–24). Perhaps most instructive were the different ways Jesus encountered people following his resurrection. No two were alike as he located them at their point of need and brought healing to their lives. Note, for example, the secondary trauma of Mary, who only wanted to know where the body had been taken (Jesus showed her the body!) (John 20:10–18); of the two companions on the road to Emmaus, who needed a biblical explanation of the event (Luke 24:13–35); of Thomas, who needed physical proof of the resurrection (John 20:24–29); and of Peter, who needed restoration and a renewed calling (21:15–19).

Proverbs 19:2 reminds us "it is dangerous to have zeal without knowledge, and the one who acts hastily makes poor choices" (NET). Understanding the nature of crisis and trauma and how to respond to them is essential for ministers, counselors, and lay leaders today. Dr. Brooke Osborn and Dr. Karen Roudkovski have written a remarkable book, which combines a biblical worldview with years of study in the field of crisis counseling and trauma, professional and practical training in counseling, and deeply personal experiences, resulting in a comprehensive understanding of the subject. Their approach is not superficial or simplistic but rich in biblical wisdom and practical advice. You will find a wealth of helpful information to guide and assist you in ministering effectively during such difficult and challenging times.

—Ian F. Jones, PhD, professor of counseling,
New Orleans Baptist Theological Seminary

ACKNOWLEDGMENTS

Brooke

To my clients, thank you for allowing me the privilege of walking with you through crisis and trauma. Your stories have changed me for the better.

To all my students, there would be no book without you. I learn so much from each of you both in and out of the classroom. You help me refine my thoughts and practices.

To my teaching assistant, Chessie, thank you for all your work during the time this book was written. You lightened my load by helping with grading and looking over chapters.

To my friend and colleague Lorien, thank you for being a constant source of encouragement and support.

To my coauthor, Karen, thank you for taking on this project with me.

To Patton and Lex, thank you for your flexibility and patience as this book was written. We have weathered our share of crisis situations together.

Karen

To my clients who have allowed me the profound honor of joining with them in their journey.

To the churches where my husband and I have served, you exemplify ministry during times of crisis.

To my students, you inspire me to persist in learning.

To my coauthor, Brooke, thank you for the invitation to join you. This book would not have been possible without your expertise, wisdom, and insight.

To Jake, Joseph, and Katerina, thank you for your encouragement while this book was being written. I am truly blessed to have such a supportive family.

To our Lord and Savior, Jesus Christ, who comforts us in all our affliction so that we are able to comfort those in affliction with the comfort we have received from you (2 Corinthians 1:4).

Part 1
Introduction

INTRODUCTION

Learning how to navigate crises is one of the most practical things we can do as we journey through this life. All you need to do to witness crisis and trauma in action is walk out your front door. As we will discuss later in the book, a crisis can be one of our greatest mission fields. We have the opportunity to meet people in some of their most vulnerable moments in life. During these times, they are often searching for answers and need to feel the presence of Christ.

We practice counseling from an integrated perspective, which means we filter everything we use through the lens of Scripture. Our theology informs our counseling practice. We strive to meet people where they are, with the realization that not everyone we encounter will be believers. We respect the decisions of nonbelievers while walking with them through their circumstances. The hope is always to be able to share the gospel, whether through meeting personal and practical needs or by achieving emotional health. Throughout this book, we use fictional case studies, along with examples from real life. When you see a real-life example, we have taken measures to change or combine features of their story to protect their anonymity. In other cases, we have sought permission to share their stories.

Throughout this book, you will notice the abbreviation *DSM-5-TR* or just *DSM*. This is short for the *Diagnostic and Statistical Manual of Mental*

Disorders, Fifth Edition, Text Revision. The *DSM-5-TR* was published by the American Psychiatric Association as a guide for diagnosing mental disorders. It describes the typical and atypical behaviors and experiences of individuals. Just because the *DSM-5-TR* is descriptive does not mean it is prescriptive. Scripture tells us how we should live in the context of these behaviors and experiences, while the *DSM-5-TR* relates the nature of mental disorders.[1] You will also notice we consult with secular resources and counseling interventions. Although we may not agree with a person's worldview or various aspects of their interventions, we believe there are components that can be beneficial when filtered through the lens of Scripture.

Our approach is also trauma informed. "Trauma informed" means we consider the pervasive nature of trauma in our practices. We promote environments where individuals feel safe and can begin to heal rather than places or practices that might re-traumatize an individual. We have chapters dedicated to describing the impact of trauma, but we also weave this information throughout the book. We desire our churches and counseling centers to be places where people can take refuge and recover.

Both of us have extensive training and experience working with those who have endured crisis and trauma. We are licensed professional counselors, who have used our expertise and experience in both the church and community. We teach at institutions that incorporate faith into licensure-track counseling programs. Brooke has worked with local child-advocacy centers in offering sexual-abuse prevention training and providing referrals to families in need of services. In recent years, Brooke's research interests have considered the impact of trauma on learning and behavior, including those with neurodevelopmental disorders. Karen specializes in working with individuals with a history of trauma at her private practice. Karen's research interests include spiritual and religious abuse and recovery.

---

[1] See Mark Yarhouse, *Talking to Kids about Gender Identity: A Roadmap for Christian Compassion, Civility, and Conviction* (Grand Rapids: Bethany House, 2023), 108.

Whether you are a pastor, ministry or lay leader, or a professional counselor, we hope this book will serve as a guide to equip you to meet people where they are and help them get to the other side of their crisis. Unlike professional counseling, crisis counseling is designed to be time-limited, lasting until the crisis is resolved. As such, we want to be prepared for an efficient and Christ-honoring response and also be ready to refer a client elsewhere if a crisis does not resolve in the short-term.

This book is divided into nine parts. Part 1 discusses the nature of suffering. When a crisis hits, many of us struggle to see the goodness of God in a fallen world, where things are not as they should be. Part 2 discusses the nature of crisis and the process of crisis intervention. Parts 3–5 cover grief and loss, suicide, and trauma.

In parts 6 and 7, we address crises common to children and adolescents and the family system. Part 8 covers crises that may impact the church. We conclude the book with considerations for how to take care of ourselves as we minister to others.

We hope this book will serve as a guide to equip you to meet people where they are and help them get to the other side of their crises. We realize that each topic covered in this book could fill the pages of an entire book by itself. We are also well aware that you never know what crisis may come your way, and you are often not afforded the luxury of being able to read an entire book before responding. Our aim is to provide a brief overview of information about each type of crisis, recommendations for response, and some additional resources should you need them. In many cases, we also provide ways to prepare in advance.

Chapter 1

Theology and Suffering

The year 2020 was full of uncertainty and so many unknowns. Being professors, we look forward to graduation and celebrating with our graduates before they move on to the next chapter of their lives. But because of COVID-19, May 2020 graduation never happened. Some of our graduates stayed to pursue other degrees or serve the city, while others moved on with the intention of celebrating graduation in December.

During this time, I (Brooke) received an email from a student who regretted that we would not be able to say goodbye in person before he and his wife moved to another state. He was going to graduate school, and his wife was planning to work as a counselor. I had taught him in our undergraduate program and written letters of recommendation for graduate school. His wife was in a graduate course I taught one semester and later worked as my teaching assistant for a year. They had come over for dinner on a few occasions. This couple had a bright future in front of them, and I was eager to see how God would use each of them.

About two months later, I received the news that he had been killed in a work-related accident. I was devastated. I reached out to his wife, though

I knew it might be a while before she was able to respond. When she did reach out via email, she mentioned a number of things related to her grief and delivered another blow. Two days before her husband died, they had found out they were pregnant after a few years of being unsuccessful. They celebrated when they found out about the baby but, like many, decided to wait before making this news public. She shared with me that the day after they found out she was pregnant was so ordinary that she does not really remember it. The following day, however, is the one she will never forget.

I also have a friend who became a widow at the age of twenty-seven after having been married for less than a year. Another close family friend spent half her marriage caring for her husband, who had brain cancer. Perhaps Bob Kellemen put it best when he said, "We live in a fallen world and it often falls on us."[1]

A crisis can bring us to our knees before we even know what hit us, and none of us is immune. During these times, some turn toward God for refuge. One of our most effective opportunities for ministry is a time of crisis. Even those who are not believers may be more receptive to the gospel during a time of despair. Whether believers or not, many people often turn toward the church in a time of crisis. For example, if a teenager at a local school dies by suicide, the school can be overwhelmed trying to handle the situation and take care of the students impacted. As a result, they may turn to the church to provide support. When people are struggling to meet their basic needs, they turn to the church. As we will discuss in a later chapter, a crisis can be a turning point, which makes it an opportune time to minister to others. As such, we should be equipped to care for those in need.

Not everyone turns toward God during a time of crisis. Some struggle to believe in a good God who could allow such evil in the world. Due to the nature of depravity in our world, some have been abused and exploited from such an early age that they do not remember being treated any differently.

---

[1] Robert Kellemen, *God's Healing for Life's Losses: How to Find Hope When You're Hurting* (Winona Lake, IN: BMH Books, 2010), 4.

Some have experienced abuse at the hands of someone in the church and want no part in anything the church or God has to offer.

When we walk with others through crisis and trauma, we should be aware that we will be confronted with the depths of evil and suffering in our world. Natural disasters blaze through, destroying everything within a matter of minutes. Human beings commit atrocities against each other, many of which are difficult to put into words. There are times when we believed God would intervene, but he didn't, at least not in the way we imagined.

We live in a world of unprecedented suffering and brokenness. These human conditions include different types and levels of social and psychological suffering, which are often minimized; neglected or, because they are beyond what people can cope with at a given time, left unattended; or addressed from out-of-context perspectives. These omissions are both unjust and costly to individuals and communities.

When helping people in crisis, we will be better able to meet them where they are in their distress if we gain a better understanding of where they come from, the major influences in their lives, and how they arrived at their current seasons of life. People often ask us if we, as counselors, ever hear things that "mess us up." The reality is, we do hear things that change us, but that is not exclusive to counselors. Anyone who enters into suffering with another person will be changed. We must consider our own background as well.

Our Worldview on Suffering

When a crisis comes, our world is shaken. A crisis may be the point at which we become aware that our beliefs do not match our response to a crisis, creating cognitive dissonance. Cognitive dissonance refers to the internal struggle we experience when our beliefs and actions are incongruent. Adjusting to the unexpected turns of life may prompt us to examine the difference between our beliefs and actions. In other words, what are we really holding on to for life? According to Mary Jo Sharp, "Our actions flow from what we really believe. Thus, if a person hasn't deeply examined his or her current beliefs and compared them to what the Bible has to say, it is possible for him or her to act contrary to the Christian ethic."[2]

In John 9:1–9, Jesus healed a man born blind. The disciples asked who sinned, the man or his parents. In other words, the disciples were saying, "Tell us this is fair because of something someone did."[3] Is this any different from our thoughts when bad things happen? Do our beliefs reflect conditional theology? In other words, are we operating out of the belief that bad things happen to those who do not follow God's plan, but if we follow all of God's rules, he will bless us? This type of theology is the struggle the disciples were having in John 9. They needed to believe this man's blindness was caused by a misstep on the part of either him or his parents. Assigning fault means we can control the outcome. If this man was born blind through no one's fault other than the nature of living in this fallen world, it is out of our control, which is frightening.

During these difficult times, we need to manage our theological anxiety. Our theological anxiety is the panic we experience when we begin to question the goodness of God. In other words, if God is good, how could he have let ____________ happen? Our emotions can be more powerful than we realize, especially when we are unaware of their existence. After all, we cannot manage emotions we are not aware we are experiencing.

Our brains have an intense need to construct a narrative out of our experience. The brain has a need to fill in the missing pieces to make a more coherent story, even if the additional pieces are not true. "When confronted with anomalies and cognitive dissonance, the brain rewrites history so that it makes more sense and can be more easily retained."[4] Coming face-to-face with the atrocities we see on this earth, people often question, "How could a good God have allowed this to happen?" or "Where was God when this

---

[2] Mary Jo Sharp, *Defending the Faith: Apologetics in Women's Ministry* (Grand Rapids: Kregel, 2012), 13.

[3] Diane Langberg, *Suffering and the Heart of God: How Trauma Destroys and God Restores* (Greensboro, NC: New Growth, 2015), 56.

[4] John Gottman, *The Science of Trust: Emotional Attunement for Couples* (New York: Norton, 2011), 150.

happened?" When this happens, our brains try to make sense of a good God who allows bad things to happen to good people.

Past "emotional injuries live in current issues when they are unaddressed."[5] This means that when we experience hurt personally or witness it firsthand in those to whom we are ministering, we want to make sure we take the time to process or work through those hurts, frustrations, disappointments, and any anger that may be present. Otherwise, we will continue to carry these negative emotions with us. When left unexamined, these negative emotions can linger and help our brains fill in the blanks when presented with cognitive dissonance. In other words, these negative emotions can override our beliefs about the goodness of God.

In the church, we tend to downplay emotions. We may label certain emotions, such as happy and excited, as "good" emotions, while anger and upset may be considered "bad" emotions. However, pushing our emotions to the side does not make them go away. Instead, they linger and color our present experience. As we discussed before, we cannot manage negative emotions if we remain unaware of their presence. Learning to recognize and label what we are feeling can help us manage our emotions so they do not continue to exert control over our present circumstances.

At a cognitive level, we may know that God has a plan for our lives and that he intends to work all things for our good. However, the nature of inherent sinfulness on this earth can make that difficult to remember at times. We become disappointed when God does not intervene in a way we thought he would. Or we may not understand why someone else got a different answer than we did. When that happens, the healthiest decision we can make is to bring those hurts and disappointments to God. After all, he's omniscient, so he already knows. Why not go ahead and bring it to the light? Placing these things in the light of our relationship with God and his Word can help us to heal and remember who God is, even when his ways may not make sense to us.

---

[5] Gottman, 214–15.

Sitting in Our Own Darkness

When we discuss grief in class, we discuss the inappropriate things people tend to say when others are suffering. Many of us have likely said something to someone in a difficult situation that we wish we could take back. Something embedded in our human nature causes our natural inclination to either avoid those in pain or find a way to alleviate it quickly. Part of ministry and counseling is having a front-row seat to watching God work during some of the darkest moments in a person's life. To sit with others in their pain, we must sit in our own darkness first, which requires courage.

Years ago, before my husband and I (Brooke) adopted our son from China, I counseled with a few families who had adopted internationally. One story I will never forget involved a preteen boy who had been with his forever family for a few years. He was having a hard time and experiencing anger that was so disruptive his family was not able to get out much because they never knew what would set him off. In many cases, his behavior was unmanageable.

His parents reached out to me because they heard I was trained in EMDR (eye movement desensitization and reprocessing) and thought it might be helpful for some of the trauma he had experienced in his orphanage.[6] This family was only going to be in the city for a few more months before they returned home. They were not aware of any EMDR-trained therapists where they lived, so they wanted to take advantage of the opportunity while in our area.

For many weeks, the parents reported constant struggles with their son. So many things revolved around him and his quickly shifting moods. Because they were moving soon, they wanted to press forward with EMDR. We worked through a few traumatic events, but the last one we worked through took my breath away.

This event concerned an older boy who had bullied my client and many of the other younger kids in the orphanage. From what my client said, the

[6] EMDR is an intervention used by licensed professional counselors for a wide range of presenting issues, including trauma. It is discussed further in chapter 10.

workers at the orphanage often looked the other way and justified it as the older kids keeping order in the institution. On this one occasion, the older boy was trying to suffocate him, and my client genuinely believed he was going to die.

As you can imagine, this was painful to process. When we made it to the end of processing the memory with EMDR, I asked my client how he was feeling. He said he was sad for the older boy. He went on to explain that in this country, a child was no longer eligible for adoption after the age of fourteen. The older boy was older than fourteen, which meant there would never be a family coming for him. In coming to terms with his own trauma, my client was able to recognize the plight of his former enemy and have empathy for this boy. When we confront our own darkness, we can enter the darkness of others, which opens the door to compassion.

Trying to connect with someone when we have not sat in our own darkness also has the potential to shift the focus to ourselves rather than being with the other person. We miss opportunities to connect with others when we are consumed by our need for control. When a terrible event happens to someone else, those of us with control issues are often looking for a formula. We want to know there is something we can do to prevent that event from happening to us.

When a tragedy strikes another person, it can be easy to bombard the person with questions. In and of themselves, questions are not bad. It often comes down to our motivation for asking them. If our motivation in asking a question is to better understand the situation and the person's perspective, then, more than likely, it is helpful. On the other hand, if our goal is to gain information about how it happened to prevent it from happening to us, then we have completely lost the other person's perspective.

In our attempts at control, we sometimes reason that if a child goes down the wrong path and makes poor choices, the fault lies with the parent. Then we try to figure out that parent's mistakes so we can prevent ourselves from ending up in that position. If someone's spouse is unfaithful, we look for what went wrong in the relationship so we can prevent that from happening in our own marriages.

The problem with this line of thinking is we are living in a fallen world, and no one leaves unscathed. There will always be things we can do to improve our marriages, our parenting, and other areas of our lives. However, we cannot have control over everyone involved. We have a responsibility to our children to be the best parents we can be, but we cannot control what they do with that. Our children have their own free will. It is the same with our marriages. We are responsible for ourselves, but we cannot control whether our spouses assume their own responsibility in the relationship.

We often spend so much time struggling with this thought process and looking for ways to maintain control that we miss the opportunity to take the other person's perspective. When we sit in our own darkness, we are forced to recognize that we do not always have control over the outcomes. We may also acknowledge our shared humanity, which means we are not immune to any struggle or trial.

How God Works in Suffering

"Every time we treat someone with dignity rather than shame, respect rather than disregard, concern rather than exploitation, kindness rather than brutality and careful attention rather than turning away—we are doing things that are the reverse of trauma and evil."[7] God heals in unique ways. In some cases, God may choose to bring complete healing, demonstrating his sovereignty over all. While in other situations, he may not choose complete healing, demonstrating his sufficiency to walk with us in the midst of suffering.[8] We are called to sit with people in their pain, not above them. Jesus began his pursuit of the Samaritan woman by expressing his own vulnerability—he asked for a drink. She had an emotional need, while his was a physical one.

---

[7] Diane Langberg (@DianeLangberg), Twitter post, September 19, 2019, 6:49 a.m., https://twitter.com/DianeLangberg/status/1174651695953002496.

[8] See Beth Moore, *Believing God Day by Day: Growing Your Faith All Year Long* (Nashville: B&H, 2008), 206–7.

"Our work is to listen, learn from, grieve with, walk with, and be changed to look more like our Lord."[9]

In this chapter, we have discussed the emotional problem of evil because that is typically a common struggle for us during a time of crisis. When a person is in pain and despair, we want to meet that person where he or she is, which means a crisis is not an appropriate time to debate the logical problem of evil. As we will discuss further in chapter 3, effective crisis intervention involves determining the location of a person and meeting him where he is. *We want to connect with his emotional experience, not offer scholarly responses to the nature of evil and suffering in the world. Regardless of how true or theologically sound our argument is, hurting people are not in a place to receive it.*

A Prayer as We Go

God, we pray that you would help us stand firm in our faith even when the world shakes us. In times of suffering and distress, help us remember that you are our deliverer. As we walk with others through darkness, we pray that your Holy Spirit will go before us and surround us. Our words are not adequate, so we ask you to comfort those in distress with a love that only you can give. We thank you for the assurance we have in you and that we will never be forsaken. Amen.

Conclusion

To have the courage to be fully present with those who are in pain and suffering, we need to be aware of how our own past is impacting our present. As Jesus was preparing to leave and send the Holy Spirit, he told his disciples in John 16:33, "I have said these things to you, that in me you may have peace. In the world you will have tribulation. But take heart; I have overcome the world" (ESV). The unfortunate truth of living in a fallen world

---

[9] Diane Langberg, *Redeeming Power: Understanding Authority and Abuse in the Church* (Grand Rapids: Brazos, 2020), 119.

is that it will fall on each of us at some point. We need to deal with hurts when they happen so we can have an unhindered relationship with God in the present.

> *If we have not personally come to know and understand the heart of our God in response to evil and suffering we will either avoid entering into the experience of evil in our client's lives or we will glibly apply the words of Scripture without an accurate representation of the God of Scripture.*
>
> —Diane Langberg, *Suffering and the Heart of God*

Additional Resources

This chapter focused more on our emotional responses to evil and suffering, rather than the logical problem of evil. If you are interested in further reading on the logical problem of evil, you might consider the following:

Evans, Jeremy A. *The Problem of Evil: The Challenge to Essential Christian Beliefs*. B&H Studies in Christian Apologetics. Nashville: B&H, 2013.

This book offers responses to the arguments from evil and includes a ministerial perspective.

Harwood, Adam. *Christian Theology: Biblical, Historical, and Systematic.* Bellingham, WA: Lexham, 2022.

Chapter 8, "Providence and Evil," focuses on the problem of evil and offers other helpful resources on the subject.

Meister, Chad, and James K. Dew Jr., eds. *God and Evil: The Case for God in a World Filled with Pain.* Downers Grove, IL: InterVarsity, 2012.

This book is a series of essays from a wide range of scholars who delve further into the logical problem of evil and reasons God may allow evil in this world.

Part 2
Crisis

Chapter 2

What Is a Crisis?

The phone rings. News of a tragic death echoes in your ear. The call is from a young father of two small children. He is in complete disbelief and confusion after receiving the news of an accident that took the life of his wife. You turn on the news, and images of unspeakable destruction flash across the screen: a nearby town torn apart by tornadoes, property destroyed, and precious lives lost. A wife visits your office in shock over her husband's betrayal, uncertain of the next steps she should take.

Crises. We all experience them. No one is immune. The nature of life is a dichotomy of joy and pain, beauty and ashes. Even Scripture is replete with examples of crises. The fall of humankind in the garden. The first murder. The flood. Plagues. Acts of violence. Sickness. Death. The metanarrative of Scripture is God's response to the crisis of the fall and humanity's need for redemption.

Experiencing a crisis is a defining moment in the life of an individual. When experiencing a crisis, the church is often one of the first places people call for help. As such, we have a tremendous opportunity to respond to those needing our assistance. When Christians are prepared to respond to crises, we can lovingly share Christ's gospel through our words and actions.

Defining the Term *Crisis*

What do we mean when we refer to a crisis? Definitions abound. Choose a field of study—psychology, health care, business, or government—and you can find an applied definition. Let's first consider the etymology of the word *crisis.*

Etymology

The term *crisis* originates from the Greek *krísis,* meaning an "act of separating, decision, judgment, event, outcome, turning point, sudden change."[1] It originally referred to "the turning point for better or worse in an acute disease or fever."[2] We now use the term more broadly than the initial medical perspective.

Merriam-Webster defines *crisis* in several ways, including phrases such as "a decisive moment," "an emotionally significant event or radical change of status in a person's life," "an unstable or crucial time or state of affairs in which a decisive change is impending," and "a situation that has reached a critical phase."[3] For this book, we define a crisis as follows:

Definition

A crisis

- is a situation beyond one's control
- threatens an individual's ability to cope

---

[1] *Merriam-Webster,* s.v. "crisis (*n.*)," accessed May 29, 2024, https://www.merriam-webster.com/dictionary/crisis.

[2] *Merriam-Webster.*

[3] *Merriam-Webster.*

- may negatively impact a person's physical, psychological/emotional, spiritual, or relational well-being
- requires a prompt decision, action, or intervention to avoid increased harm

Stress, Crisis, and Trauma

Stress

Stressors. Stressful life events. We experience stress as part of daily life. Stress may occur when we have more commitments than time, miss a work deadline, argue with a spouse, or drive in inclement weather. Job loss, health conditions, and financial challenges are stressors. Often, when coping and problem-solving skills are engaged in response to the stressor, the situation is resolved and does not escalate to a crisis. In other situations, the stressor may be unrelenting despite our best attempts at grappling with the issue.

Crisis

A stressor may become a crisis when the event or series of events overwhelms the individual's ability to cope, thus negatively impacting functionality.[4] At times, prolonged stressors, such as a chronically ill family member, can reach a crisis point. Initially, the individual may have the resources to cope with the chronic situation, but those resources may become depleted over time. Some situations, such as an unexpected death or tragedy, immediately surpass a typical stress response and become a crisis.

---

[4] See Kristi Kanel, *A Guide to Crisis Intervention*, 6th ed. (Boston: Cengage, 2018), 9.

Trauma

The crisis may become a trauma if an individual's safety or perceived safety becomes threatened and the situation overwhelms an individual's ability to cope, causing long-term negative consequences. The *Diagnostic and Statistical Manual of Mental Disorders* defines trauma as "exposure to actual or threatened death, serious injury, or sexual violence."[5] We will explore trauma and its impact in part 5.

Each person's history, support system, and coping skills bring a subjective nature to the impact of stress, crises, and trauma. This subjectivity occurs in the perception of threat, the methods of coping, and the extent of harm experienced. We should consider each experience as unique because each individual is unique.

Types of Crises

Crises occur globally, nationally, regionally, locally, and individually. People across the globe experienced the crisis of COVID-19. Some may recall receiving the news of a widespread shutdown of in-person education and jobs. Perhaps you remember the eerie feeling of walking into a grocery store, mask on, shelves bare, confusion in the eyes of those around you, whispers of the unknown, and predictions of what was to come.

On September 11, 2001, the United States experienced a national crisis. Many Americans recollect hearing the news of 9/11. I (Karen) remember that morning as though it happened two weeks ago rather than over two decades ago. While watching a news show, I viewed the live coverage as the shocking events unfolded. Wanting to connect with others, I called my family and friends to tell them to turn on the news so we could discuss what was happening. That evening, I met others at the church where my husband

[5] American Psychiatric Association, *Diagnostic and Statistical Manual of Mental Disorders*, 5th ed., Text Revision (*DSM-5-TR*) (American Psychiatric Association, 2022), 301. Hereinafter APA, *DSM-5-TR.*

was pastoring so we could experience the comfort of togetherness and pray as we faced the unknown.

Regional crises abound as well. Tornadoes in the South and Midwest demolish entire neighborhoods in minutes. Flooding, landslides, and wildfires ravage portions of California. Hurricanes along the Gulf Coast and Florida destroy towns and communities. We read of worldwide wars, refugee crises, famines, and a host of other tragic events. While we were writing this book, the world was shocked by the massive fatalities of an earthquake that impacted Turkey, Syria, and nearby countries. The earthquake and numerous aftershocks left a heartbreaking death toll of almost 46,000 people.[6]

Some crises are localized to a specific church, school, or community. When I (Karen) was thirteen years old, my church felt the devastating loss of our beloved pastor in a car accident. The entire church was swept into a wave of grief while our pastor's wife and children faced the harrowing experience of the sudden, unexpected death of their husband and father.

Some crises occur within a family or on an individual level, such as a chronic illness, infidelity, a health diagnosis, or financial crisis. The impacts can be pervasive even though they occur within the family unit. Like a pebble tossed into a lake, the impact ripples throughout the various systems to which the individual belongs, beginning with the closest relationships and moving outward.[7]

We can classify crises into two broad categories: natural and human caused. Natural disasters include illnesses or weather/geological events, such as tornadoes, tropical storms, hurricanes, droughts, wildfires, tsunamis, landslides, floods, and extreme temperatures. Human-caused disasters may be intentional, such as mass shootings, war, biological warfare, and assault. Alternatively, human-caused disasters can be accidental, such

---

[6] See Reuters, "Turkey's Earthquake Death Toll Rose to 45,968—Interior Minister," Reuters, March 4, 2023, sec. Middle East, https://www.reuters.com/world/middle-east/turkeys-earthquake-death-toll-rose-45968-interior-minister-2023-03-04.

[7] See Richard K. James and Burl E. Gilliland, *Crisis Intervention Strategies*, 8th ed. (Boston: Cengage Learning, 2016), 10.

as motor vehicle accidents, chemical spills, building/bridge failures, and nuclear accidents. Recently, there has been an increased potential for a technological crisis, such as a disruption of services or a data breach. Some crises are a combination of natural and human caused. For example, after hurricanes swept through our area of South Louisiana, some individuals were financially scammed by dishonest individuals posing as repairmen. Those individuals felt the impact of both natural (hurricane) and human-made (financial scam) disasters.

Danger and Opportunity

The Chinese word for *crisis* is composed of two characters: "danger" and "opportunity."[8] A crisis can be considered a "dangerous opportunity." A crisis may present the possibility of danger, distress, and decline. However, a crisis also may be considered an opportunity for growth and change. We will explore both aspects.

Crises can lead to immense stress, and the impact of stress is cumulative. The more stress an individual experiences, the greater the potential for a holistic negative impact on the person's psychological/emotional, relational, physical, and spiritual well-being.

Do not underestimate the spiritual struggles that may accompany a crisis experience. Those spiritual struggles may create additional distress. Based on the analysis of hundreds of research studies encompassing a variety of religious and spiritual traditions, Pargament and Exline conclude that for some individuals, "Spiritual struggles are consistently associated with a variety of indicators of distress and disorientation."[9] Spiritual struggles are associated with "symptoms of psychiatric disorders and PTSD, suicidality,

[8] Kanel, *A Guide to Crisis Intervention*, 3.

[9] Kenneth I. Pargament and Julie J. Exline, *Working with Spiritual Struggles in Psychotherapy: From Research to Practice* (New York: Guilford, 2021), 63.

symptoms of physical illness, a weakened immune system, perhaps greater risk of mortality, and social problems."[10]

While it is important to recognize a crisis may lead to a spiritual struggle, experiencing a crisis does not inevitably lead to long-term spiritual struggles. The connection between severe difficulties and spiritual struggles is modest.[11] The crisis can present a "potential for growth and positive transformation."[12]

Due to the tendency of a crisis to lead to decline or growth, a crisis may be considered a turning point. Consider how a crisis may initiate change.

A Spiritual Turning Point

On March 11, 2020, the World Health Organization declared COVID-19 a global pandemic, a worldwide crisis. That same month, the number of Google searches for "prayer" reached the "highest level ever recorded" and continued to be 10 percent higher than average for the remainder of the year.[13]

Faith and spirituality assist an individual with coping, resilience, and growth when facing a crisis.[14] A crisis prompts an inward focus on one's faith to help the individual cope with what is happening, especially in the areas of intrinsic faith practices, such as prayer and one's relationship with God.[15] Jeanet Bentzen notes, "People are more likely to rank themselves as a religious person, say they find comfort in God, and to state that God is

---

[10] Pargament and Exline, 80.

[11] See Pargament and Exline, 81–83.

[12] Pargament and Exline, 85.

[13] Jeanet Sinding Bentzen, "In Crisis, We Pray: Religiosity and the COVID-19 Pandemic," *Journal of Economic Behavior & Organization* 192 (December 2021): 541, https://doi.org/10.1016/j.jebo.2021.10.014.

[14] See Anka Roberto et al., "Impact of Spirituality on Resilience and Coping during the COVID-19 Crisis: A Mixed-Method Approach Investigating the Impact on Women," *Health Care for Women International* 41, no. 11/12 (November 2020): 1321, 1326, https://doi.org/10.1080/07399332.2020.1832097.

[15] See Bentzen, "In Crisis, We Pray," 543.

important in their lives when hit by earthquakes, tsunamis, and volcanic eruptions. This holds for people from all backgrounds. And the increased religiosity lasts for generations."[16]

Importance of Faith Communities

When experiencing a crisis, we often seek solace from others in our faith communities. After 9/11, many churches nationwide gathered for prayer services, providing a corporate opportunity for prayer and support and furthering the potential positive impact of using one's faith to cope.

People often turn to their church in times of crisis. For example, women who are experiencing spousal abuse may approach a minister or someone in their church before seeking other forms of help.[17] In a financial crisis, people may seek the help of a church for assistance with food, housing, utilities, or other financial needs. Churches may provide shelter, resources, and volunteers in response to natural disasters. Christians experiencing relational crises may turn to their church for counsel. A health crisis may prompt requests for prayer and practical support. After a death, one's minister is often one of the first calls the family will make.

The church needs to remember its role in offering spiritual care along with practical support. In addition to physical needs, spiritual support during a crisis is a "core need" of many individuals.[18] Goodwin and Kraft note, "Faith and communities of faith are inextricably linked to people's

---

[16] Bentzen, 545.

[17] See Maxine Davis and Maxine Johnson, "Exploring Black Clergy Perspectives on Religious/Spiritual Related Domestic Violence: First Steps in Facing Those Who Wield the Sword Abusively," *Journal of Aggression, Maltreatment & Trauma* 30, no. 7 (2021), 953.

[18] See Ellen Goodwin and Kathryn Kraft, "Mental Health and Spiritual Well-Being in Humanitarian Crises: The Role of Faith Communities Providing Spiritual and Psychosocial Support during the COVID-19 Pandemic," *Journal of International Humanitarian Action* 7, no. 1 (December 2022): 2, https://doi.org/10.1186/s41018-022-00127-w.

experiences of crises and their ability to cope and recover."[19] Spiritual care in crisis is not having all the answers but acknowledging the struggle, providing a space to explore questions, offering spiritual and practical support, and providing a healthy supportive community.

A Timely Response

A timely response is critical in responding to a crisis. An event is considered a crisis because of the threat to one's ability to cope and the need for some type of immediate response. If someone in crisis contacts you, this needs to be prioritized. Scheduling an appointment with someone in crisis should not be delayed. If someone's safety is compromised, as with suicidal ideation or cases of abuse, take swift and immediate action, contacting the proper professionals and authorities. If there is no immediate safety concern, yet the individual is in crisis, schedule a meeting with him or her within forty-eight hours, preferably within twenty-four hours. If you cannot meet with the person personally, have another trusted individual meet with him or her to provide prompt care.

Conclusion

Countless times in churches and Bible studies, I have heard the following statement or one similar: "You either just got out of a troublesome time, are currently experiencing troubles, or are about to enter a time of trouble." Those making this statement are referring to times of crisis. None of us is immune to experiencing a crisis. Despite the potential to overwhelm, a crisis is often a turning point. Learning to respond to a crisis is a critical component of effective ministry.

---

[19] Goodwin and Kraft, 2.

Chapter 3

The Process of Crisis Intervention

Crisis counseling differs from traditional professional counseling in that it is time-limited and specific to helping a person navigate a crisis. As you will see in this chapter, most crisis interventions involve being able to understand and clarify the situation to help the individual find the appropriate resources. In general, crisis intervention should not be long-term. Instead, crisis intervention should be aimed at helping the person find stability in the midst of a difficult situation. For example, a family who has lost everything they own in a house fire is likely to have a long road ahead of them in terms of dealing with the insurance company and rebuilding. Crisis interventions are designed to help this family find stability while they continue to deal with the aftermath of the fire. In this case, crisis intervention may include helping them secure temporary housing, meeting other immediate needs such as clothing, and listening as they grieve their losses. They will continue to have needs in the months to come, but the needs are unlikely to be as intense.

To walk with a person through a crisis, we must practice: EMPATHY.

E Establish Safety	M Meet Them	P Perspective Taking	A Attune	T Talk	H Help	Y You
Physical Safety: Meet basic needs. Ensure physical safety. Emotional Safety: Do they feel safe?	Location: In relation to self, others, and God. Is there a trauma response: fight, flight, or freeze?	Consider their perspective without judgment.	Lean in closer to listen and connect.	They talk, you listen. Ask good questions. Understand the purpose of your questions.	Resources, practical needs, counseling. Prepare a community resource guide. Know when to refer.	Notice how you are responding. Do your own work. Take care of yourself so you can care well for others.

Let's look at each of these in more detail.

Establish Safety

The first thing we need to do in a crisis situation is establish safety, both physical and emotional. Physical safety includes the basic needs such as food, shelter, and clothing. Having shelter means not just a place to stay but a safe place to stay. If someone is currently in an abusive relationship, make sure he or she has a safety plan, as discussed in chapter 18. If child abuse is involved, report it to the appropriate authorities (see chapter 25). Emotional safety is also essential. The individual should feel comfortable expressing his or her struggles and needs without fear of judgment.

Meet Them Where They Are

Location tells us where things are situated and is a crucial determining factor in where people move, where businesses open, and the strength of the economy. The three dimensions of location in crisis counseling involve the location of the person in relationship to self, the location of the person in relationship to others, and the location of the person in relationship to God. To engage in crisis intervention, we must first determine the location of the counselor, then the location of the client. The first crisis addressed in Scripture occurred in the garden. After Adam and Eve had eaten the forbidden fruit, their eyes were opened. In Genesis 3:9, God asked them, "Where are you?" Of course, God knew exactly where they were, but he wanted them to reflect on where they were. They were no longer in right relationship with God.[1]

Location of the Counselor

As counselors, we need to determine our location in relationship to ourselves. What level of awareness do we possess about past events in our lives or about current stressors and crisis situations? Are these things impacting our ability to care well for those around us? Before we are able to help others effectively, we must be emotionally healthy. None of us is immune to struggles or crisis events, but we must engage with our own mental health if we want to connect with others.[2]

In addition to considering our own mental and emotional health, we should consider our relationship with others. Do we have a healthy and solid support system in place? Is there accountability? In working with those in crisis, we can easily become so caught up in helping them develop a support network that we neglect nurturing our own.

We should consider our own relationship with God. Many crisis events bring us face-to-face with the evil in the world and the atrocities humans commit against one another. Have we addressed any doubts we may have about our faith? Where are we on our spiritual journeys? We want to make

---

[1] See Ian Jones, *The Counsel of Heaven on Earth: Foundations for Biblical Christian Counseling* (Nashville: B&H Academic, 2006), 31–32.

[2] In this book, you'll notice several opportunities for self-reflection. We believe it is important to reflect on our own experiences to help others effectively.

sure we are taking time alone with God to confess any sin, discuss doubts or questions we have about our faith, or restore ourselves.

Location of the Client

Where is the individual in crisis located? Beginning with physical safety, assess the person's immediate needs of lodging, food, and clothing. Determine whether he or she is experiencing abuse or entertaining suicidal thoughts, and report appropriately. We cannot help a person work through a crisis until basic needs are met.

Consider his current level of functioning. Is he sleeping and taking care of himself? Are there areas where he could use some additional assistance or resources? Assess for practical help such as meal preparation and childcare assistance.

From a trauma perspective, is she in a state of fight, flight, or freeze? The fight stage of trauma response is a person in a state of self-preservation. She is pumped with adrenaline, ready to stand her ground and attack if needed. This person may need someone to help her calm down and think through her decisions before acting on them.

A person in a state of flight is often seeking to avoid. She may replay the traumatic memories, engaging in rumination. Rumination may increase her anxiety levels, or she might become hypervigilant. She may also immerse herself in perfectionism to gain some control and isolate herself from others. This person is trying desperately to escape the perceived threat. Depending on the situation, this person might benefit from some calming strategies, social support, and a sense of safety being established.

The freeze state is when a person may feel numb emotionally. He may feel stuck and unable to process the situation or make decisions. In some cases, physical activity may help the person get unstuck.

Assess how the crisis may have strengthened or weakened their relationships with others. Determine the strength and reliability of their support systems and look for ways to bolster them. Identify how the current crisis may have impacted their relationship with God. During times of suffering, some say they feel closer to God than at any other time in life. They have drawn themselves to him, and his strength sustains them each day. Others struggle to find God in the midst of crisis.

Perspective Taking

According to Theresa Wiseman, part of empathy is staying out of judgment.[3] Empathy is about connecting with another person's emotional experience. We cannot connect deeply with other people if we are judging them for their mistakes or the handling of their current situations.

In my (Brooke) Introduction to Counseling class, we talk about people we know, love, and respect who become ensnared in sexual sin. This person's sin may escalate, and eventually it becomes public. In looking at the devastation left behind, we are often in a state of shock because we had no idea the person was struggling. We wonder why he or she never came to us.

There could be a number of reasons why those struggling deeply in private choose not to approach us, but I would like for us to consider whether we are approachable. We never know what the person next to us is struggling with, and we may not be aware of how comments we make can bring further shame on him or her. For example, let's say I have a friend struggling with pornography. She is convicted that what she is doing is wrong, but she is not sure where to seek help. She finally works up the courage to talk to me. But before she can, she overhears my conversation with a coworker, in which I say that I do not understand how anyone could ever struggle with pornography. Maybe I throw out a sarcastic remark making light of the situation. She then decides I am not a safe person to confide in, and she continues struggling with her sin in secret.

Another possibility is that many of us live in a perpetual state of chaos. We take on more responsibilities than we can handle, leaving us stretched

---

[3] See Theresa Wiseman, "A Concept Analysis of Empathy," *Journal of Advanced Nursing* 23, no. 6 (June 1996): 1162–67, https://doi.org/10.1046/j.1365-2648.1996.12213.x.

thin and depleted. Every time people see us, we are in a hurry or complaining about how busy and stressed we are. Those who are struggling might consider us safe and compassionate people, but they do not want to burden us when we already seem beyond our limits.

We should continually evaluate whether we are approachable to those around us. Although some may use fear of judgment and our busyness as a reason not to seek help, we believe there are many who desperately want help. They just need someone to see them and love them in spite of their sin. There are also cases where an individual's sin may not be the cause of her crisis, but she may feel weak for not being able to handle it herself. We can be a safe place for her to ask for help.

Attune

Outside of the counseling world, we do not often hear the word *attune*. In some ways, being attuned might be thought of as giving more attention to detail or becoming acclimated or accustomed to something or someone. As it does for many people, public speaking makes me nervous. My husband always tells me that I (Brooke) am so calm under pressure that no one even realizes how anxious I am. Several years ago, I was scheduled to speak at a small event. I would be speaking about a topic that had directly and devastatingly impacted people in the group. I was concerned about balancing the content matter with sensitivity for those who had been recently wounded. I tried to remind myself that no one would realize how concerned I was about how my message would land. Afterward, my husband asked if everything was fine because I seemed so nervous. I responded with "I thought you said no one notices." His response was that other people didn't notice. However, we had been married for over ten years at the time, which gave him much experience with being attuned to how I was feeling.

You might think of attuning to another person as leaning in closer so you can hear better. We are not just listening to the content of others' words; we are connecting with their emotional experiences. In graduate school, we took a course on techniques and skills in counseling where we discussed how to make empathic statements along with other interpersonal relationship skills such as active listening and asking good questions. We learned the generic "You feel ______ because of ______," so we tend to associate empathy with a feeling word.

As therapists-in-training, many of us were more focused on trying to say the right thing to our clients or not making things worse. This often brought about anxiety, which shifted the focus to ourselves, rather than those we were serving. Instead of leaning in closer to the other person, we were leaning into ourselves, which made empathy impossible.

Empathy and sympathy are often confused and misunderstood. Sympathy is about being sorry that something happened to a person. When extending sympathy, we are often thinking about how we would feel if we experienced what is happening to the other person. Sympathy drives disconnection. On the other hand, empathy is imagining being in that person's shoes and experiencing the situation as they would. Empathy allows a person to feel understood, fueling connection. In *Atlas of the Heart*, Brené Brown explains further:

> Empathy is not sympathy—in fact, using the near enemy concept, we can definitely consider sympathy the near enemy of empathy. Rather than being a tool for connection, sympathy emerged in the data as a form of disconnection. Sympathy is removed: When someone says, "I feel sorry for you," or "That must be terrible," they are standing at a safe distance. Rather than conveying the powerful "me too" of empathy, it communicates, "not me," then adds, "But I do feel sorry for you."[4]

According to Theresa Wiseman, empathy involves four things: perspective taking, staying out of judgment, recognizing emotion, and communicating emotion.[5] Taking the perspective of another person means

---

[4] Brené Brown, *Atlas of the Heart: Mapping Meaningful Connection and the Language of Human Experience* (New York: Random House, 2021), 124.

[5] Wiseman, "A Concept Analysis of Empathy."

we consider the impact that person's background, previous experiences, and current situation have on her perspective in the current situation. Something in our human nature seems to orient us toward doing rather than being.

Perspective taking does not mean we analyze and interpret what the person is saying. Instead, we note and accept.[6] Accepting what a person is saying does not necessarily mean we are in agreement. Rather, it means we respect her perspective on the situation without judgment or argument. Arguing with another person's perspective or minimizing her experience will likely lead to her isolating herself and not receiving help.

Talk

They talk, we listen. David Yeiter says, "How we come to define a problem will largely determine how we will approach it and solve it."[7] Identifying the surface-level problem is usually straightforward; the underlying problem is not as easy to detect. If we help someone resolve the current crisis, what is the likelihood of it resurfacing? If we are addressing the underlying cause of the crisis, it is unlikely it will present again. If we do not address the underlying issue, we are likely to continue helping the person put out fires rather than preventing the fire from being started in the first place.

For example, let's say you have a family come to you multiple times throughout the year needing financial assistance from the benevolence fund. If they had only come to you on one occasion, you might think they hit a rough patch and needed help this once. Because they have come multiple times in the last year, you question whether giving them money each time is really solving anything. To look below the surface would be to determine their money-management skills. If money management is the issue, we might recommend a financial course that would give them skills in this area. Or do they have a low-paying job? Assist them in exploring how they

[6] See P. Burnard, "Sharing a Viewpoint," *Senior Nurse* 7, no. 3 (1987): 38–39.

[7] David Yeiter, *Lessons in Listening* (Toronto: Inclusion, 2022), 9.

might get a job that pays enough to support their family. If getting a higher-paying job were easy, they likely would have already done so. Consider using benevolence funds for further training or schooling, so they can obtain a more sustainable job.

Provide space for the client to feel heard by asking questions strategically and avoiding interruption. Use open questions that invite explanations and broader responses, instead of closed (yes/no) questions. Excessive questioning may stifle the flow of conversation.

To determine whether your question is open or closed, anticipate the likely responses. If you believe you will only get a one- or two-word response, chances are it is a closed question. If you believe the question can facilitate further discussion, it is probably an open question. An example of a closed question would be "Do you have any hobbies?" An open-ended question might ask, "What kind of hobbies do you have?" Or, in the form of a statement, "Tell me about your hobbies."

Both open- and closed-ended questions have a purpose. Open-ended questions are best to facilitate a discussion, to learn more about the situation, and to reduce interjections by the counselor. When you need factual information quickly and concisely, closed-ended questions are best.

Asking too many closed questions may inadvertently cause the client to feel as though he is being interrogated, and he may become defensive. The use of "why" questions can also cause a client to become defensive. If he knew "why," he probably would not be coming to us for help in the first place.

Throughout the conversation, consider reflecting back to the client what you are hearing to ensure you understand. After the client has answered some questions and explained his or her situation, confirm: "What I'm hearing you say is . . ." Reflecting assists in understanding them well.

Help

Now that we have taken the time to listen, connect, and sit with clients in their crisis, we want to consider a plan of action. Consider the immediate, most pressing needs, including meal preparation, financial assistance, or connecting them with a professional counselor or support group.

We want to consider what kind of support system they have and how we may need to help them expand it. If they are currently involved in a church, we want to see how we can mobilize their church or other community resources. In my (Brooke) Crisis Counseling class, one of the assignments is for students to complete a "Community Resource Guide." The purpose of this guide is to think about the various resources people in our church and community may need. We want to be aware of and begin building relationships with the resources. If a church member or a person from the community needs assistance, we have a wide range of resources that can be utilized without having to take time tracking these things down. Some examples of what could be included in this resource guide are listed in the appendix.

If you are not trained as a professional counselor, you want to exercise caution engaging in long-term counseling with church or community members. A good guideline might be that if you cannot resolve the crisis in three counseling sessions, you probably need to refer to a professional. You may still choose to disciple, encourage, and support the person throughout the crisis, just not in the capacity of long-term counseling. There may be times when the individual is reluctant to seek professional counseling. You might consider checking in with him after the first appointment or throughout the process. This is also where it might be helpful to have built relationships with professional Christian counselors in the area. This way, you'll know you are sending him to someone you trust. A list of questions to ask prospective counselors is included in the appendix.

Along with checking in with him after his first counseling session, it might be helpful to check in again several weeks later. In some cases, he may not feel the counselor is a good fit for him or the cost may prohibit him from continuing. Depending on what he is working through, counseling may be hard, and he may need encouragement to continue.

You

Be mindful of your inner experience when responding to the person. For example, are we allowing her to do most of the talking? Or are we continually interjecting and disrupting her thought process? Allow the person to take ownership of her situation by working through her own decision-making rather than pushing her in the direction you think is best.[8]

In addition to our inner experience, we want to be aware of how our previous life experiences may be impacting our ability to help. We should consider whether we are leaning in to listen or jumping to conclusions based on our own life experiences.[9] We also need to realize that what worked for us and helped us endure our situation may not work the same for another. This is why we should be aware of several different approaches to a crisis. Interventions and techniques may work differently for each person. Their experience should be at the forefront of our minds.

We believe in the importance of doing our own work and being mindful of how we have been impacted by crisis and trauma. Throughout this book, we will have a few opportunities for you to consider how you may have been impacted, both past and present, by grief and the stress of ministry. We would encourage you to take the time to reflect on your own life to make sure you are in a place to serve others longer and well. In reflecting on his work with those who have disabilities, David Yeiter stated, "One of the things I discovered is that real listening takes courage. Rogers would say, '*If you really understand a person in this way, if you are willing to enter his private world and see the way life appears to him, you run the risk of being changed yourself. . . . The risk of being changed is one of the most frightening prospects most of us can face.*'"[10]

---

[8] See John Thomas and Lisa Sosin, *Therapeutic Expedition: Equipping the Christian Counselor for the Journey* (Nashville: B&H Academic, 2011), 156.

[9] See Thomas and Sosin, 156.

[10] Yeiter, *Lessons in Listening*, 12.

A client in crisis may come to you as a result of circumstances outside of his or her control. It could be a natural disaster, a human-made disaster, or a health crisis. In other cases, a client might be in a state of crisis because of choices he or she has made. None of us is immune to crisis, whether of our own doing or a result of things outside of our control. We always want to meet people where they are without judgment. As Beth Moore says, "Even if I blow it, I can choose to follow [God] the rest of the way. It's never too late to start following his lead in a crisis."[11] We do not want to absolve people of the consequences of their actions, but we do want to walk with them as they experience them.

Conclusion

Navigating a crisis situation is not always easy or straightforward. Practicing EMPATHY along the way can serve as a guide to ensure we are serving others well during difficult times and taking care of ourselves. We will always encounter crisis situations, whether personal or professional. The more effective we are at ministering to others in times of crisis, the more efficiently a resolution can be achieved that serves everyone involved with care and compassion.

[11] Beth Moore, *Praying God's Word Day by Day* (Nashville: B&H, 2006), 105.

Chapter 4

The Effects of Social Media

Americans are a social media active society with approximately seven accounts per user and averaging over two hours daily.[1] If you use social media, you likely get at least some news content from one or more social media sites. You may even be involved in community, church, interest, or professional groups on social media. Because of the prevalence of social media usage, we need to incorporate its use in our crisis response strategies.

My family and I (Karen) evacuated our home in South Louisiana during a recent hurricane. We sought information from our community Facebook page during and after the storm. The news was the most recent and most local to our home. The New Orleans news stations typically do not broadcast from my neighborhood, but my neighbors will post updates I can access in real time. Soon after Ida's landfall, local churches began to post

[1] See Belle Wong, "Top Social Media Statistics and Trends of 2024," *Forbes*, May 18, 2023, https://www.forbes.com/advisor/business/social-media-statistics.

information about volunteer crews helping with cleanup efforts, such as tree removal. Had we been physically unable to clean up the several downed trees on our property, we could have requested assistance from one of these teams through social media. We could also see photos and information from local government, fire and rescue, and people in our community to assess whether we had safe property access as we planned our return home.

Social Media Usage and Demographics

Social media users report using various platforms for different reasons and interacting with diverse audiences.[2] For example, some use Facebook to connect with family and friends and TikTok for educational entertainment. Others turn to TikTok journalists, who have accounts that share a summary of recent news. The usage of social media as a news source appears to be growing. Austin et al. state, "In 2009, for the first time, American adults reported the Internet was their preferred source for information and the most reliable source for news."[3]

Pew Research identified how much of their news Americans "regularly" receive from various social media sites:[4]

- Facebook: 30 percent
- YouTube: 26 percent
- Instagram: 16 percent

---

[2] See Colleen McClain, Lee Rainie, and Peter Bell, "Life on Social Media Platforms, in Users' Own Words," Pew Research Center: Internet, Science & Tech, June 7, 2023, https://www.pewresearch.org/internet/2023/06/07/life-on-social-media-platforms-in-users-own-words.

[3] Lucinda Austin, Brooke Fisher Liu, and Yan Jin, "How Audiences Seek Out Crisis Information: Exploring the Social-Mediated Crisis Communication Model," *Journal of Applied Communication Research* 40, no. 2 (May 2012): 190, https://doi.org/10.1080/00909882.2012.654498.

[4] See "Social Media and News Fact Sheet," *Pew Research Center's Journalism Project*, https://www.pewresearch.org/journalism/fact-sheet/social-media-and-news-fact-sheet.

- TikTok: 14 percent
- X: 12 percent
- Reddit: 8 percent
- Nextdoor: 5 percent
- LinkedIn: 5 percent
- Snapchat: 4 percent
- WhatsApp: 3 percent
- Twitch: 1 percent

Demographics impact these numbers. For example, women report higher usage of Nextdoor, Facebook, Instagram, and TikTok for getting news, while men report higher use of Reddit, X, and YouTube.[5] Age also influences where people go for news. For example, people aged 30–49 are more likely to use Facebook and Nextdoor than the 18–29 demographic.[6] As such, consider posting to multiple platforms based on the demographics you are trying to reach.

During a crisis, people use social media for "insider information" from people who have firsthand knowledge of the event and may be sharing the information before traditional news channels.[7] In the example at the beginning of the chapter, I (Karen) shared how my local Facebook group provided my family "insider information" after Hurricane Ida.

Another reason people use social media during a crisis is to check in with their family and friends.[8] Brynielsson et al. note, "If the message is received through a friend or family member who is considered trustworthy, the information is more likely trusted than if the information is received through a media outlet."[9]

[5] See "Social Media and News Fact Sheet."

[6] See "Social Media and News Fact Sheet."

[7] See Austin, Liu, and Jin, "How Audiences Seek Out Crisis Information."

[8] See Austin, Liu, and Jin.

[9] Joel Brynielsson et al., "Informing Crisis Alerts Using Social Media: Best Practices and Proof of Concept," *Journal of Contingencies and Crisis Management* 26, no. 1 (March 2018): 6, https://doi.org/10.1111/1468-5973.12195.

Benefits of Social Media During a Crisis

Using social media during a crisis provides a vast array of benefits. You might use social media for any or all of these activities:

- to post information and make announcements
- to provide quick, accessible, and free news that is not being reported elsewhere or is not readily available
- to check in with each other
- to find out who needs assistance
- to organize volunteers
- to host meetings or church services when dispersed
- to provide support
- to facilitate a sense of connectedness

Drawbacks of Social Media Use

While social media has multiple benefits, there are numerous drawbacks:

- Some people may lack access to social media or may choose to avoid using social media.
- Misinformation, rumors, and gossip can spread, and they can spread quickly via social media.
- Social media is not an adequate replacement for in-person interaction.
- Social media does not provide a complete picture of someone's life. Simply because someone presents well and appears happy on social media does not mean the person is immune from significant private struggles.
- People may post private information about themselves or another person. Or they may post information that should not be shared on social media. For example, in one community Facebook group, someone posted a picture of a fatal car accident soon after the

accident and before the family was notified. After that, the group had more strongly enforced rules about not posting pictures or specifics about accidents.

- Without speaking in person, you lose the nuance of a conversation. We can inadvertently offend others because we are not communicating in person and cannot see their reactions. For example, you cannot see facial expressions, posture, or how another person responds to your words. You also cannot hear tone of voice. Do they sound hurt? Offended? As a result of this lack of nuance, there could be misunderstandings.
- Social media posts can lead to interpersonal conflict. People can be harsher with their words on social media than in in-person conversations. They might attack others or make divisive statements.
- People are not always aware of the posting rules, which should be monitored.
- Social media has time demands. For example, the information should be updated and monitored regularly.

The Importance of Guidelines

Because of social media's drawbacks and the potential for social media itself to become a crisis, guidelines for managing social media during a crisis are essential. Seeger notes that a universal goal for crisis communication should be to "reduce and contain harm."[10] Keep this goal in mind as you consider the following:

---

[10] Matthew W. Seeger, "Best Practices in Crisis Communication: An Expert Panel Process," *Journal of Applied Communication Research* 34, no. 3 (August 2006): 234, https://doi.org/10.1080/00909880600769944; World Combined Sources, "Poll: Online News Sources Top All Others," People's World, June 17, 2009, https://www.peoplesworld.org/article/poll-online-news-sources-top-all-others.

Types of social media used:

- Which social media platforms will you use? For what purpose are you using them? What audience do you want to reach?

Guidelines for management and monitoring:

- Who will be responsible for posting?
- Who will monitor comments?
- How will inappropriate, disrespectful posts and comments be handled?
- How often will you post during a crisis? You need a regular posting schedule.

Guidelines for what to post:

- What is your purpose in posting?
- What type of crisis is being addressed?

Adapting your communication strategy to the stage: How can social media be used to help people prepare for a crisis?[11] Identify areas of potential risk and possible resources.

- How can social media be used during a crisis?
- How can social media be used after a crisis?

Social Media and Children

For many years, there has been concern about what preteens and teens share about themselves online. Parents often warn their children that what is shared online may follow them into adulthood, impacting their future. However, there is also a growing concern among researchers about parents sharing information about their children through social media platforms.

[11] Seeger, 237.

Sharenting

A common practice among parents who are active on social media is to post photographs or stories about their children. This sharing is often done without their child's permission or knowledge about what is being shared.[12] A new term—*sharenting*—has emerged, which combines the terms *parenting* and *sharing*. Sharenting occurs when a parent or guardian shares photographs, videos, or stories about their children on an online platform like Facebook or Instagram.[13]

Parents or guardians may share for various reasons, many of which are supportive and helpful for the parent.[14] They may share to connect with others, stay in touch with family and friends, convey their pride and affection toward their children, receive validation for their parenting, obtain support in the challenge of parenting, ask for advice about a parenting-related issue, celebrate accomplishments, or create a digital scrapbook of memories.[15]

Parents or caregivers might share birthday celebrations, academic accomplishments, family adventures, humorous anecdotes, or sports achievements. The intention may be to only share with a limited group of "friends" or "followers." But consider: What if a friend or relative reposts the picture? A photo or story can be unintentionally spread beyond the

---

[12] See Mary Jean Amon et al., "Sharenting and Children's Privacy in the United States: Parenting Style, Practices, and Perspectives on Sharing Young Children's Photos on Social Media," *Proceedings of the ACM on Human-Computer Interaction* 6, no. CSCW1 (March 30, 2022): 1–30, https://doi.org/10.1145/3512963.

[13] See Keltie Haley, "Sharenting and the (Potential) Right to Be Forgotten," *Indiana Law Journal* 95, no. 3 (July 2020): 1005–20.

[14] The authors recognize that some parents share for financial gain on "monetized" posts, but that is outside the scope of this chapter.

[15] For a summary of the research related to why parents or guardians "sharent," see L. Lin Ong et al., "Sharenting in an Evolving Digital World: Increasing Online Connection and Consumer Vulnerability," *Journal of Consumer Affairs* 56, no. 3 (September 2022): 1106–26, https://doi.org/10.1111/joca.12462.

intended audience.[16] This is just one concern about posting information about minors online.

Social media sharenting may have a negative impact on parents. They might experience discouragement from comparing themselves to the highly curated images of others who appear to "have it all together." Or they may experience gossip or judgment for something shared. However, sharing may impact the child or teenager even more negatively.

The potential negative consequences of sharenting on minors are sobering.[17] The minor may experience identity theft or digital kidnapping. Personal information, such as health conditions or the child's location, may be exposed. They may be embarrassed, shamed, or humiliated by what is shared online. The breach of privacy may impact their development of "self-identity, autonomy, and trust."[18] Minors trust their parents. How might this trust be impacted if a parent shares personal or embarrassing information that the child would like to keep private? Future consequences of shared content cannot be predicted nor controlled. For example, will this impact their future college choice or career? Sharing information might expose the minor to online or in-person bullying.

Churches need policies for sharing content that includes photographs of minors on their websites or social media. Permission forms need to be signed by parents who consent to have their child's picture posted. Even with permission, it can be challenging to know which children have parental permission and which do not. One local church in our area provided different colored wristbands to children. Those whose pictures could be posted wore yellow bands, and those who did not have permission wore orange bands. The social media coordinator could then ensure no photos were posted of those whose parents had not signed the permission form.

---

[16] See Ong et al., "Sharenting in an Evolving Digital World."

[17] See Haley, "Sharenting and the (Potential) Right to Be Forgotten" for a discussion of the negative impacts of sharenting.

[18] Haley, 1010.

We must exercise caution and wisdom when sharing images and stories about children and teenagers online. Consider the following general recommendations for sharing:[19]

- Be aware of the privacy settings on your social media platforms.
- Avoid sharing information about a child's current location.
- Avoid posting pictures or stories about children other than your own without permission from their parents or guardians.
- Avoid sharing images of minors in any state of undress.[20]
- Ask the child or teenager if he or she is comfortable with the picture or information you want to share. But keep in mind that even if minors consent to the information shared, they are likely unaware of the potential negative consequences.
- Ask yourself:
    - What is the purpose of sharing the information?
    - Is this information embarrassing, shaming, or humiliating (both currently and in the future)?
    - Does this post reveal personal information the child or teen may want to remain private (e.g., health conditions, learning challenges, relationship status)?
    - How might this sharing impact the child's future?

When did you establish an "online presence"? Now, most children have an online presence at birth or even before birth with the sharing of pregnancy announcements and ultrasound photographs. As a result, we need to prioritize the well-being and safety of those in our care.

---

[19] See the following article for a list of seven "best practices" for online sharing: Stacey B. Steinberg, "Sharenting: Children's Privacy in the Age of Social Media," *Emory Law Journal* 66, no. 4 (July 2017): 839–84.

[20] See Steinberg.

Conclusion

Social media is often one of the first places we turn to in a crisis. We want to get local updates, check in with family and friends, and have a sense of connection. This chapter overviewed the benefits and challenges of social media use during a crisis. Additionally, we considered a current issue in social media, the topic of "sharenting." The overarching guidelines of social media use are to distribute correct and helpful information in a timely manner, respect the privacy of others, and consider the consequences of what is shared.

Part 3
Grief

Chapter 5

The Human Experience of Grief

Be careful. The undercurrent is powerful," my mom's voice cautioned as I (Karen) waded into the ocean. I glanced at the breathtaking, rocky Oregon coastline and breathed in the crisp, salty air. The icy water lapped around my ankles. Disregarding her warning, I waded in deeper. I recall thinking to myself, *How can water that is barely above my ankles be dangerous?* Suddenly, something pulled at my legs. I yelled, "Mom, something is grabbing my ankles!" As I started running for shore, my small legs fought the undertow threatening to knock me off my feet and swallow me into the crashing wave. I escaped the grasp of that powerful undertow but will never forget its grip on my legs.

The experience of grief is like waves in the ocean. Some waves are small, while others are powerful, knocking us over. At times, invisible undertows pull us back into the sea of grief quickly and deeply. A song, an anniversary, a birthday, or even something seemingly as simple as food or a scent can engulf us, grabbing us in the undertow of grief.

Death and loss are inevitable. The pain of losing someone we love can be excruciating. I've often heard it said that emotional pain rivals physical pain. The language used to describe grief gives us insight into its depths. Anguish. Despair. Heartache. Yearning.

This chapter will identify numerous ways we experience grief and loss throughout our lifetimes. We will define the terms *grief*, *mourning*, *bereavement*, and *lament*. We will explore the neurobiology of grief and the impact of grief. Finally, we will discuss several types of grief often ignored by society: anticipatory grief, traumatic grief, complicated spiritual grief, ambiguous loss, and disenfranchised grief. Finally, we will review prolonged grief disorder.

Defining Terms

We use various terms when describing the experience of loss. The terms *grief*, *mourning*, and *bereavement* are often used interchangeably. *Lament* is less used but still a vital term to consider, particularly for persons of faith. In this chapter, I will introduce the term *lament*. In the next chapter, I will focus on how lament may be incorporated as a tool for processing the grief experience.

Grief

Grief is the holistic experience of how an individual responds to loss. By holistic, we are referring to the potential impact of grief on all aspects of life: emotional/psychological, cognitive, behavioral, physical, relational, and spiritual. Experiencing symptoms of grief is an expected response to loss. Jesus wept at the death of his friend Lazarus. He experienced grief over the death of someone he loved while knowing he would raise Lazarus from the dead. Despite that knowledge, he expressed grief (see John 11). Ministering to those who are grieving requires us to acknowledge that grief is a normal part of life.

Mourning

While grief is our reaction to loss, mourning is our process of adjusting to the loss.[1] The mourning process and mourning rituals are influenced heavily by culture. As such, cultural awareness and sensitivity are significant when ministering to grieving people. Culture impacts how we express emotion, what we communicate about death, our funeral and burial traditions and rituals, whether there is a prescribed period of mourning, how people refer to and talk about the deceased, views about dreams involving the deceased, how the community responds, how the family responds, and the spiritual/religious practices and views about death.[2]

Bereavement

Bereavement is "the state of having suffered a loss."[3] You may hear someone described as a "bereaved" individual. We often pray for "the bereaved" in our churches and communities, referring to those who have experienced the loss of a loved one.

Lament

Lament is a means by which we can communicate our pain, suffering, and doubts to God. Lament is valuable for Christians to consider and incorporate in the mourning process. We will examine the process of lament in the next chapter.

---

[1] See J. William Worden, *Grief Counseling and Grief Therapy: A Handbook for the Mental Health Practitioner*, 5th ed. (New York: Springer, 2018), 27.

[2] See Robert A. Neimeyer, ed., *New Techniques of Grief Therapy: Bereavement and Beyond* (New York: Taylor & Francis, 2022), 48.

[3] Therese A. Rando, *Grief, Dying, and Death: Clinical Interventions for Caregivers* (Champaign, IL: Research, 1984), 16.

Neurobiology of Grief

When you consider the experience of grief, does it seem like some abstract, intangible experience? While intangible, grief also occurs tangibly on a biological and physical level. We feel grief's quantifiable nature in our bodies when the emotional pain consumes us in overwhelming waves, our stomachs clench, and we gasp for breath through our tears. We sense grief's impact on the physical structure of our brains through the utter bewilderment that fills our minds when we realize for the thousandth time that the person we love will not walk through the door. Our brains forget and remember over and over again. It's exhausting. Sometimes, we question our sanity. Why does this occur?

A well-known phrase in the field of neuroscience is, "Neurons that fire together wire together."[4] Neurons are a type of cell located in your brain and the other parts of your nervous system. Neurons in your brain share information via electrical signals or chemicals (neurotransmitters) with other neurons and various cells throughout your body. This communication is how we learn, develop habits, predict behavior, and function. This communication allows for automatic behaviors. When did you last need directions for driving to work from home or look for an instruction sheet on tying your shoes? Your neurons fire together so seamlessly and wire together so strongly that you barely think about those mundane tasks.

The neurons of your brain wire together in relationships as well. We form attachment bonds with our loved ones. Neuroscientists have identified regions of our brains that can track closeness to others. Those to whom we are attached are mapped out in our brains.[5] Your brain maps out that your spouse returns from work at 6 p.m. You know his pattern of taking off his

---

[4] This concept was presented in the groundbreaking research of Donald Hebb, often considered the father of neuropsychology.

[5] See Mary-Frances O'Connor, *The Grieving Brain: The Surprising Science of How We Learn from Love and Loss* (San Francisco: HarperOne, 2023).

shoes, walking through the house, calling your name, kissing you, and asking about your day. Your expectation of this is wired into your brain. You have come to expect it.

After a loss, our brains do not have the circuitry to understand what happened. It is simply incomprehensible the person no longer exists in physical form in our lives. The attachment bonds persist. Our brains are forced to begin the slow, emotionally painful process of rewiring to integrate the information that our loved ones are no longer within physical reach while still existing in our minds. We struggle to integrate the knowledge that he will no longer return from work as our brain has learned to expect. Mary-Frances O'Connor, an expert in the neurobiology of grief, summarizes the experience: "It is because your loved one existed that certain neurons fire together and certain proteins are folded in your brain in particular ways. It is because your loved one lived, and because you loved each other, that means when the person is no longer in the outer world, they still physically exist—in the wiring of the neurons of your brain."[6]

Keep this information in mind when we examine how to respond to someone who is grieving. We do not "get over" grief. Slowly, over time, our brains reorganize and restructure. But we are forever changed by the presence of the lost loved one. They are forever imprinted in our brains.

Impact of Grief

Grief can impact every area of our lives. There is no checklist of symptoms that everyone will experience the same way. Following are some commonly reported grief impacts; the list is not exhaustive:

---

[6] O'Connor, 49.

Emotional	Cognitive	Behavioral/Physical
Shock	Questioning	Withdrawing socially
Sadness	Self-blame	Avoidance of reminders
Fear	Forgetfulness	Restlessness
Anxiety	Difficulty focusing	Crying
Guilt	Confusion	Changes in eating patterns
Anger	Rumination	Tightness in throat/chest
Loneliness	Hallucinations	Stomach issues
Helplessness	Dreams	Tiredness/exhaustion
Relief	Thinking, "Am I crazy/losing my mind?"	Insomnia/sleep issues
Yearning	Awareness of one's mortality	Fluctuation in appetite
Emptiness/ numbness	Disbelief	Lack of motivation

People to whom you minister may have some or all of these symptoms as well as additional, unlisted symptoms.

The Many Faces of Grief and Loss

Grief is experienced not only in death but in a variety of painful and unwanted losses or changes. Loss can result from a variety of experiences:

- job loss or demotion
- retirement
- decline in health
- news of an incurable or terminal illness of yourself or a loved one

- empty nest
- divorce
- loss of a friendship
- loss of property (i.e., loss of a home to fire or foreclosure)

Recognizing Types of Grief and Loss

In working with grief, it is helpful to be aware of the various types of grief society may not acknowledge.

Anticipatory Grief

Anticipatory grief is when an individual grieves before the loss of his or her loved one. Family and friends of those dying of a terminal diagnosis experience anticipatory grief. This form of grief is particularly difficult for parents of terminally ill children. The term can also refer to a terminally ill patient grieving his or her own impending death.

Traumatic Grief

Traumatic grief is when trauma accompanies the grief. Some examples of traumatic grief may be the unexpected loss of a family member to a violent death or the loss of a child during childbirth. Those experiencing traumatic grief may have questions such as, "Why did this happen?" or "How could this have been prevented?"

Complicated Spiritual Grief

Related to the experience of traumatic grief is the concept of complicated spiritual grief, which may be experienced by the family and friends of someone who dies from a violent death. Burke and Neimeyer define complicated spiritual grief as "a sense of discord, conflict, and distance from God, and at times from members of the survivor's spiritual community."[7] The sudden loss and manner of death can precipitate a spiritual crisis that entails "resentment and doubt toward God," "dissatisfaction with the spiritual support received," and "substantial changes in the bereaved person's spiritual beliefs and behaviors."[8] In complicated spiritual grief, people may ask questions about the nature of God, God's love toward them, and where God is in the midst of suffering.

Ambiguous Loss

The term *ambiguous loss* was coined and defined by Pauline Boss. Boss defines the term as "a loss that remains unclear."[9] Boss identified the concept in the 1970s while investigating family stress and observing families who were intact, but the father was psychologically absent. This type of loss was also noted in studies of military families with a loved one missing in action.[10] Boss and other researchers later expanded the concept to include multiple types of ambiguous loss.

The ambiguity of this type of loss makes it difficult for loved ones to achieve a sense of resolution. Boss states, "The basic theoretical premise is that ambiguous loss is the most stressful loss because it defies resolution and creates confused perceptions about who is in or out of a particular family. With a clear-cut loss, there is more clarity—a death certificate, mourning rituals, and the opportunity to honor and dispose of remains. With ambiguous loss, none of these markers exists."[11]

---

[7] Laurie A. Burke and Robert A. Neimeyer, "Complicated Spiritual Grief I: Relation to Complicated Grief Symptomatology Following Violent Death Bereavement," *Death Studies* 38, no. 4 (April 2014): 259, https://doi.org/10.1080/07481187.2013.829372.

[8] Worden, *Grief Counseling and Grief Therapy*, 49.

[9] Pauline Boss, "Ambiguous Loss Theory: Challenges for Scholars and Practitioners," *Family Relations* 56, no. 2 (April 2007): 105, https://doi.org/10.1111/j.1741-3729.2007.00444.x.

[10] See Pauline Boss, "Ambiguous Loss Research, Theory, and Practice: Reflections after 9/11," *Journal of Marriage & Family* 66, no. 3 (August 2004): 551–66, https://doi.org/10.1111/j.0022-2445.2004.00037.x.

[11] Boss, 553.

There are two types of ambiguous loss. In the first type, the individual is physically absent but psychologically present, also referred to as "leaving without a goodbye."[12] One example is a missing person and uncertainty about whether the person is dead or alive. The person may be presumed dead, but there is no evidence. This loss may occur in a disappearance, kidnapping, or disaster. Ambiguous loss occurred on a large scale after the 9/11 attacks when multitudes of families and friends faced the devastating uncertainty of the fate of their missing loved ones.[13]

A second type of ambiguous loss is when an individual is psychologically absent but physically present. In other words, "goodbye without leaving."[14] Examples of this are with individuals who have experienced traumatic brain injury,[15] serious mental illness,[16] shaken baby syndrome/abusive head trauma,[17] addiction, dementia, severe cognitive impairment,[18] or chronic physical illness.[19]

In some situations, both types of ambiguous loss are experienced. For example, refugees awaiting asylum have been forced away from their homes and families (physically absent) but may also be psychologically absent due

---

[12] Boss, "Ambiguous Loss Theory," 105.

[13] See Boss, "Ambiguous Loss Research, Theory, and Practice."

[14] Boss, "Ambiguous Loss Theory," 105.

[15] See Jeffrey S. Kreutzer, Ana Mills, and Jennifer H. Marwitz, "Ambiguous Loss and Emotional Recovery after Traumatic Brain Injury," *Journal of Family Theory & Review* 8, no. 3 (September 2016): 386–97, https://doi.org/10.1111/jftr.12150.

[16] See Anne M. Williams-Wengerd and Catherine Solheim, "Grief Experiences in Parents of Adult Children with Serious Mental Illness," *Journal of Family Theory & Review* 13, no. 4 (December 2021): 528–49, https://doi.org/10.1111/jftr.12434.

[17] See Kimberly A. Powell and Amber Sorenson, "Ambiguous Loss after Shaken Baby Syndrome/Abusive Head Trauma: Parental Management of Dialectical Contradictions of Grief," *Communication Quarterly* 68, no. 3 (July 2020): 243–64, https://doi.org/10.1080/01463373.2020.1759112.

[18] See Neimeyer, *New Techniques of Grief Therapy*, 65–66.

[19] See Pauline Boss and Barbara A. Couden, "Ambiguous Loss from Chronic Physical Illness: Clinical Interventions with Individuals, Couples, and Families," *Journal of Clinical Psychology* 58, no. 11 (November 2002): 1351–60, https://doi.org/10.1002/jclp.10083.

to the stresses of the asylum-seeking process and the traumatic events that prompted the need to seek asylum.[20] Youth in foster care also experience complex, non-death ambiguous losses.[21]

Disenfranchised Grief

Disenfranchised grief refers to losses overlooked or silenced by society, such as a miscarriage or an empty nest.[22] The ambiguous losses we discussed previously may also be classified as disenfranchised because they are often overlooked or minimized by society. Mitchell summarizes five categories of disenfranchised loss:[23]

1. The significance of the loss is not recognized by society.[24] This occurs with non-death losses such as a move, retirement, or an empty nest. Death losses, such as a miscarriage, often go unrecognized.
2. The relationship is not acknowledged.[25] An example of this is the multiple losses sustained by those in foster care. The loss of a friend may also be minimized by society.
3. The type of loss is not acknowledged.[26] This can occur when someone leaves an abusive situation. The reaction may be "You are better off" without recognizing the severing of the relationship is a loss.

---

[20] See Damir S. Utržan and Andrea K. Northwood, "Broken Promises and Lost Dreams: Navigating Asylum in the United States," *Journal of Marital and Family Therapy* 43, no. 1 (January 2017): 5, https://doi.org/10.1111/jmft.12188.

[21] See Monique B. Mitchell, "'No One Acknowledged My Loss and Hurt': Non-Death Loss, Grief, and Trauma in Foster Care," *Child and Adolescent Social Work Journal* 35, no. 1 (February 2018): 1–9, https://doi.org/10.1007/s10560-017-0502-8.

[22] See Kenneth J. Doka, *Disenfranchised Grief: New Directions, Challenges, and Strategies for Practice* (Champaign, IL: Research Press, 2002).

[23] See Mitchell, "'No One Acknowledged My Loss and Hurt,'" 4–6.

[24] See Mitchell, 4.

[25] See Mitchell, 4.

[26] See Mitchell, 5.

4. An individual's grieving is overlooked, such as the grief of a child or an individual with cognitive disabilities.[27]
5. A community rejects the individual's grieving style.[28] This may include judgment or rejection of an individual's grieving process when he or she does not display the stereotype of what grief "should" involve.

When we minister to those with ambiguous and disenfranchised losses, we can provide care and practical help to those whose grief is largely ignored by society.

Prolonged Grief Disorder

Prolonged grief disorder was added to the 2022 update of the *Diagnostic and Statistical Manual* and is described as a "prolonged maladaptive grief reaction that can be diagnosed only after at least 12 months (6 months in children and adolescents)."[29] It is characterized by at least one month of daily or almost daily "intense yearning/longing for the deceased person" and/or "preoccupation with thoughts or memories of the deceased."[30]

Symptoms may present as follows, with diagnosis requiring at least three of the following to be present nearly every day for at least one month:

- Disruption in identity
- Disbelief about the death
- Avoidance of reminders that the loved one is dead
- Intense emotional pain
- Difficulty engaging in previous relationships, activities, interests, or planning for the future

---

[27] See Mitchell, 5.

[28] See Mitchell, 6.

[29] American Psychiatric Association, *Diagnostic and Statistical Manual of Mental Disorders*, 5th ed., Text Revision (*DSM-5-TR*) (American Psychiatric Association, 2022), 323. Hereinafter APA.

[30] APA, 323.

- Emotional numbness
- Feeling life is meaningless
- Feelings of intense loneliness[31]

To qualify for a diagnosis, these symptoms need to clearly exceed social, cultural, or religious norms and significantly impair functioning. Additionally, to qualify as prolonged grief disorder, they must not be attributed to another mental disorder, substance use, or a medical condition.

Concerns have been raised about the consideration of prolonged grief as a mental-health diagnosis. One may argue that it is unhelpful to pathologize grief, and this is a valid concern. On the other hand, the medical diagnosis enables individuals to receive medical coverage for the treatment of grief that is interfering with daily functioning over an extended period.

At times, grieving individuals will experience depression in addition to their grief response. There are some distinctions between grief and depression. Depression is more generalized than grief. Additionally, grief does not typically cause a loss of self-esteem in the way depression does. Another distinguishing factor of depression is that depressed individuals tend to have more negative appraisals of themselves and the world in general.[32] Finally, depression often seems to occur without warning, while grief is a normal response to loss.

Factors That Impact Grief

As mentioned previously, individuals experience grief in various ways. Researchers have identified certain factors that impact our experiences of grief. In his book *Grief Counseling and Grief Therapy*, Worden comprehensively discusses these factors or "mediators" of grief.[33] If the factors within these three groups are present, the grief experience may be complex.

---

[31] See APA, 335.

[32] See Worden, *Grief Counseling and Grief Therapy*, 37–38.

[33] Worden, 56–73.

Relational

The following questions are intended to explore the relational factors with the deceased individual that may impact grieving. Difficulties within the relationship or unresolved conflict may complicate the grief experience.

- What was the type of relationship (i.e., child, spouse)? Typically, the closer the relationship, the more intense the grief.
- Were there any unresolved or regretted conflicts in the relationship?

Situational

The following questions are intended to explore situational factors that may complicate the grieving process:

- Did the individual die by natural causes, accident, suicide, or homicide?
- Was this a sudden, unexpected, or violent/traumatic death? These types of deaths may cause additional difficulties in grieving, particularly those lost to a violent or traumatic death.
- Was the death considered preventable?
- Have there been multiple losses in a short period of time?
- Was the death an ambiguous or disenfranchised loss?

Individual

Consider the following questions to explore personal factors that impact grief:

- Is there any unresolved grief from previous losses?
- What coping skills does the individual have?
- Are there any unhelpful thinking patterns, such as rumination or self-blame?
- What is the individual's support system?

- What resources are available to the bereaved?
- What is the belief system of the bereaved?

Consider these questions when exploring the impact of grief so you can tailor interventions to the individual.

Conclusion

In this chapter, we defined various terms to describe the grieving process. The study of neurobiology provides insight into the painful process of grief and the holistic symptoms experienced by the bereaved. We explored types of grief that are often overlooked. Finally, we considered relational, situational, and individual factors that impact the grieving process. In the next chapter, we will examine theoretical models for understanding how we grieve.

Chapter 6

How We Grieve

The art of weaving tapestries fascinates me (Karen). Piles of thread are transformed into complex, intricate works of art. The process of grieving reminds me of weaving a tapestry. The type of fabric, colors, pattern, and size vary from person to person. The fabric may represent the type of loss you experienced, and the colors display your physical and emotional responses. The pattern you weave is based on your distinct mourning process. Your tapestry may include a large amount of red and orange thread, while another person's tapestry may include more blues and purples. There is no one correct color or design for a tapestry and no one correct way to grieve. There is no timeline for completion. You continue to add to the design throughout your life, typically working on it a lot at first and then less as time passes.

This chapter will explore several theories for understanding grief from a therapeutic perspective and identify common themes of the various approaches. Finally, we will explore the biblical practice of lament.

Models for Understanding Grief

Models exist to help us understand the process of grief, typical grief responses, and how we reconstruct life after loss. Models also assist those who are grieving by normalizing their experience. We will get an overview of some representative examples of grief models to provide a deeper understanding of how people experience the journey of grief.

Bowlby's Attachment Perspective

Attachment theorist John Bowlby developed one early grief model. Attachment is the emotional bond or connection you have with another person. These bonds begin in childhood through attachment with primary caregivers and are affected by whether or not those relationships are secure. Those early attachments impact adult relational attachment and coping. Bowlby theorized four stages in the grief process:[1]

1. **Numbness.** A person may feel shock or numbness after hearing of the death. Bowlby noted that this phase can be interrupted by "outbursts of extremely intense distress and/or anger," lasting from a few hours to a week.[2]
2. **Yearning and searching for the deceased.** This phase includes intense emotions, including extreme pining and distress that may last for months or years.[3]
3. **Disorganization and disorientation.** Life feels disorganized and disoriented after loss. The role once filled by the deceased is now vacant, leaving the bereaved trying to figure out how life will now

[1] See John Bowlby, *Loss: Sadness and Depression,* Attachment and Loss 3, rev. ed. (New York: Basic Books, 1982), 85.

[2] Bowlby, 85–86.

[3] See Bowlby, 86–93.

look. If the individual who is grieving has a history of insecure attachment, this stage may be complicated.[4]

4. **Reorganization.** This occurs when the bereaved adjusts to life without the deceased.[5]

Bowlby's insights provide the framework for understanding that grief is an attachment injury, and individuals with a history of attachment injuries may have a complicated grieving process.

Kübler-Ross

Elisabeth Kübler-Ross developed what is arguably the most well-known grief model based on her interviews with terminally ill patients during the 1960s. She introduced the model in her 1969 book *On Death and Dying.* You are likely familiar with this model due to its pervasive presence in pastoral and counselor training. Her model consists of five "stages":

1. Denial
2. Anger
3. Bargaining
4. Depression
5. Acceptance

Kübler-Ross contributed notable research and a grief model. She also emphasized dying people's experiences, needs, and dignity. Despite acknowledging the importance of her work, grief experts emphasize the model has limitations.[6]

---

[4] See Bowlby, 93–96.

[5] See Bowlby, 93–96.

[6] See Charles A. Corr, "Elisabeth Kübler-Ross and the 'Five Stages' Model in a Sampling of Recent Textbooks Published in 10 Countries Outside the United States," *Omega: Journal of Death and Dying* 83, no. 1 (May 2021): 33–63, https://doi.org/10.1177/0030222819840476.

One limitation of the model is that the research was conducted with terminally ill individuals. These individuals were grieving their own mortality and impending death. The model was also applied to the family members of the terminally ill and expanded to describe the process for those who are grieving the loss of a loved one.[7]

Stage models, in general, are critiqued due to the lack of empirical evidence that grief recovery follows a sequential pattern of certain stages.[8] Using a stage model might indicate a particular progression one must go through to have a "normal" grief experience. While stage model theorists may intend the models to be descriptive, they are often interpreted as prescriptive for a "normal" grief-response timeline, which is unhelpful for the grieving individual who may think he or she is grieving incorrectly.[9] There is no "right way" or particular order in which one must progress through grief. Some individuals may not experience one or more stages and may have experiences of grief beyond the five presented by Kübler-Ross or other stage models.

Based on contemporary research, grief experts are moving away from "stage" models to "process" and "task" models.[10] We will explore additional models that provide a better understanding of the grief experience. No model is a perfect representation, but all have points of importance in understanding the complexities of grief.

---

[7] See Margaret Stroebe, Henk Schut, and Kathrin Boerner, "Cautioning Health-Care Professionals: Bereaved Persons Are Misguided through the Stages of Grief," *Omega: Journal of Death and Dying* 74, no. 4 (March 2017): 461, https://doi.org/10.1177/0030222817691870.

[8] See Stroebe, Schut, and Boerner, 461.

[9] See Charles A. Corr, "Should We Incorporate the Work of Elisabeth Kübler-Ross in Our Current Teaching and Practice and, If So, How?" *Omega: Journal of Death and Dying* 83, no. 4 (September 2021): 716, https://doi.org/10.1177/0030222819865397.

[10] Corr, "Elisabeth Kübler-Ross and the 'Five Stages' Model," 57.

Worden's Four Tasks of Mourning

Task or process models of grief differ from stage models. Stage models indicate a certain progression, while task or process models provide greater flexibility in understanding the grief process. Worden developed a model outlining the four tasks of mourning:

> **Task 1:** Accept the reality of the loss. This includes intellectual and emotional acceptance that the individual is gone and will not return.[11]
> **Task 2:** Process the pain of grief. This involves feeling and processing feelings. The intensity of pain will vary among individuals.[12]
> **Task 3:** Adjust to a world without the deceased.[13] Worden notes three areas of adjustment: external, internal, and spiritual. External adjustments are ways the loss impacts daily life. Internal refers to how the loss affects one's sense of "self-definition, self-esteem, and sense of self-efficacy."[14] Spiritual adjustments are how the loss impacts "beliefs, values, and assumptions about the world."[15]
> **Task 4:** Find a way to remember the deceased while embarking on the rest of one's journey through life.[16] This involves remembering and staying connected with the deceased while moving forward with life. Worden notes this is often the most challenging task for grieving individuals to accomplish, thus potentially becoming a stuck point.

When considering these tasks, remember these are not linear stages such that we begin with task 1 and progress through task 4, checking off each task as "completed" when done. Instead, while there is a general order to the tasks, a grieving individual may revisit each task numerous times and even

---

[11] See J. William Worden, *Grief Counseling and Grief Therapy: A Handbook for the Mental Health Practitioner*, 5th ed. (New York: Springer, 2018), 43–46.

[12] See Worden, 46–47.

[13] See Worden, 47–50.

[14] Worden, 48.

[15] Worden, 47.

[16] See Worden, 50–52.

work on multiple tasks simultaneously. Working on each task is essential in working through grief.[17]

The Dual Process Model (DPM)

Process models recognize grief as nonlinear. Consideration is given to the holistic impact of the grief experience and the integration of the loss into one's life. We will focus on one process model, the dual process model (DPM), developed by Margaret Stroebe and Henk Schut.[18] The model was built on several previous models and provides a comprehensive, holistic understanding of grief.[19]

According to the dual process model, the bereaved face two main categories of life stressors in their everyday experience of coping with grief:

1. **Loss orientation.** This includes processing stressors related to the actual loss.[20] We typically consider these areas "processing the grief" or "grief work." In this orientation, the grieving individual is focusing on the loss. The bereaved may long for his or her deceased loved one and their life together, mourning what was lost.[21]
2. **Restoration orientation.** This aspect includes processing stressors and changes caused by the loss.[22] For example, if the spouse of a

---

[17] See Worden, 43.

[18] See Margaret Stroebe and Henk Schut, "The Dual Process Model of Coping with Bereavement: Rationale and Description," *Death Studies* 23, no. 3 (May 4, 1999): 197–224.

[19] See Jennifer Fiore, "A Systematic Review of the Dual Process Model of Coping with Bereavement (1999–2016)," *Omega: Journal of Death and Dying* 84, no. 2 (December 2021): 415, https://doi.org/10.1177/0030222819893139.

[20] See Margaret Stroebe and Henk Schut, "The Dual Process Model of Coping with Bereavement: A Decade On," *Omega: Journal of Death and Dying* 61, no. 4 (May 2010): 277, https://doi.org/10.2190/OM.61.4.b.

[21] See Stroebe and Schut, "The Dual Process Model of Coping with Bereavement: Rationale and Description," 212–13.

[22] See Stroebe and Schut, "The Dual Process Model of Coping with Bereavement: A Decade On," 277.

> stay-at-home mom dies, the widow will likely need to seek employment to provide for her family. Additionally, the family may need to relocate to a less-expensive home to reduce mortgage and home-ownership expenses. The family must also adjust to having one parent available for the children rather than two parents.[23]

Stroebe and Schut assert that an individual moves in and out or "oscillates" between the stressors of the two orientations (loss and restoration). At times, the bereaved may focus on the loss. At other times, the focus is on restoration and readjusting to life.

Moving back and forth (oscillating) between the two is viewed as necessary for adaptive coping. Over time, the individual will spend more time in the restoration orientation.[24] Stroebe and Schut emphasize, "One cannot cope the whole time. It is exhausting to do so a lot of the time; time off is needed, where nonbereavement related activities are followed or when the person simply relaxes and recuperates."[25]

After developing the original theory, Stroebe and Schut adjusted it to include the concept of stressor "overload," in which a person perceives they can no longer cope. In the loss orientation, this may occur if an individual experiences multiple consecutive losses. In the restoration orientation, this may happen if there are too many stressors related to engaging in life after the loss. Adding the concept of overload enhanced this theory by emphasizing the need to assess for preexisting stressors and to address the complications of overload when working with the bereaved.[26]

Research indicates the DPM provides a picture of how we grieve. Cantwell-Bartl summarizes the strengths of this model as one that

---

[23] See Margaret Stroebe and Henk Schut, "Overload: A Missing Link in the Dual Process Model?" *Omega: Journal of Death and Dying* 74, no. 1 (November 2016): 99, https://doi.org/10.1177/0030222816666540.

[24] See Stroebe and Schut, "The Dual Process Model of Coping with Bereavement: A Decade On," 282.

[25] Stroebe and Schut, "Overload: A Missing Link in the Dual Process Model?" 99.

[26] See Stroebe and Schut, "Overload."

"encompasses individual ways of coping, different styles of grieving, periods of rest from grieving, and a biopsychosocial perspective."[27]

The model has been researched and found effective with various ages and types of grief. A few examples are working with perinatal loss,[28] the death of a spouse,[29] grieving children,[30] parents of a child with a life-threatening disability,[31] and non-death (or non-life-threatening) losses such as reentry of missionaries.[32]

Meaning Reconstruction

Another significant aspect of grief is making meaning of one's life after loss, also known as "meaning reconstruction." Neimeyer asserts, "A central process in grieving is the attempt to reaffirm or reconstruct a world of meaning that has been challenged by loss."[33] The ability to make meaning of the loss

---

[27] Annie Cantwell-Bartl, "Grief and Coping of Parents Whose Child Has a Constant Life-Threatening Disability, Hypoplastic Left Heart Syndrome with Reference to the Dual-Process Model," *Death Studies* 42, no. 9 (October 2018): 570, https://doi.org/10.1080/07481187.2017.1407380.

[28] See Ellen Shannon and Brett D. Wilkinson, "The Ambiguity of Perinatal Loss: A Dual-Process Approach to Grief Counseling," *Journal of Mental Health Counseling* 42, no. 2 (April 2020): 140–54, https://doi.org/10.17744/mehc.42.2.04.

[29] See Marie Lundorff et al., "How Do Loss- and Restoration-Oriented Coping Change across Time? A Prospective Study on Adjustment Following Spousal Bereavement," *Anxiety, Stress & Coping: An International Journal* 32, no. 3 (May 2019): 270–85, https://doi.org/10.1080/10615806.2019.1587751.

[30] See Darlene Green, Kacie Karafa, and Stephanie Wilson, "Art Therapy with Grieving Children: Effect on Affect in the Dual-Process Model," *Art Therapy: Journal of the American Art Therapy Association* 38, no. 4 (October 2021): 211–15, https://doi.org/10.1080/07421656.2020.1823197.

[31] See Cantwell-Bartl, "Grief and Coping of Parents Whose Child Has a Constant Life-Threatening Disability," 569–78.

[32] See Susan Selby et al., "Cross-Cultural Re-Entry for Missionaries: A New Application for the Dual Process Model," *Omega: Journal of Death and Dying* 62, no. 4 (2010): 329–51, https://doi.org/10.2190/OM.62.4.b.

[33] Robert A. Neimeyer, "Meaning Reconstruction in the Wake of Loss: Evolution of a Research Program," *Behaviour Change* 33, no. 2 (June 2016): 66, https://doi.org/10.1017/bec.2016.4.

mediates the risk of complicated grief.[34] Meaning reconstruction focuses on an individual's life narrative or life story.

Meaning reconstruction provides an opportunity to process two narratives. The first narrative is the "event story" of the loss and how that impacts life moving forward. The second narrative is the "backstory" of an individual's relationship with the deceased, including the attachment history and unfinished business.[35] The opportunity to explore the backstory is helpful in all forms of loss but can be particularly useful in sudden or traumatic loss.[36] For the Christian, there is an opportunity to explore how God was working in one's life before the loss and how he continues to work after the loss.

Common Themes

We gained helpful knowledge from all the models we overviewed. Let's review some common themes and strengths of the models. Then, we will incorporate the spiritual aspect of grief more fully through the lens of lament.

Common themes of the models are the response to loss, processing the grief, and integration of the loss into daily life.

- Response to the loss (emotional/psychological, physical, relational, spiritual)
  - — Shock, disbelief, confusion: "Can this really be happening?"
  - — Overwhelming emotion: "How will I make it through this pain?"
  - — Questioning, anger: "Why did this happen?"

[34] See Robert A. Neimeyer, "What's New in Meaning Reconstruction? Advancing Grief Theory and Practice," *Grief Matters: The Australian Journal of Grief & Bereavement* 23, no. 1 (January 2020): 4.

[35] See Robert A. Neimeyer, ed., *New Techniques of Grief Therapy: Bereavement and Beyond* (New York: Taylor & Francis, 2022), 4.

[36] See Neimeyer, "What's New in Meaning Reconstruction?" 8.

- Sense of abandonment
- Processing grief
    - Realization of the loss
    - Identifying and processing emotion
    - Working through unresolved relational issues
- Integration of the loss into the life of the bereaved
    - The need to continue daily life while processing grief
    - Meaning making
    - Adjusting to life after loss
    - Remembering the deceased

From the dual process model, we learned that the grieved individual moves (or oscillates) between the tasks of processing grief and integrating the loss.

Biblical Perspective of Grief and Lament

Lament provides a space and structure to express complex, agonizing, and bewildering thoughts and emotions to God. Lament allows us to express our complaints, struggles, confusion, and requests. By doing so, we reduce the negative impact of holding those thoughts and feelings inside ourselves.

Lament is a way to pray and petition God in times of crisis. Ellington describes prayers of lament: "Such prayers are born from devastation when safety is replaced by turmoil. We find them in those places where our defenses against chaos have been breached and our resources for coping overwhelmed. Feelings of pain, fear, confusion, and outrage drive lament prayers. They are the fruit not of quiet reflection, but of pressing need."[37]

[37] Scott A. Ellington, *Risking Truth: Reshaping the World through Prayers of Lament*, Princeton Theological Monograph Series 98 (Eugene, OR: Pickwick, 2008), 155.

Lament is an act of faith and hope when we feel abandoned and hopeless. Prayers of lament allow us to experience loss within our relationship with our Creator.

We see Jesus lamenting over Jerusalem (Matthew 23:37–39; Luke 13:34–35) and over the death of Lazarus (John 11:33–35). Throughout the Psalms, we see expressions of individual and corporate lament, providing a rich theology of suffering.[38]

Complaint is a significant aspect of lament. We tend to avoid the concept of complaint, but we need to consider its use as part of a healthy grief response. In Scripture, we see the Israelites chastised by God for their complaints (Numbers 11–14). Yet, throughout Scripture, we also see examples of individuals expressing their complaints to God. Kellemen distinguishes between the two forms of complaint seen in Scripture. He states, "Biblical complaint complains *to* God about the fallen world. Ungodly complaint complains *about* God and accuses Him of lacking goodness, holiness, and wisdom."[39]

Prayers of lament move us toward increased intimacy with God. Torr summarizes the structure of lament while noting that not all steps are present in every passage:[40]

1. Address: Make your address to God.
2. Complaint: Communicate your emotions and thoughts.
3. Confession of trust: The lamenter expresses trust in God.
4. Petition: Express to God your request.
5. Vow of praise: A commitment is made to praise God.

---

[38] See Ann Ahrens, *Suffering, Soul Care, and Community: The Place of Lament in Corporate Worship* (Eugene, OR: Wipf & Stock, 2023).

[39] Robert Kellemen, *God's Healing for Life's Losses: How to Find Hope When You're Hurting* (Winona Lake, IN: BMH Books, 2010), 32.

[40] Stephen C. Torr, "A Winnicottian Approach to Biblical Lament: Developing a True Self in the Midst of Suffering," *Journal of Psychology and Theology* 47, no. 1 (March 2019): 52, https://doi.org/10.1177/0091647118795184.

Let's examine a brief psalm of lament (Psalm 13) and observe the structure. Note that the order is different, but all stages of lament are present.

David begins by addressing God.

> How long, LORD? (v. 1)

Next, he launches his complaint in a series of four questions expressing his sense of abandonment, anxiety, and defeat.

> Will you forget me forever?
> How long will you hide your face from me?
> How long will I store up anxious concerns within me,
> agony in my mind every day?
> How long will my enemy dominate me? (vv. 1–2)

He petitions God with a request.

> Consider me and answer, LORD my God.
> Restore brightness to my eyes;
> otherwise, I will sleep in death.
> My enemy will say, "I have triumphed over him,"
> and my foes will rejoice because I am shaken. (vv. 3–4)

David confesses his trust.

> But I have trusted in your faithful love;
> my heart will rejoice in your deliverance. (v. 5)

He vows to praise God.

> I will sing to the LORD
> because he has treated me generously. (v. 6)

In Scripture, we see both individual and corporate expressions of lament. Integrating corporate lament in worship can assist Christians in learning how to utilize this practice in their grief journeys. Lament is a valuable tool to incorporate in ministering to grieving people.

Five Things to Remember about Grief

1. Grief is not linear. There are no clearly defined, neat stages.
2. Grief is hard work and can be overwhelming at times.
3. Grief impacts every area of life: spiritual, emotional/psychological, physical, and relational.
4. Grief may take longer than expected. While the bereaved may improve over time, an anniversary or reminder of the person can engulf the individual in a fresh wave of emotions.
5. Lament is a biblical, helpful way to express one's grief to God.

Conclusion

In summary, each person weaves his or her unique tapestry of grief. Grief models assist us in understanding grief and normalizing the experiences of the bereaved, but there is no one-size-fits-all description. There is no substitute for considering the uniqueness of each individual and how that impacts his or her grieving process. In the next chapter, we will explore practical ways of ministering to the bereaved.

Chapter 7

Helping Those Who Are Grieving

Grief is unpredictable, with no two experiences alike. For the first few years, it can be a roller coaster with many ups and downs. We are mistaken to compare our journeys through grief with another person's. Our grief journeys are so intricately woven together in such a way that many factors influence the intensity and duration of our grief.

Years ago, I (Brooke) had a client, whom I will call Sharon, who lost her husband. She would come in for counseling consistently, then I wouldn't hear from her for a few months. One day, she would randomly schedule an appointment, then come frequently for a while, then vanish again for a few months. There came a time when we discussed what was going on. It turns out Sharon would quit counseling because she felt she needed to "be okay" without it. When I asked her about her expectations for so soon after her loss, she referenced a few people in her life, including a neighbor who had also lost her husband. After six months, Sharon's neighbor had already moved on and begun dating. My client reasoned that if her neighbor could move on in six months, she should have already moved on since it had been a year. She also expressed frustration at well-intentioned friends who had begun trying to set her up on dates. Each one's journey through grief differs and should occur on that person's timeline. We never know what other factors might be impacting a person's grief or even if the person is doing as well as she appears.

Dealing with Our Own Grief

In preparing to help others heal from their losses in life, we need to make sure we have dealt with our own losses and are prepared for the intense emotions that accompany grief. Before ministering to others, we encourage you to reflect on the following:

- The first death you remember, your age, and feelings at the time
- The first funeral you attended, your age, and what you remember
- The most recent death you experienced and how you coped
- The most difficult loss and why
- The most difficult death you have experienced in your life and why it was so difficult
- How you typically cope with loss
- How you know when your grief is resolved
- When you think it is appropriate to share your experience of grief with others[1]

After reflecting on these experiences, it may be helpful to process your experiences with a friend, mentor, or in some cases, a counselor. Working through your own experiences with grief produces a greater awareness of how your own losses impact you. This awareness will serve you well when you are ministering to others who have stories that are personal to you.

---

[1] Adapted from Norman Wright's *The Complete Guide to Crisis and Trauma Counseling* (Ventura, CA: Regal, 2011), 241–42.

The Power of Presence

In Job 2:11–13, Job's friends were off to a solid start. They came from a distance to be with their friend in his time of need because they cared for him. They mourned with him and were present with him in his suffering without speaking for a week. In chapter 4, however, the situation shifts when one of Job's friends begins speaking out. Job's friend appears to rationalize the situation by making assumptions about the cause of Job's suffering. I'm not sure this was helpful to Job in that moment.

We can search for answers, but most of the time, we'll come up short. There are things we will never understand while living on this earth. When tragedy strikes, there are no words sufficient to bring comfort. In many cases, in our desire to fix things or alleviate the pain, we may unintentionally say things that are offensive. In some cases, those who are grieving are looking for permission to feel the way they do or to have their feelings normalized. Or they are simply looking for someone to be present with them in their distress.

Remember: it is better to say nothing than to say something inappropriate. There seems to be something about our human nature that causes us to say things that are inappropriate and insensitive. Most of us have been on both the giving and receiving end of this.

There was a lady who lost her husband and was trying to start the process of moving forward without him. Her first Sunday back at church, she went into the couples' small group that she and her husband had attended together. Someone asked why she was in the couples' class. These were her people. She was looking for a place where she felt comfortable with familiar faces. This question was not helpful.

Avoid Clichés

Stay away from clichés, even the faith-based ones. Remarks such as "At least she's in a better place" or "God needed another flower for his garden" are not helpful in the grieving process. These comments often come from a place of trying to alleviate the pain and our own discomfort around someone else's suffering. When grief is stifled, the healing process is hindered. Giving others space to express their pain and sadness can allow them to process their feelings in a healthy manner.

During times of grief and loss, Romans 8:28 is often given as a source of encouragement. While it is true that God does work all things together for good for those who love him, in the early stages of grief, people are still trying to make sense of their situation at an emotional level. They are not in a place to process at a logical level. They need someone to connect with their emotional experience, validate it, and help them normalize their journey through grief.

Designate Someone to Help with Communication

While text messaging can be an efficient method for communication, receiving a large volume of texts can be overwhelming. During a time of loss, people reach out via texting with the best of intentions. They want to communicate their care and concern for us and offer help. Although these gestures may bring comfort, we can easily become overwhelmed by the obligation of responding to each person. In the aftermath of grief, we typically do not have the emotional bandwidth needed to respond to every single text.

A designated spokesperson for the family can help mitigate confusion and overwhelm from the concerned people around them. The family can appoint a single person who will be responsible for communicating plans, needs, and relevant details to family and friends. This will allow for a more organized approach to serving the family in their time of need without placing undue burden on them.

Do Not Expect Them to Reach Out for Help

One of the most well-intentioned statements we make to people in grief or crisis is "If you need anything, call me." Few people will actually take us up on this, even if we are sincere. In some cases, they may not have positive experiences with people following through on their offers to help. Other times, they may not be sure what kind of help they can request. When we say "anything," do we mean a trip to the grocery store, babysitting the kids, yard work . . . literally anything? They may be afraid of asking for too much. It might be beneficial to encourage them to make a list of helpful tasks that someone could complete for them. I (Brooke) have a friend who does this well. During her husband's yearslong health struggles, she would put together a list of ways her friends and family could help, leading up to and following a major surgery or medical procedure. I loved being able to look at the list, determine what I could commit to that week, and follow through. I knew I was helping in a way she needed.

Think about the Long-Term

People often check in frequently with the bereaved in the beginning, then move on with their lives. Many times, though, it is at this point that reality begins to truly hit the bereaved and they need our help the most. Unfortunately, they are left feeling alone to navigate the complexities of grief. To mitigate this, we can put a monthly notification on our calendars for the first few years to check in with them. These reminders will help us to continue caring for the bereaved in their moments of need.[2]

Realistic Expectations during the Grieving Process

As illustrated by the example in the introduction to this chapter, we cannot compare our grief journeys to another person's. Each person's grief will look different depending on the type of loss, the nature of the loss, the relationship with what was lost, and other life circumstances coinciding with the loss. With the understanding that our grief journeys are likely to vary, we want to encourage the bereaved to have realistic expectations for

---

[2] See Wright, 245.

the grieving process. Time frames for healing and recovery may vary for each person.

Journaling

Expressive writing related to losses we have experienced is most beneficial when it is directed. When there is no direction for journaling, those who have experienced losses may not write about topics that are healing. In some cases, journaling may lead to maladaptive coping behaviors or a downward spiral of despair. Having a person journal about how he has made sense of the loss can reduce his level of grief, depression, or PTSD. A person may reflect on how she made sense of the loss at the time it happened and how that compares with how she makes sense of it now. She may also consider the impact of her worldview on her loss, especially as it relates to her theological beliefs. Reflecting on how the loss has changed the trajectory of a person's life, along with how the future might look different, can be an important component in making sense of the loss.[3]

Another helpful journaling activity involves discovering the treasure in grief and loss.[4] For example, you can use the following journal prompts:

- How have your priorities changed as a result of the loss?
- What have you noticed about your resiliency during this difficult time?
- What have you been surprised by in how you have navigated the grief journey?

We also want to reflect on lessons in love and living that we learned from the loss, along with any increase in gratitude. Being able to journal about

[3] See Wendy Lichtenthal and Robert Neimeyer, *Techniques in Grief Therapy: Creative Practices for Counseling the Bereaved*, ed. Robert Neimeyer (New York: Routledge, 2012), 165–66.

[4] See Peter Scazzero, *Emotionally Healthy Discipleship: Moving from Shallow Christianity to Deep Transformation* (Grand Rapids: Zondervan, 2021), 110–11.

how we have made sense of a loss and look for any hidden treasure can lead to growth following a loss.[5]

Designated Crying Time

In the weeks following a loss, there is much business that needs to be addressed, including many decisions that have to be made. During these days, many report feeling as though they cannot stop crying long enough to take care of anything. Crying is a typical response of grief, and as such, we do not want to stifle its expression.

As people are trying to pick up the pieces and find their new normal in life, we can help them balance the process and expression of grief with the need to complete important tasks. One way to address this is to encourage them to have a designated crying time each day. Have the person set aside time each day just to cry. For some, thirty minutes is sufficient, while others may require more or less time. In going through their daily tasks, if they feel as though they are about to break down, they can remind themselves to save it for their designated crying time later. This allows them to take the time to grieve without stifling its expression while being able to accomplish other things. Many clients have reported that this helped them to focus during the day while still being able to express their sadness.

Be on the Lookout for the Following

Excessive Busyness

Although it can be a good sign when the bereaved begins to resume daily life activities, there should be a balance between taking time to grieve and returning to life. A person may keep themselves busy to avoid dealing with the intense emotions that come with grief. If you notice signs of excessive working or business trips, you might examine this behavior with your client.

---

[5] See Lichtenthal and Neimeyer, *Techniques in Grief Therapy*, 165–66.

Impulsive Decision-Making

As discussed in chapter 2, a crisis can serve as a turning point in life. A major loss can cause us to reevaluate our priorities, which can lead to major life changes. For some, this may be a career change, a move to another state, or a major sale or purchase, perhaps of a house or a business. Depending on the circumstances, some major changes may be unavoidable. Quick decisions may be necessary due to finances or other extenuating circumstances. When possible, we want to encourage a waiting period before making a life-changing decision.

In the aftermath of grief, we often feel as though we are surrounded by a fog and unable to see clearly. Although difficult, waiting for the fog to clear allows time for God to prepare us for the next chapter in life. As Peter Scazzero says in *Emotionally Healthy Discipleship*, "Waiting on God in the midst of loss defies human instincts and quick solutions. It runs contrary to Western culture and our own bent toward self-will. That is why we so desperately need the Holy Spirit to sustain us in these times."[6]

A Return to Old Sins and Bad Habits

As with any crisis, the intensity of grief can send the bereaved into relapse. If there are past struggles with substance use, pornography, or other maladaptive coping mechanisms, the temptation to return to old patterns will likely be stronger in the face of grief or crisis. During this time, we should encourage the bereaved to increase their support in this area. They can find an accountability partner or support group to help them develop a plan for when they are tempted to engage in these unhealthy behaviors. We also want to work with them on increasing healthy coping mechanisms, such as exercise, journaling, or relying on their support team from church.

---

[6] Scazzero, *Emotionally Healthy Discipleship*, 123.

A False Narrative about the Person Lost

When we lose someone we love, it is easy to fall into one of two extremes. Either we overly idealize the person and put him or her on a pedestal, or we vilify the person and remember the negative. We all have both good and bad in us. None of us is perfect.

To balance the memories of the deceased, encourage the bereaved to consider the following:

- the things about the person they want to keep and pass on
- the things they would like to change
- the things they want to discard

This activity can help the bereaved reflect on the good things they remember about the person, along with the less-than-desirable attributes possessed by the deceased.

Other Considerations

Conflicted Grief

Occasionally, after losing a loved one, we may discover something about the person that does not line up with what we thought we knew about him or her. Perhaps there were secrets that were disclosed after the person's death, or the person may have been caught in sin and took his or her own life as a result. These situations are devastating, to say the least, complicated by the fact that we are unable to confront the person for clarity.

For some of us, we are able to better reconcile the cognitive dissonance between who we thought the person was and their secret sins if we can understand why. Clarification of the person's actions does not resolve the discord, but it does help us to understand and, in some cases, have compassion. In this situation, closure is unlikely. Years ago, I was part of a community processing a similar situation. One of our community leaders was well-respected and loved by everyone. Following his death, we discovered secrets that were contrary to the person known by the community. In the aftermath of the discovery, someone close to the deceased remarked that he was having a hard time because he really thought he knew this person, but he was not sure anymore. My colleague spoke to this person and said, "Why couldn't he be both?"

Up until that moment, I had never thought much about that, but it does speak to the reality of our fallen world. As Richard Winter says, "Accepting that we are glorious ruins, with great dignity and profound depravity, is part of the tension of living in a fallen world."[7] We all have secret sins, although some are more socially acceptable than others, but we have a Savior who will perfect us when we meet him face-to-face.

Conclusion

Grief can be a long and winding journey. Resolving our own losses will equip us to walk more effectively with others through loss. Words are often inadequate in helping those who are grieving. Our presence can be the best source of comfort while we use wisdom in when to speak and what to say.

Additional Resources

Kellemen, Robert. *God's Healing for Life's Losses.* Winona Lake, IN: BMH Books, 2010. This short book discusses a biblical response to grief and includes directed journaling prompts.

[7] Richard Winter, *Perfecting Ourselves to Death: The Pursuit of Excellence and the Perils of Perfectionism* (Downers Grove, IL: InterVarsity, 2005), 156.

Part 4
Suicide

Chapter 8

Assessing, Preventing, and Responding to Suicide

There are moments in life that are impossible to prepare for. We can rehearse and agonize all we want, but when that moment comes, none of our preparation seems sufficient. Few incidents in life create as many unanswered questions and regrets, nor as much confusion and devastation, as suicide.

Not too long ago, I (Brooke) was asked to attend a special-called meeting to work alongside other counselors in helping a church, including its staff, process a recent suicide. A young man had hung himself at church during the Wednesday night activities. A few of the staff members had found the young man and attempted to resuscitate him but failed. Half of the church staff who had been present when the incident occurred were also some of my undergraduate students, which means they were young and, in some cases, newly married. I found myself wondering how I would have handled this situation at their age.

In the following days, weeks, and months, they would work through the grief and trauma that followed. Their entire church and ministry staff had been traumatized by the event. They were trying to take care of themselves, while ministering to their church family, including the family of the young man who had taken his own life. It is also worth mentioning that this church and many of its members were still dealing with the devastation left behind by Hurricane Ida, the category 4 storm that had ripped through southern Louisiana a few months earlier.

Research conducted in 2017 indicated that around 69 percent of pastors had heard about one or more suicides in their local communities in the previous year, with almost 40 percent saying the suicide had been connected to their church. Of 1,000 pastors surveyed, only 41 percent reported having any formal training in suicide prevention. Unfortunately, among Protestant churchgoers, about 55 percent believe people are more likely to gossip about the suicide than to reach out to the family in support.[1] The church should be a safe haven for those who are contemplating suicide and those who have survived the loss of a loved one due to suicide.

Who's at Risk?

In 2019, there were 47,511 deaths by suicide, which is about one every eleven minutes. It was the second-leading cause of death for those 10–34 years of age, fourth for 35–44, fifth for 45–54, and the eighth-leading cause of death for ages 55–64. Some occupations may carry a higher risk of suicide, especially those with high stress, low job security, and low pay.[2]

Among females, the highest suicide rate was for those aged 45–64, while 75 and older held the highest rate among men.[3] Those who graduate

---

[1] See "Suicide and the Church," Lifeway Research (2017), 7, 9, 23, http://research.lifeway.com/wp-content/uploads/2017/09/Suicide-and-the-Church-Research-Study-Report.pdf.

[2] See "Suicide and Occupation," Centers for Disease Control and Prevention, https://www.cdc.gov/niosh/stress/suicide/index.html.

[3] See "Suicide Is a Leading Cause of Death in the United States," National Institute of Mental Health, updated June 2022, https://www.nimh.nih.gov/health/statistics/suicide#part_10459.

from college and those who have been married are at a lower risk than those who didn't finish college or never married. Also at greater risk are those who live below the federal poverty threshold.[4] Previous research indicated that Protestants have the highest suicide rates in the US, followed by Roman Catholics and Jewish individuals. However, studies have indicated that greater religious devotion decreases the risk of suicide.[5]

The Faces of Suicide

Examine the life of any person with suicidal thoughts, and you are likely to find a person stuck in a pit of despair, feeling completely hopeless. How does a person come to feel so hopeless that he desires to take his own life? This feeling often begins with an accumulation of negative life events. These events are accompanied by a downward spiral of negative thought patterns and self-blame with a feeling of inability to change the situation. Moving out of this dark place requires hope.[6]

In *Atlas of the Heart*, Brené Brown offers the following explanation of hope: "We need hope like we need air. To live without hope is to risk suffocating on hopelessness and despair, risk being crushed by the belief that there is no way out of what is holding us back, no way to get to what we desperately need. But hope is not what most of us think it is. It is not a warm, fuzzy emotion that fills us with a sense of possibility. Hope is a way of thinking—a cognitive process."[7] Hope is what allows us to conceptualize alternatives and plan for the future. It helps us adjust and get back on track

---

[4] See Robert Herpen, "CDC: Geographic, Socioeconomic Factors Linked to Suicidal Behaviors in Adults," Healio.com, January 6, 2022, https://www.healio.com/news/psychiatry/20220106/cdc-geographic-socioeconomic-factors-linked-to-suicidal-behaviors-in-adults.

[5] See Robin Gearing and Dana Alonzo, "Religion and Suicide: New Findings," *Journal of Religion and Health* 57 (May 7, 2018): 2478–99. Available online at https://link.springer.com/article/10.1007/s10943-018-0629-8.

[6] See Brené Brown, *Atlas of the Heart: Mapping Meaningful Connection and the Language of Human Experience* (New York: Random House, 2021), 101–3.

[7] Brown, 97.

when things do not go as planned. Determining a person's level of hopefulness and finding ways to inspire hope are key components of suicide assessment and intervention.

It is difficult to pinpoint one specific cause of suicide. Often, a person's decision to take his or her own life is made up of an intricate set of factors. There is no magic formula. Although a family may have multiple members who die by suicide, a genetic predisposition for suicide has not been identified. However, there are a number of environmental factors that increase a person's risk of suicide, along with unmet psychological needs. Certain protective factors may decrease the likelihood a person with risk factors may die by suicide.

For some people, a recent loss, such as the death of a spouse, a child, or a best friend, could trigger thoughts of suicide. A major financial or job loss can also be critical. In this situation, the risk may increase if the loss is sudden or unexpected. When helping those who are recovering from a loss, we should be alert to comments such as "I told the Lord that if I didn't wake up tomorrow, I would be fine with that."

Any person who has lost physical ability, especially those left with chronic, relentless pain following an accident or medical crisis, may also be at risk. Because she is unable to do many of the things she did previously, she may struggle with finding purpose in life. She may believe herself to be a burden to her family and that they would be better off without her. Those who lack mental capacity whether due to a brain injury or mental-health condition may also be at risk. Substance use can reduce mental capacity and increase the intensity of suicidal thoughts. More than one in three people who die from suicide are under the influence of alcohol at the time of their death.[8]

When a person is in a deep place of desperation and hopelessness, suicide has been used as a form of revenge. Suicide is also not uncommon

[8] See "Risk of Suicide," National Alliance on Mental Illness, https://www.nami.org/About-Mental-Illness/Common-with-Mental-Illness/Risk-of-Suicide.

following a conflictual breakup; in some cases, this may include a murder-suicide.[9] There are also a number of psychological needs not being met. The person's need for love, acceptance, or belonging has been averted.[10] We see this with victims of bullying and divorce.

In recent years, we have seen suicides by leaders who are avoiding shame, defeat, humiliation, or disgrace, such as ministry leaders who have fallen into a pit of sin. We see this in the news when major scandals have been exposed. They could not see another way out, other than suicide.

Helping the Suicidal Person and the Affected Family

Engage and Connect

We want to be intentional, calm, and understanding with the suicidal person. In this moment, he or she needs empathy and validation. It is not the time to argue with the individual. If we engage in a debate with someone considering suicide, we risk losing both the debate and the person. Rather than trying to show him or her why things are not as bad as they seem or how you know things will get better soon, it is better to ask constructive questions. This will help to clarify the nature of the situation and ways we can offer support.

Assess and Prevent

Following are some simple assessments that can help determine a person's risk of suicide. If a person has attempted suicide before, the DIRT assessment should be used.

---

[9] See Tim Clinton, Archibald Hart, and George Ohlschlager, *Caring for People God's Way: Personal and Emotional Issues, Addictions, Grief, and Trauma* (Nashville: Thomas Nelson, 2005), 349.

[10] See Edwin Shneidman, *The Suicidal Mind* (New York: Oxford University Press, 1996), 25.

DIRT

D—Dangerous

How dangerous was the previous suicide attempt? Previous suicide attempts should not be minimized; however, higher levels of lethality, such as a firearm, indicate a higher risk for another attempt. In essence, the greater the danger in the attempt, the higher the current level of risk that the suicide is going to occur. A more lethal attempt, such as the use of a firearm, would elevate the risk significantly.

I—Impression

In reflecting on the previous suicide attempt, what was the person's expressed perception of the event? Did she honestly believe her actions would end her life? Or was it intended to be a cry for help? If the person seemed surprised to be alive after the attempt, then the present level of risk is much higher.

R—Rescue

Was the person in a situation in which he was likely to be rescued? It could be that the attempt took place shortly before he knew his wife would be home or his coworker would return from lunch. In these cases, there was a possibility that a person could come in and call for help before it was too late. It may also be the case that the person had everything for his plan in place and then called for help. Or maybe he overdosed on some type of medication and then called for an ambulance. If the probability of being rescued was high, or if the person participated in his own rescue, the present risk level is lower.

T—Time

How long ago was suicide attempted? The more recent the attempt, the higher the current level of risk. A person may show signs of improvement after a suicidal crisis, but that does not mean the threat is over. The person who attempted suicide in the last week or month remains at a high level of risk. However, if a person states that she attempted suicide ten years ago, you may consider her a low risk unless other DIRT indicators are high. Being suicidal once does not necessarily mean being suicidal forever.

If a person has never attempted suicide before and is having suicidal thoughts, the SLAP assessment should be used.

SLAP[11]

S—Specificity
Does the person have a plan? If a person expresses that he has experienced intense or obsessive thoughts of suicide, we might ask, "Have you thought about a plan for suicide?" Or, "Have you thought about how you might harm yourself?" A person who has thought through methods for suicide, thought about how to acquire the means to follow through on his plan, or secured the elements needed is at an elevated risk level. If we are working with someone who has expressed having suicidal thoughts, we might ask if he has thought about how he would commit suicide. The more detailed a plan he has, the more he has thought through suicide.

L—Lethality
Will the method of choice result in death? How quickly will the person die if he does what he plans on doing? For example, in most cases, a firearm will hasten death more quickly than an overdose. The higher the level of lethality in the plan, the greater the degree of risk.

A—Availability
Does she have the means to carry out her plan immediately? Does the person have firearms in her home? Is there medication or other substances around on which she can overdose? The more readily available the implement to be used, the higher the degree of risk.

P—Proximity
How physically and geographically close is the person to others who could rescue him if necessary? What are the chances the person will be found? Does that appear to be part of his plan? The greater the distance he is from those who could rescue him in an emergency, the greater the degree of risk.

---

[11] The SLAP assessment was developed by Dr. Kenneth Morris.

* * *

Based on these two assessments, here is a breakdown of the overall risk levels.

Low Suicide Risk

SLAP indicators are low when a person has no previous attempts and a great support system. This person is communicative and willing to commit to a safety plan (see appendix). In this situation, we explain to her the need for a verbal safety commitment. We record this conversation in our notes and follow up at the next session. This record could be as simple as a document with the date and the statement "________ reports having suicidal thoughts, but has agreed not to act on them." Keep this document in a locked filing cabinet. If the person is resistant to a verbal safety commitment, then the risk level is elevated to "moderate" status.

Moderate Risk

When a person has frequent thoughts of suicide and previous self-harm gestures, he may be considered a moderate risk. He has an adequate support system and is concerned with his own safety. He may be more reserved and less communicative than someone at a lower risk. However, he is still willing to commit to safety.

We should explain the need for a safety contract to the person. A safety contract is a form where the person states what he will do if he is having obsessive or recurrent suicidal thoughts. It almost always involves calling and/or spending time with a friend, going for a walk, or engaging in some other activity to redirect his focus.

In addition to a list of friends and support people, the contract also has a list of numbers, including a crisis line and the nearest emergency room. Some counselors have a witness sign the contract or have a generic safety contract for the client to complete with a list of his support system contacts.[12] Other counselors encourage the client to write out the entire safety

[12] A sample safety contract can be found in the appendix.

contract to help him understand his commitment more fully. As always, we record this action in our regular notes and follow up at the next meeting. If the person refuses to commit to a safety contract, then the risk level is significantly elevated.

Significant Risk

For a person to be at a significant risk for suicide, she has expressed clear threats of self-harm. The person is resistant to offers of help and is unable to assure safety. In many cases, this person may have prior suicide attempts and does not have much of a support system.

In this case, an immediate safety intervention is needed, which involves calling 911 and taking the person to the emergency room. We explain the need for safety and the process to the client, if possible. Stay with the person until help arrives and ensure that she is isolated from potential sources of harm. Once help arrives, facilitate the transition to the transport team. Follow up to confirm she arrived safely. Hospitals typically will not release the person unless they have an aftercare plan in place, which may involve scheduling an appointment with her counselor. Document every intervention in your notes.

When It's a Phone Call

I (Brooke) am one of those people who would prefer to have serious conversations in person. I always feel it is much easier to discuss and reason in person. A person's facial expressions and body language provide invaluable information about the discussion at hand. The emotional climate of the room can also help us assess a person's current emotional state. So, how do we apply the information from the previous sections to receiving a phone call from someone contemplating suicide?

As soon as you receive a phone call from anyone who appears to be in crisis, ensure that you have the appropriate callback number in the event you are disconnected, along with his physical address. If you determine the person to be suicidal, you need to immediately dispatch the police or an ambulance. You also want to get as much information as you can about where he is located within the physical address, such as the garage or a second-floor bedroom. In the event the person acts on his suicidal thoughts, you want to be able to give as many details as possible to first responders. A few minutes can make a difference in whether a person lives or dies, so being able to help locate the person quickly and efficiently is important.

In some cases, the person may be uncooperative or refuse to provide her location. In these moments grounding exercises can be an effective way to help a person calm down and refocus to become more aware of her surroundings. The 5-4-3-2-1 exercise is simple and widely used. We ask a person to tell us five things she sees, four things she feels, three things she hears, two things she smells, and one thing she tastes. You might also ask her to look out the window and tell you what she notices outside. In addition to grounding, this might provide some clues about her location. Taking the time to ground her can provide clarity to her thought processes and allow her to more effectively communicate what she is feeling. This will aid you in helping her conceptualize alternatives to suicide and, hopefully, will assist in getting the information needed to offer appropriate help.

One day when I (Brooke) was sitting in a chapel service, I glanced down at my phone to see a text message coming through: "I am thinking about ending it all." The message was from a lady I had met through one of the ministries at our church. She had been reading the Bible we had given her, and I had been trying to answer her questions as she sorted through some faith issues. I jumped up immediately and went outside to call her.

When I tried to call, her phone had been disconnected, which was disconcerting. Fortunately, I had her address from a few weeks earlier, when we had made arrangements to pick her up for Bible study. She had canceled at the last minute, so I had never been to her house, but her address was still in my phone. Because I left the chapel service, I was low on options for assistance at that moment. I immediately called my husband and explained to him that I was about to text him an address and wanted him to call 911 and ask them to do a welfare check. After texting him the address, I texted her and got a response. It turns out she was being evicted and had nowhere to go with her four children. Her phone had been cut off, but she had found Wi-Fi, allowing her to text me.

With the help of a local ministry that manages a shelter for women and children, she was able to make it through this time of crisis. She still had a long road of recovery ahead of her, but we were able to get her through those few days of desperation and into a place with hope. Managing a suicidal crisis via texting is not something we covered in my graduate school training, but having the basic principles of assessing and responding to a suicidal crisis prepared me to adapt to the situation before me.

The Importance of Hope

Do they have hope? As mentioned earlier, when people are able to conceptualize alternatives, it means they still have hope that there is a way out of the present situation. We cannot improve without hope.

One of my (Brooke) most challenging experiences with helping a client find hope in the midst of despair came during my internship in graduate school. A young woman with a terminal illness and progressively worsening paralysis was transferred to my counseling practice. The doctors told her there would be nothing they could do once the disease reached her lungs and other vital organs. I had only been working with her for a few months when I received a call from her one day that she had gotten a gun from a family member and was thinking of taking her life.

I froze for a moment. My client had already exceeded her life expectancy. How could I help her conceptualize positive alternatives for the future? She had intermittent support from her family, who loved her and desired to be there for her in her time of need, but were exhausted from their caregiving responsibilities. My client felt isolated from many of her friends, who had gone off to college or moved away to pursue job opportunities while she was awaiting death.

Thankfully, I remembered her nieces were planning to visit that weekend. She loved planning fun activities for them and spending time with them while they were in town. I reminded her that she was about three days away from their visit and asked if she could hold on until then. We determined all the preparations that were needed and made a plan for completing each of those items. I checked in with her periodically over the next few days about how the preparations were going. During that time, her family removed the guns from their home.

At our session the next week, my client told me she was not sure how she could have gotten to such a desperate place the week before. She mentioned she wanted to be there for her nieces as long as she could and did not want to do anything to cut that time short. This experience taught me that helping another person conceptualize her alternatives does not necessarily mean looking a few years into the future. Sometimes, we just need enough hope to get us through the next few days.

Other Considerations

When assessing for suicide, it is important to discuss the topic openly. If we are hesitant to use the word *suicide*, it might communicate to people that we are uncomfortable having this conversation with them. They may discontinue the conversation with us and still be at a high risk. It could also cause a lack of clarity in the conversation. If we ask a vague question, such as "Are you thinking of harming yourself?" it could cause confusion since the term *self-harm* typically applies to cutting. People who cut are not necessarily suicidal. Being direct in our conversations about suicide can aid us in having a thorough assessment and more efficient response.

We should always facilitate the removal of the means a person wants to use to kill himself. This could include removing weapons from the home or having another family member lock up medication or other items that could be ingested. Usually, we will be working with those who are contemplating suicide or are formulating a plan. In rare cases, we may be in the same room as the person when he is trying to take his own life. If we do find ourselves in this unusual situation, we want to try to guide the weapon away from him rather than try to physically remove it. For example, we might ask him to put the weapon down and walk away or slide it over to us.

When someone discusses suicide with you, consider whether they express concern about those who would be left behind. In general, people with little, if any, concern over the impact of their actions on others are more likely to act on their suicidal thoughts. In cases of extreme desperation, they may be looking for revenge or hoping to cause pain or embarrassment for their families. Because of this, it is important to exercise caution in mentioning the family as a source of support until we have assessed the situation.

Theology and Suicide

Living in a city where the dominant religious affiliation is Catholicism, we frequently encounter clients who report having suicidal thoughts but assure us they would never follow through on them because they do not want to spend eternity without God. We also do not want to assume that just because someone is a Christian, he will not commit suicide. Theological beliefs regarding suicide will inevitably come up when working with those in crisis, so we should give some thought on how to engage these belief systems.

In moments of crisis, the most important thing is for us to meet people where they are. Respect the fears that may block suicide, without using these fears to manipulate them. In other words, if a person says he will not commit suicide because he does not want to go to hell, we respect that fear in the moment, even if we disagree with it, and we do not engage in a theological debate. At the same time, if we know that a person comes from a cultural or religious background with a doctrinal belief that suicide results in eternal separation from God, that belief should not be used as a fear tactic to prevent suicide.

A crisis is not typically a good time to engage in theological debates. When we are in crisis, the logical part of our brains, which helps with long-term planning and decision-making, shuts down, while the part of our brains responsible for fear and emotion is in overdrive. Thinking clearly and rationally is difficult. There's a fog obscuring our view. In a moment of crisis, we need to connect with the person and validate his experience. Engaging in a debate may mean we lose the person.

Best Practices for Suicide Intervention in Your Ministry

Train Everyone, Including the Office Staff

One of our colleagues mentioned his experience of directing a counseling center at another institution that was a training facility for graduate and doctoral counseling students. The secretary, who was responsible for answering the phone and taking down information from prospective clients, took a call from someone contemplating suicide. When she tried to put him on hold to connect a counselor, the caller said he would hang up if she transferred him to someone else.

This experience prompted a decision to offer training to everyone who worked at the counseling center, even if they were not counselors planning to have direct contact with clients. This also led to the creation of an office manual with step-by-step protocols to help those without counseling experience to navigate crisis situations. Having a clear plan in place that is communicated to everyone in your church or ministry setting will allow for a more efficient crisis response.

Work within Your Own Church

Pastors should do their best to avoid counseling someone outside of their own congregation. In terms of moral, ethical, and legal risks, there is little, if any, protection for a pastor counseling outside of his church.[13] People often reach out to churches or counseling centers when they are in a state of crisis. So, it is likely that many church leaders may encounter a person in crisis

[13] See Clinton et al., *Caring for People God's Way*, 345.

who is not a member of their church. In these cases, it is best for the pastor to help stabilize the crisis and make an appropriate referral.

One of the associate pastors at my church does this well. When he encounters crisis situations, especially those involving non–church members, he is quick to refer to a mental-health professional. After he refers, he continues the relationship with the person in crisis. On many occasions, he has invited the individual to his Bible study group, the men's prayer breakfast, or even lunch. This helps alleviate the issue of the person feeling like he is being pushed off on someone else.

Be prepared in advance to offer referrals and other resources to those in crisis. In my (Brooke) crisis counseling class, the students complete a community resource notebook. For this assignment, students identify local crisis resources, including mental-health professionals, utility/food assistance, legal aid, shelters, addiction services, inpatient treatment centers, and other relevant services. This guide is designed to be practical and put to use instantly, but it also serves as a framework for future ministry opportunities. A sample can be found in the appendix.

Work from a Written Policy

When working in a ministry setting, it is important to have a plan for crisis situations before they occur. Otherwise, critical errors can occur in the process. Step-by-step procedures for ourselves and our staff will guide decision-making throughout a suicidal crisis, including consultation and referral. A well-written policy demonstrates that you are resolute in your efforts to care for those who are contemplating suicide.[14]

Every professional and pastor needs to be capable of delineating their boundaries of expertise and the extent of their involvement. When dealing with suicidal crises, ministry leaders should consult with a knowledgeable mental-health professional. The mental-health professional can guide the pastor through the suicidal crisis and, when necessary, help him make

---

[14] See Clinton et al., 344–45.

decisions about referral options. Referral may not be necessary with close consultation to confirm and add to clinical decision-making on behalf of the person in crisis.[15]

When Suicide Intervention Fails

One of the most difficult and frustrating things about counseling is that not everyone will improve. Despite our best efforts, a client or church member may choose to take his or her own life. If a suicide occurs within your ministry setting, take time off and get counseling yourself. Losing a client is never easy. Walking with a client in the darkness and then learning that he has taken his own life is gut-wrenching. Take the time to grieve and heal. And remember that the family members and friends left behind are struggling to understand how their loved one came to the decision to end his life. They are wrestling with questions that will likely remain unanswered. Assist the victim's family in accessing counseling or debriefing services.[16]

Conclusion

Life on this earth is hard. At times, it leaves us hopeless and pushes us into a seemingly bottomless pit of despair. These moments offer us the opportunity to bring hope to the hopeless. We should ensure that we are prepared to assess for suicide and intervene when necessary.

> *I waited patiently for the LORD, and he turned to me and heard my cry for help. He brought me up from a desolate pit, out of the muddy clay, and set my feet on a rock, making my steps secure.*
>
> —Psalm 40:1–2

[15] Clinton et al., 344–45.

[16] Clinton et al., 354.

Part 5
Trauma

Chapter 9

Overview of Acute Trauma and PTSD

Generally, a crisis is a short-term situation. We all encounter minor crisis situations each day. When a large-scale crisis comes our way, we utilize our coping strategies and hope to resolve the situation soon. An accumulation of crisis situations or a crisis that remains unresolved may result in trauma.

Defining Trauma

At its most basic level, trauma is a wound. A trauma occurs "when a sudden, unexpected, overwhelmingly intense emotional blow or series of blows assaults a person from the outside. Traumatic events are external, but they quickly become incorporated into the mind."[1] Trauma is an event outside

[1] Scott Floyd, *Crisis Counseling: A Guide for Pastors and Professionals* (Grand Rapids: Kregel Ministry, 2008), 42.

of what is normally expected in the life of an individual that breaks past normal coping and defense mechanisms and causing strong emotional pain.

The *DSM-5-TR* defines trauma as "exposure to actual or threatened death, serious injury, or sexual violence."[2] SAMHSA (Substance Abuse and Mental Health Services Administration) defines trauma as "an event or circumstance resulting in physical harm, emotional harm, and/or life-threatening harm" and "has lasting adverse effects on the individual's mental health, physical health, emotional health, social well-being, and/or spiritual well-being."[3]

A crisis situation may become a traumatic event when an individual's safety or perceived safety is threatened, and the situation overwhelms an individual's ability to cope, causing long-term negative consequences. Multiple factors impact coping, so the impact is different for every person.

The Prevalence of Trauma

Most individuals experience a potentially traumatic event at some point in their lifetimes, and all of us will come into contact with survivors of trauma. Consider the following traumatic experiences, all of which are prevalent in our churches, communities, and society at large:

- abuse of any type (physical, sexual, psychological/emotional, spiritual)
- physical assault
- sexual assault
- fire
- combat
- terrorism
- domestic violence

---

[2] *Diagnostic and Statistical Manual of Mental Disorders*, 5th ed., Text Revision (*DSM-5-TR*) (American Psychiatric Association, 2022), 301.

[3] "Trauma and Violence," SAMHSA, https://www.samhsa.gov/trauma-violence.

- natural disaster
- life-threatening accident
- bullying
- being a victim of a crime
- traumatic loss
- serious and/or life-threatening illness
- childhood abuse and/or neglect
- witnessing the trauma of another individual (e.g., if you are a police officer, first responder, or in another position that assists in trauma recovery)

Despite the widespread occurrence of traumatic events, not everyone who experiences a traumatic event will develop post-traumatic stress disorder (PTSD). According to one estimate, approximately 6 percent of people in the United States will experience PTSD in their lifetimes.[4] However, an individual does not have to develop PTSD to be impacted negatively by the traumatic event.

The *DSM-5-TR* offers two diagnoses for trauma: acute stress disorder (ASD) and post-traumatic stress disorder (PTSD). Both disorders share the same criteria except for the duration of symptoms. With ASD, the symptoms last for less than a month, while PTSD symptoms last longer than a month.

For example, if a local bank is robbed, each employee or customer will have a different experience following the event. Consider these two stories:

Cindy is a fifty-one-year-old bank teller. During the robbery, she was next to Jerome, a twenty-five-year-old male and fellow bank teller, who was assaulted and forced to hand over the money. In the first few weeks following the incident, both Cindy and Jerome were shaken by the event. They had difficulties sleeping at night and would often awake with nightmares. Returning to work proved difficult as they were both triggered each time

---

[4] See National Center for PTSD, "How Common Is PTSD in Adults?," U.S. Department of Veterans Affairs, last updated February 3, 2023, https://www.ptsd.va.gov/understand/common/common_adults.asp.

they heard the doors open. Within a few weeks, Cindy began normalizing. She was finally able to sleep through the night without nightmares. She began to settle back into work, and she was not afraid to come into work or go out in public.

Things were different for Jerome. For the next several months, sleep continued to prove difficult. Jerome was afraid to go out in public. When he returned to work, he was triggered by a customer with a similar profile to the robber. He yelled at the customer to leave, prompting his supervisor to mandate that he seek help. Because Jerome's symptoms lasted for several months with no relief, he would likely have been diagnosed with PTSD.

Post-Traumatic Symptoms

Stressor

A stressor is the triggering event. In the last several years, it seems we have seen an increase in both natural disasters and violent crime. Another stressor may be childhood abuse and neglect. For those who have served in the military, it might be combat trauma. In some countries, and at certain points in US history, terrorism may be a triggering event. In the scenario above, the bank robbery was the stressor.

Intrusion Symptoms

A person may experience distressing memories and have a difficult time letting go. These memories are distracting and, in some cases, debilitating. Nightmares and flashbacks make sleep difficult and may cause people to feel as though they are reliving the event. Places, events, and people may trigger trauma reminders, which lead to emotional distress and physical reactivity. For some, physical reactivity can include being startled easily, trouble eating or sleeping, fatigue, palpitations, or rapid breathing.

Avoidance

In some cases, avoidant symptoms may include not talking about the event or trying not to think about it. It could also mean avoiding people, places, or activities that remind the person of the event. This may seem doable at times. However, there are a number of situations in which this may interfere significantly with daily living. Consider a child who experienced abuse in the bathtub and begins refusing to take a bath. Or a lady who, after being in a serious car accident, avoids the interstate at all costs, extending a twenty-minute work commute to an hour. The problem with avoidance is that people can only push it down for so long before it comes out. In some cases, it may not resurface until another traumatic event occurs.

Negative Alterations in Cognition and Mood

After experiencing a traumatic event, some people may struggle to recall key aspects of the incident. Their perspective of themselves and the world may be negatively skewed with inappropriate or excessive blame on themselves or others for causing the event. They experience sadness and find it difficult to experience joy, even in activities that once brought them enjoyment. They feel isolated and may isolate themselves because they do not believe anyone else would understand their experience.

Alterations in Arousal and Reactivity

A person may be "on edge," be hypervigilant, or have a heightened startle reaction. Jerome, the bank teller, was triggered by the customer with a similar profile to the robber. As a result, he yelled at the customer. The person may also engage in risky or destructive behavior, such as substance abuse or promiscuous behavior. Difficulties with sleeping or concentrating are likely to be present as well.

What Increases the Likelihood of a Person Experiencing PTSD?

Biological Predisposition

When our bodies experience stress, we have an increased state of arousal. Research has indicated that some people may overreact to moderate stressors, which predisposes them to develop PTSD. Abnormal activity of cortisol (stress hormone) and the neurotransmitter norepinephrine have been found in trauma survivors. In other words, the constant overreacting causes dysfunction in the brain, and as a result the symptoms of PTSD persist.[5]

Previous Experiences

Previous traumas, especially those that are unresolved, can increase the likelihood of someone experiencing PTSD when a new trauma hits. In some cases, such as early childhood trauma, a person may not have the capacity or resources to address and heal from the event, so it remains unresolved until a new event triggers it. In adulthood, a person may keep himself so busy and distracted that he does not deal with what has happened. The trauma is often lurking underneath and resurfaces when another event occurs.

After Hurricane Katrina hit New Orleans, an expert in trauma counseling came to train local counselors on how to help those impacted by Katrina. He mentioned that many people who came for counseling because of hurricane-related losses and stress would then mention in passing that they had previously experienced another trauma, such as abuse. Mental-health professionals in the area found this to be true more often than not. I (Brooke) did not move to New Orleans until a few years after Katrina, and I found this to be true with many of my clients as well.

---

[5] See Amy Lehrner and Rachel Yehuda, "Trauma across Generations and Paths to Adaptation and Resilience," *Psychological Trauma: Theory, Research, Practice, and Policy*, 10, no. 1 (January 2018): 22–29, https://doi.org/10.1037/tra0000302.

Personal Styles

A person's emotional situation at the time of a trauma can influence her response to the event. If a person is already in the middle of a crisis when trauma strikes, she is more vulnerable. Looking back over the last several years, we have seen many examples of this. In August 2020, south Louisiana, like many places, had hospitals at capacity due to the recent wave of COVID-19 cases, then they saw multiple hurricanes threatening the area, including Hurricane Laura, the strongest hurricane to make landfall in Louisiana. The continual presence of stressors and crises depletes a person's ability to cope with the current situation, making her more susceptible to experiencing PTSD.

The amount of control a person believes he has over his life can impact a trauma response. The more a person believes his life is controlled by external forces, the more susceptible he is to intense trauma responses. He believes that what happens will happen, regardless of his actions. The mentality is "If I have no control over the outcome, why exert any effort at changing or improving the situation?" However, if a person believes he has control over what happens to him, he is more likely to make positive changes, including the utilization of coping strategies that equip him to manage the traumatic event more effectively.[6] Additionally, being able to make meaning from one's experiences, even those related to suffering, can serve as a protective factor.

Support Systems

Following a trauma, a person may feel isolated, alone, and as though no one else could understand his experience. Having people who are there to offer support makes a significant difference in a person's healing and recovery process. In some cases, these are the people who help him find a counselor or other appropriate resources. Or they may offer practical assistance by running errands or bringing meals.

[6] This information is based on the "Locus of Control" work by Julian Rotter.

Being able to share with someone who has had a similar experience can also be life-giving. It has been noted that years ago, storytelling was a healing experience among the military. These days, we can usually get someone in and out of a war zone quickly. Years ago, it could have taken weeks for a person to make it home when traveling by ship. During this time, many of the soldiers were able to exchange stories with those who had been there and experienced it all firsthand.[7] Today, many in our military come home and are surrounded by those who were not there and do not quite understand, which can complicate healing.

Nature of the Trauma

Although a number of things related to the event may determine whether a person is traumatized by it, three key factors are influential. The first is a person's placement relative to the trauma. We Americans were all impacted negatively by events such as the September 11 attack on the World Trade Center (WTC) and the COVID-19 pandemic. The people who were most likely to experience long-term trauma symptoms were those closest to these events. For example, first responders at the WTC attack, those who escaped the building, and those who were nearby to witness the event in person were some of the most vulnerable. With COVID-19, healthcare workers in the ER, ICU, or code teams were confronted directly with the severity and uncertainty of the pandemic, along with those who were hospitalized.

Another key factor involves the threat of death. In other words, how close were you to the trauma, or did you believe that you would lose your life as a result of the trauma? The September 11 attacks and COVID-19 illustrate this well, along with victims of violent crime. The same might be

---

[7] See Karyn Purvis et al., "Trust-Based Relational Intervention (TBRI): A Systemic Approach to Complex Developmental Trauma," *Child & Youth Services* 34, no. 4 (December 2013): 360–86, https://doi.org/10.1080/0145935X.2013.859906.

true for abuse survivors whose lives and those of their family members or friends were threatened.

The third key factor that influences a person's trauma response is whether the event was a human-made or natural disaster. As the name implies, a human-made disaster is something preventable caused by people. Some examples include various forms of abuse and violence. A natural disaster is something outside of our control, such as a hurricane, tornado, or earthquake.

Typically, human-made disasters, also referred to as interpersonal trauma, impact people at a deeper level than natural disasters because they often could have been prevented. In some cases, human-made disasters may also reflect a form of betrayal. With abuse, this could mean being betrayed by someone you trusted or who was supposed to protect you. Certain acts of violence could indicate a community or society that is no longer safe. The guilt and regret over human-made disasters and whether we could have done something to change the outcome can be influential in whether a person develops PTSD.

Complex PTSD and Developmental Trauma Disorder

When something happens to a person that cannot be articulated in words, it is difficult to encapsulate that person's experience into a single diagnosis. As a result, some clinicians have begun discussing the need to include additional diagnoses to reflect the range of experiences created by trauma, such as developmental trauma disorder, which describes the experiences and behaviors of a person who has experienced chronic trauma throughout their lives, rather than a one-time traumatic event.[8] This diagnosis will be discussed further in chapter 11.

[8] See Bessel van der Kolk, "Developmental Trauma Disorder: Toward a Rational Diagnosis for Children with Complex Trauma Histories," *Psychiatric Annals* 35, no. 5 (2005): 402–6.

Similar to developmental trauma disorder, complex PTSD (CPTSD) has similar symptoms to PTSD, but also includes struggles with emotion regulation, relationships, and identity. CPTSD results from multiple or long-term traumatic events. Although experts disagree about whether CPTSD warrants a diagnosis distinct from PTSD, chronic trauma does appear to impact people differently than a one-time traumatic event, as we will discuss in chapter 11.

How Do You Know If Trauma Has Been Resolved?

At trauma recovery trainings I (Brooke) have attended, there is typically a discussion related to how a person knows whether his or her trauma has been resolved. I once met a clinician who believed her trauma had been resolved as a result of years of therapy. She later discovered through our training that she was still experiencing some avoidant symptoms related to her past trauma. Trauma recovery can be an ongoing process, and there are some key indicators that can help a person gauge her progress.

One indicator of trauma resolution is establishing a sense of safety and stability. Living in a constant state of fear is debilitating, which makes it difficult for a person to heal and recover. Establishing a sense of safety and stability may involve changes in environment or relationships.

Another indicator is being able to recognize and manage triggers related to the trauma. Sometimes a person may experience a trauma trigger and not recognize it. When this happens, a traumatized person can have a strong reaction that is out of proportion for the situation. Jerome, from the beginning of this chapter, was triggered by a customer coming into the bank, but was unaware of it. This led to an intense response that caused his supervisor to intervene. Awareness of triggers, together with a safety plan, can help a person manage his or her responses. If a person knows certain places or times of year that are difficult, it is beneficial to prepare for these times.

Even after completing recovery work, a person may still experience triggers from time to time, but the important thing is that he or she is aware of the triggers and takes the needed steps to address them. For some, addressing triggers could involve journaling or a conversation with a friend or mentor. Others may want to check in with their counselor. In facilitating sexual-abuse prevention classes, I have frequently had people who realized they still had a few unresolved issues after listening to the content of the course materials.

Post-traumatic growth (PTG) may also be indicative of resolved trauma. PTG describes the transformation that may take place following trauma. As those with lived experiences (LE) heal and recover, they may experience a change in their perceptions of themselves, their relationships, and their philosophies of life.[9]

As part of these changes, clients will improve their capacity for self-compassion. The experience of trauma, especially interpersonal trauma, can cause a person to question her worth and lead to a downward spiral of self-criticism and self-degradation. The practice of self-compassion allows for a person to use the same kindness and understanding for herself that she would for a friend. In other words, we need to be gracious with ourselves when we make mistakes or experience setbacks. Being able to set and maintain appropriate boundaries is another indicator that past trauma has been resolved. In many cases, the aftereffects of trauma leave a person feeling she cannot say no or that her desires do not matter. In chapter 11, we will discuss further the implications of healthy boundaries in the healing process.

People who are healing also have the opportunity to reflect on the strengths, resources, and values they have developed as a result of their trauma-recovery process. Then they can employ these resources moving forward, thriving and serving others.[10] Being able to make meaning from what has happened and channel the pain into helping others can be a critical component to the healing process.

---

[9] See Richard G. Tedeschi and Lawrence G. Calhoun, "The Posttraumatic Growth Inventory: Measuring the Positive Legacy of Trauma," *Journal of Traumatic Stress* 9, no. 3 (July 1996): 455–71, https://doi.org/10.1002/jts.2490090305.

[10] See Kim Etherington, "Supervising Helpers Who Work with the Trauma of Sexual Abuse," *British Journal of Guidance & Counselling* 37, no. 2 (April 2009): 179–94, https://doi.org/10.1080/03069880902728622.

Conclusion

Many factors influence a person's response to trauma. When a traumatic event occurs, quick interventions mitigate long-term effects of trauma, such as PTSD. When symptoms of PTSD are present, encourage the person to find an experienced trauma counselor familiar with evidence-based treatment models. In resolving past trauma, post-traumatic growth can take place for both the person with lived experience and the helper. Taking the time to reflect on what we have learned and how we have grown through the process can help us make meaning from tragedy.

Chapter 10

The Impact of Trauma on the Brain and Body

In the past, when it comes to trauma, our society mostly dismissed the long-term impact of trauma. We spoke of the importance of resiliency and letting go of the past. Over the last few decades, the long-term impact of trauma on our brains and bodies has come to the forefront of medical research. The groundbreaking adverse childhood experiences (ACEs) study published in 1999 made it clear to the medical community and our society that trauma does not resolve on its own. When left unresolved, trauma has long-term implications on our physical, mental, and emotional health.

Throughout this chapter, we will follow the Smith family and consider the impact of trauma on their lives. Allen, Meg, and their two children, fourteen-year-old Anna and eight-year-old David, watched in horror as flames engulfed their home. When the fire began, Allen was home with David while Meg and Anna were out running errands. After calling 911, Allen phoned his wife. Meg and Anna rushed home and stood helplessly in a neighbor's yard, watching the flames claim their home and possessions. We will follow their journey as we overview what is happening in the brains and bodies of those who need support during a crisis or a potentially traumatic event.

For the Smith family, Allen and David's lives were in danger. Their home caught fire while they were inside, and they narrowly escaped the rapid spread of flames. Both Allen and David are susceptible to the impact of trauma.

Trauma can also occur even when a person is not in direct danger of losing one's life, so Meg and Anna may also experience trauma due to the emotional toll of watching their home and possessions be consumed by fire and realizing their lives could have been endangered. There is also the toll of realizing "We could have lost Dad and David too."

Trauma and the Brain/Body Connection

Neurobiology is the study of the "structures and processes of the nervous system."[1] A basic understanding of neurobiology assists in recognizing the holistic impact of trauma. When someone is in crisis, his body and brain respond differently than if he were in a state of safety, security, or rest. Let's briefly examine the impact of trauma on the brain and body.

Different Structures of the Brain Serve Different Primary Functions

The brain's structures are interconnected, so the functions of each cannot be clearly divided. But there are some basic functions of each structure. We will review a few of these structures and functions as they relate to trauma.

Left and Right Hemisphere. You may be familiar with the concepts of a left and right hemisphere of the brain, and you may have heard someone

[1] "Neurobiology," American Psychological Association, https://dictionary.apa.org/neurobiology.

refer to themselves as "right brain" or "left brain" dominant. Our entire brain works together, but each hemisphere has associated tasks. Our left hemisphere is primarily engaged in analytical and logical tasks, such as language and math. Our right hemisphere engages primarily in tasks that are more creative or related to emotion, such as music and art.[2]

Bessel van der Kolk, author of *The Body Keeps the Score*, pulls from neuroscience and attachment theory in his understanding and treatment of trauma. He notes, in memory, the left brain stores the facts, details, and words to describe an experience, while the right brain stores what the experience felt like—the "sound, touch, smell, and the emotions they evoke."[3] Siegel and Bryson describe the reason for this distinction. The right brain is "more directly influenced by the body and lower brain areas, which allow it to receive and interpret emotional information."[4] That brings us to the concept of the "upstairs" and "downstairs" areas of the brain.

"Upstairs" and "Downstairs." In simple terms, think of your brain as having two separate sections: "upstairs" and "downstairs."[5] Your "upstairs" brain is your cortex, or "thinking" brain. The "downstairs" brain is your limbic system or "emotional brain." When people experience a crisis or trauma, they typically respond from their "downstairs" brain. Communication with the "thinking" brain is temporarily suspended to allow for a fast response to the event. For example, when you see a snake on a pathway, do you need to spend several minutes considering your options about what you should do? No, you can respond quickly, thanks to how your brain is designed.

When you engage with people in the midst of experiencing a crisis or trauma, be aware that they may be communicating and responding from

---

[2] See Bill McHenry, Angela M. Sikorski, and Jim McHenry, *A Counselor's Introduction to Neuroscience* (New York: Routledge, 2014), 24–25.

[3] Bessel A. van der Kolk, *The Body Keeps the Score: Brain, Mind and Body in the Healing of Trauma* (New York: Penguin Books, 2015), 44–45.

[4] Daniel J. Siegel and Tina Payne Bryson, *The Whole-Brain Child: 12 Revolutionary Strategies to Nurture Your Child's Developing Mind* (New York: Delacorte, 2011), 16.

[5] See Siegel and Bryson, 37–65.

their "downstairs" brain, so your job is to focus more on helping them establish safety, stabilization, and regulation before they will be ready for planning, strategizing, or anything else requiring the "upstairs," logical left brain.

Our Brains Are Constantly Scanning for Danger

Two structures of our "downstairs" brain, the amygdala and hippocampus, work together to scan and evaluate potential threats. Much like the fire alarm in the Smith family home, we have a "fire alarm" in our brains. This fire alarm is our amygdala. The amygdala appraises our environment and experiences to assess for danger. The amygdala processes potential danger far more quickly than our prefrontal cortex.[6] It can override our cortex (our "thinking" or "upstairs" brain) to take control of both our actions and our reactions.[7] This is why we can act before thoroughly analyzing a situation.

The hippocampus works with the amygdala in threat assessment by linking previous experience with what is currently happening.[8] For example, if you are hiking in the mountains and see a bear on the trail, your brain immediately senses the potential danger without thoroughly evaluating and examining the situation. I think we can agree this is a very good design! If we see a bear, there is no need to evaluate whether there is a potential danger. Based on previous information or experience, we know bears can be dangerous. If you have experienced a prior encounter with a bear, you are likely vigilant in scanning the area for bears. You might even experience a fear response if a squirrel runs in front of you because your brain has a memory that might link any unexpected rustle of leaves to a potential bear.

Suppose an individual has a previous history of trauma. In that case, there will be an increased likelihood that her body will respond to anything resembling a potential threat by linking past and present experiences.

---

[6] See van der Kolk, *The Body Keeps the Score*, 60–61.

[7] See Louis J. Cozolino, *The Pocket Guide to Neuroscience for Clinicians*, 1st ed. (New York: W. W. Norton, 2020), 45.

[8] See van der Kolk, *The Body Keeps the Score*, 60.

Our Brains Are Part of Our Nervous System, Allowing for a Whole-Body Response

Neurobiology involves more than just our brains. Our brains are part of the nervous system. The central nervous system consists of the brain and spinal cord. The peripheral nervous system is composed of the autonomic nervous system and the somatic nervous system. The nerves of the peripheral nervous system run from the brain and spinal cord throughout the body, allowing for communication between the brain and body. The autonomic nervous system is divided further into the sympathetic nervous system and the parasympathetic nervous system. (See diagram below.) Under actual or perceived threat, the sympathetic nervous system activates in what is commonly referred to as a "fight or flight" (or "freeze") reaction. The parasympathetic nervous system, also called "rest and digest," helps calm us by reducing arousal, heart rate, breathing, and muscle tension.[9] Our entire bodies are engaged in the response to a potential trauma.

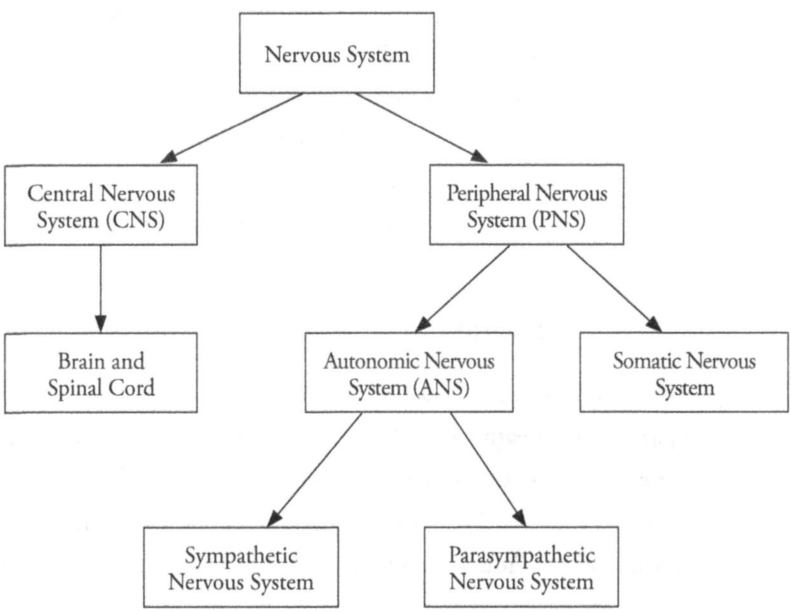

[9] van der Kolk, 79.

When Our Brains Sense Danger, We Can Respond Quickly

When your amygdala senses danger, your entire nervous system is impacted and works to protect you. As discussed previously, the autonomic nervous system engages in a "whole-body response."[10] Stress hormones cortisol and adrenaline are released throughout our bodies so we can respond quickly, increasing our heart rate and blood pressure. At times, you might hear this referred to as going into "fight or flight." While many do fight or take flight (run away from the danger), in some situations, such as intimate partner violence, the victim may seek to appease the perpetrator as a means of seeking safety. Or, in the case of sexual assault, the victim may dissociate or "freeze."

When Allen heard the fire alarm in his home, his amygdala and hippocampus instantly evaluated the situation as potentially dangerous. When he smelled smoke in his house, his autonomic nervous system engaged to respond to the crisis. Stress hormones were released throughout his body as he called out David's name and rushed toward his son's room. Allen's heart pounded as he picked up his son and ran out the door, his sympathetic ("fight or flight") nervous system fully engaged. Eventually, his parasympathetic nervous system began to regulate his body and reduce his heart rate. But because the stress of losing his home was ongoing, he remained more physiologically elevated than before the fire. Long-term, chronic stress set in over the next several months as he dealt with the ramifications of losing his home.

Trauma and Memory

Memory is sometimes likened to a filing cabinet, with different memories stored as separate files neatly tucked away in a time-stamped, sequential order. In some instances, this description seems to work. Think back to yesterday. How did you spend your day? What did you have for dinner? Did you interact with others? You can most likely describe your day in quite a bit of detail.

---

[10] van der Kolk, 60.

Now, think back to this day one month ago. You probably noticed that some of the files are not accessible because the file cabinet illustration for memory is not how the brain actually works. Instead of neatly pulling a file for a particular day, your brain recalls memory based on associations with your senses, emotions, ideas, or images.[11] When you think about a day one month ago, you've likely forgotten many events of the day, but you may be able to remember events associated with your senses, emotions, ideas, or images. You might remember your tasty meal if you ate at a new restaurant you've wanted to try for months. Or you may remember a meaningful conversation with a friend. Perhaps you recall seeing an awe-inspiring sunset. As time passes, significant memories such as a special anniversary meal, a dream vacation to Europe, or a wedding are remembered with greater detail than mundane memories of what you wore to work last month.

The above exercise helps you access your "explicit memory," a "conscious recollection of a past experience."[12] Another type of memory is "implicit memory," which does not require conscious awareness. For example, adults tie their shoes based on implicit memory. Many of your day-to-day tasks are based on implicit memory of how to do them. Additionally, implicit memory makes predictions about what might happen in certain circumstances. Trauma memories may be both explicit and implicit. When a person has unprocessed trauma memories, they are often stored as implicit memories and connected more to our senses and emotions. One goal of trauma therapy is to process these implicit memories. We will explore three implications of the way trauma is stored in memory.

Trauma Memories Are Non-linear and Nonverbal

Van der Kolk notes two main differences between how people described positive versus traumatic experiences. First is how the memories are organized. Trauma memories are encoded, stored, and recalled differently than

[11] See Siegel and Bryson, *The Whole-Brain Child*, 76.

[12] Siegel and Bryson, 71.

other memories. Rather than being neatly filed away in sequential order, trauma memories are stored as though your file cabinet of memories was picked up by a tornado and strewn about the house. Whereas nontraumatic memories typically have a sequential flow when recalled, traumatic memories are disorganized. Details may be remembered but in a nonsequential order. Secondly, traumatic memories are associated with physical sensations more than with words. The senses (such as smell), emotions, images, and sounds can be overwhelming when triggered.[13]

For example, your sense of smell is strongly correlated to memory. At times, this correlation is pleasant. You might walk into an apple orchard bakeshop, smell the fragrant cinnamon apple aroma, and be instantly transported to the comfort of your grandmother's kitchen. Conversely, the triggered memory may be unpleasant or a traumatic flashback. Allen and David remember the fire whenever they hear an alarm or smell smoke. Since the fire, when Meg's phone rings, her stomach lurches, her body remembering the phone call that their home was on fire.

Trauma Survivors May Be Hypervigilant for Potential Danger

Let's put together what we have discussed so far. Our brains and bodies do not function separately. They are interconnected in a way that assists in protecting us from danger. Implicit memory informs our warning system to predict what might happen in a particular circumstance, and the limbic system can take charge based on these predictions. However, when there is a history of trauma, this warning system can become hypervigilant in the effort to protect us. As a result, we may experience "false alarms" of danger.

Allen and David experienced numerous "false alarms" after the fire. Anytime a car alarm sounded in his office parking lot, Allen's body jolted to attention, his heart rate increased, and he experienced difficulty concentrating for the next hour. Young David would jump in his seat during the school bell and experience difficulty concentrating. Each hour that the

[13] See van der Kolk, *The Body Keeps the Score*, 195–96.

class bell rang, David's nervous system released a fresh wave of stress hormones, repeatedly engaging his "downstairs" brain and disrupting communication with his "upstairs" brain. Solving math problems, reading his assignments, and focusing on what the teacher said was not physically possible for David with these sounds constantly engaging his sympathetic nervous system. During a fire alarm drill at school, he froze, unable to leave his seat, and began weeping uncontrollably. The school counselor recommended his parents take him to see an outside counselor to help him process the trauma.

Traumatic Memories May Feel as Though They Are Happening in the Moment

Triggered. You have probably heard this word. Over the past several years, the growing pervasiveness of the term has unfortunately minimized its meaning. But for the survivor of trauma, the term has overwhelming significance.

Because traumatic memories are not time-stamped and we experience them on a physiological level, they may be triggered by a seemingly unrelated event in the present. They can occur or be triggered any time after the initial event, even decades later.

Allen is triggered by the sound of the car alarm. David is triggered by the school alarm. Meg is triggered by her phone ringing because of the sheer panic she felt when she received the phone call from Allen that their home was engulfed in flames. Anna is triggered by smoke, bringing her back to the night of the fire when the air was heavy with the smell of loss.

Understanding the concept of trauma "triggers" provides critical insight into ministry and counseling with trauma survivors.

Let's examine a few additional examples of trauma triggers. A survivor of trauma will likely have multiple trauma triggers, so I am only highlighting the one that is most interfering with daily functioning in the lives of the following individuals.

At twenty years old, John was in a car accident that almost took his life. At twenty-five, John holds his breath, grips the steering wheel, and fights panic as he drives, avoiding it if possible. He recently lost his job because he missed too many days due to difficulty driving.

At seventeen years old, Mary was sexually assaulted. At thirty-two, Mary gags at the scent of a particular musky cologne and jumps when anyone touches her unexpectedly. Recently, she began experiencing intrusive memories and panic attacks.

Throughout her childhood, Linda hunched in the corner of her room, waiting for the screaming, crying, and crashing to stop, with the ticktock of the grandfather clock in the background. At forty-eight, Linda can barely tolerate being in a room with a ticking clock and often avoids social settings where she might hear this sound.

As already discussed, trauma triggers often correlate with the senses: a scent, a sound, a taste, or a bodily sensation. As professional counselors, we have seen countless trauma survivors make the connection between a dysregulating event in the present and an implicitly stored traumatic event in their past. At times, survivors know what is triggering. But frequently, there are dysregulating reminders or situations that the survivor does not connect to the original trauma. Because trauma is not time-stamped, it can feel like the trauma is occurring in the present moment, even if it happened years or decades earlier.

Long-Term Impact of Trauma

Most people who experience a traumatic event do not develop post-traumatic stress disorder. Still, even without a clinical diagnosis, they may experience a negative impact as a result of the traumatic event. When we say that someone has experienced trauma or has a history of trauma, that terminology indicates some degree of long-term impact.

An individual who has a history of trauma may experience emotional dysregulation. This dysregulation might be seen as becoming quickly overwhelmed and unbalanced emotionally (a "fight or flight" response) in day-to-day life. The individual may have difficulty calming oneself. Or someone might become emotionally numb and shut down (or "freeze").

A person might experience hypervigilance (or hyperarousal) and be constantly on guard for potential danger. This hypervigilance can occur 24/7 and impact sleep.[14] Chronic stress caused by the traumatic event and increased emotional arousal can negatively impact an individual's physical well-being. Many individuals notice the physical symptoms before noticing the emotional impact of stress.

Professional Treatment of Trauma

Formal training in trauma therapy is needed to work in a safe and healthy manner with those with lived experiences. In the event a ministry professional needs to refer, it might be helpful to be aware of some of the evidence-based trauma therapy models.[15] While talk therapy is effective, when it comes to trauma, a person typically cannot "talk" themselves out of a trauma response. We previously discussed how trauma is experienced on a neurobiological level. There are two basic categories of therapeutic approaches: "top-down" and "bottom-up." In "top-down" treatment, the focus is on what occurs in the cortex (your "thinking brain"). The goal is to challenge and change thoughts and behaviors to impact emotions and improve overall well-being.

Trauma-focused cognitive behavioral therapy (TF-CBT) is an example of a "top-down" approach. TF-CBT is a highly researched and effective treatment option that involves helping clients identify emotions and thoughts associated with the trauma. Then, the counselor and client work together to challenge and reframe these thoughts.[16] For example, if you have a person who was raped when she was drunk, one of her negative cognitions may

---

[14] See chapter 3 of Center for Substance Abuse Treatment (US), "Understanding the Impact of Trauma," in *Trauma-Informed Care in Behavioral Health Services* (Substance Abuse and Mental Health Services Administration [US], 2014), https://www.ncbi.nlm.nih.gov/books/NBK207191.

[15] Evidence-based therapy models are practices that have been heavily researched and found effective for treating a specific diagnosis.

[16] For more information about TF-CBT or to see the research on its efficacy, visit https://tfcbt.org.

be that she blames herself for what happened to her. Her therapist could help her think through the difference between regret and responsibility. She may regret that she got drunk, which made her vulnerable, but it was not her fault she was raped. The fault resides with her perpetrator. Along with addressing emotions and cognitions related to the trauma, the client will ultimately construct a trauma narrative that will likely be revised multiple times to include more information and details from the event. The client will then be given the opportunity to read through the narrative multiple times until she can do so with little to no distress.

To treat the impact of trauma, you might consider a "bottom-up" approach. In "bottom-up" approaches, the entire brain and body are considered and engaged in treatment. Eye movement desensitization and reprocessing is one example of a "bottom-up" approach. EMDR uses dual attention stimuli to help people alleviate the emotional distress and heal from past trauma. The stimuli could involve moving eyes from left to right, tapping, or alternating sounds in each ear. EMDR focuses on a number of elements, rather than one component of the clinical picture. These elements may address the emotions, thoughts, attitudes, behaviors, and physical sensations. Other therapy models may zero in on one of these parts, while EMDR seeks to address them all simultaneously.[17] From our perspective, EMDR is one of the most efficient ways to process trauma, with many clients reporting improvement after only a few sessions.[18] A professional counselor can work with the person to determine the most appropriate treatment approach.

---

[17] See Francine Shapiro and Margot Silk Forrest, *EMDR: The Breakthrough "Eye Movement" Therapy for Overcoming Anxiety, Stress, and Trauma* (New York: Basic Books, 2004), xix–xx.

[18] For more information about EMDR or to see the extensive research on its efficacy, visit the website of the EMDR Institute, Inc., at https://www.emdr.com/what-is-emdr.

Conclusion

In this chapter, we followed the Smith family as we overviewed the neurobiology of trauma, the impact of trauma, and how trauma relates to memory. While reading, some of you may have made a connection between something that occurred in your past and a current trigger. If this happened, we encourage you to find a trusted friend or counselor with whom you can share your story. Or you may have recalled one or more individuals in your ministry who struggle with the impact of trauma. Perhaps there are some counseling referrals you need to make so these individuals can receive professional trauma therapy. Our church pulpits and pews are filled with countless people impacted by trauma. In the next chapter, we will turn our attention to recommendations for trauma-informed ministry care for those with a history of trauma.

Chapter 11

Chronic Childhood Stress

In 1998, Vincent Felitti and his colleagues published the original research study on adverse childhood experiences (ACEs) in the *American Journal of Preventive Medicine*. Over the last two decades, this research has influenced further study and practice in the public health field. Various researchers and clinicians have expanded the list of ACEs. However, the original study considered childhood exposure to abuse (psychological, physical, and sexual), household dysfunction (substance abuse, untreated mental illness, domestic violence), and criminal behavior (incarceration of a family member). A person who experienced one ACE was highly likely to experience at least one more.[1]

In the original ACEs study, researchers were looking for a relationship between early childhood adversity and risk factors for several of the leading causes of death in adults, including ischemic heart disease, cancer, stroke, chronic bronchitis, emphysema, diabetes, hepatitis, and skeletal fractures.

[1] See Vincent Felitti et al., "Relationship of Childhood Abuse and Household Dysfunction to Many of the Leading Causes of Death," *American Journal of Preventive Medicine* 14, no. 4 (1998): 245–58.

Those with ACEs were more likely to experience risk factors such as smoking, obesity, physical inactivity, depressed mood, suicide attempts, alcoholism, drug abuse, a high lifetime number of sexual partners, and history of sexually transmitted diseases.[2]

The connection between ACEs and the leading causes of death appears to be related to the coping mechanisms of those with lived experiences.[3] When children grow up in chronic stress with little support, they look for ways to cope. Because many of them have not witnessed healthy coping strategies, they are likely to turn to maladaptive coping. This might include anything that could numb the pain they are experiencing, such as substance abuse, overeating, or sexual activity. They may have also developed a core belief that they are not worth caring for, so they do not practice healthy lifestyle habits such as appropriate diet, exercise, and sleep. ACEs appear to contribute significantly to risk factors for the leading causes of death.

We will now consider the risk factors for childhood victimization and the long-term implications of ACEs when left unaddressed. Individual risk factors may include young children who typically have few independent skills, along with children who may have some type of special need that places additional stress and strain on their parents or caregivers. Parents with their own prior history of child abuse, along with any substance abuse or mental-health issues in the home, can increase the likelihood of abuse or neglect. Parents who are young and have a lower educational level may not have the skills needed to parent effectively. They may not be attuned to the needs of the child and may have little understanding of appropriate developmental tasks for young children.[4]

Violence within the home and neighborhood can also be a risk factor. Research has found that homes with intimate partner violence increased

---

[2] See Felitti et al.

[3] See Felitti et al.

[4] See CDC, "Risk and Protective Factors," Centers for Disease Control and Prevention, February 22, 2024, https://www.cdc.gov/child-abuse-neglect/risk-factors/index.html.

the likelihood of other forms of abuse occurring. Living in a disadvantaged neighborhood with residential instability and high unemployment rates is also a risk factor.[5]

In a previous chapter, we discussed the two diagnoses offered by the *DSM-5-TR* for trauma: acute stress disorder (ASD) and post-traumatic stress disorder (PTSD). Many in the trauma-counseling field express concern about putting people who have experienced a one-time traumatic event into the same category as someone who has endured multiple traumas, along with those who have extensive histories of trauma and neglect, especially in the early years of life. Some trauma experts question whether PTSD is the best diagnostic fit for those who grew up with chronic trauma in the home or their neighborhood.[6] Consider the following case studies.

Amy is a thirty-three-year-old woman who works as an elementary school teacher. She had a relatively stable upbringing, raised by both of her parents. Her parents were not perfect, but she always knew she was loved. She had teachers at school and youth leaders at church who invested in her and encouraged her along the way. One day on the way to work, a driver in the oncoming lane fell asleep at the wheel and veered into her lane. Quick thinking on Amy's part prevented a head-on collision with the driver, but the car accident was still serious. She was transported to the hospital, where she stayed overnight for observation. She was later released with relatively minor injuries. Following this experience, she had a difficult time sleeping, called in sick to work frequently, and avoided driving. Through the employee-assistance program offered by the school, she met with a counselor to process the accident. In the weeks and months that followed, most of her trauma symptoms abated. She started sleeping more soundly, was able to resume work productively, and began driving again. Depending on

---

[5] See "Risk and Protective Factors."

[6] Bessel van der Kolk, "Developmental Trauma Disorder: Toward a Rational Diagnosis for Children with Complex Trauma Histories," *Psychiatric Annals* 35, no. 5 (2005): 402–6.

how long the symptoms lasted, Amy might have been diagnosed with either ASD or PTSD.

On the other hand, Jenny is a twenty-five-year-old female who works at a local strip club. Her dad left when she was four. After he left, her mom had a series of live-in boyfriends, one of whom sexually abused her. In a few instances, she witnessed abusive behavior toward her mother. On a few occasions, her mom would go on a trip with her boyfriend and leave Jenny alone to watch her siblings. Jenny never knew when her mom would return or what state she would be in if she did. After a series of failed relationships, Jenny's mom told her, "Men will always abuse you and take advantage of you, so you might as well get paid for it." After all the years of watching her mom in her failed relationships, along with her own series of abusive boyfriends, Jenny believes she has learned how to make a man happy, and she brings it into her work at the strip club. But after seeing so many married men come into the clubs, Jenny is inclined to agree with her mom's perspective on men. She spends much of her time under the influence of substances to cope with the pain and emptiness she feels.

Under the current edition of the *DSM,* if Jenny were to see a mental-health professional, she would likely be diagnosed with PTSD. However, the nature of her trauma and the type of help needed to heal and recover would look extremely different from Amy's experience. In the first scenario, Amy had a relatively positive perspective on how the world works. Because she had such a strong support system growing up, she is likely to reach out for help and trust others to be there for her. Amy knows what it is to have hope that things can get better, while Jenny has only seen things go from bad to worse. Because of their lifestyle choices, Jenny and her mom only received judgment from the church. They never received any form of kindness or compassion from school, church, or home. As such, Jenny does not trust others to help, and she has no hope of her situation improving.

Some members of the National Child Traumatic Stress Network developed a proposal for a developmental trauma disorder diagnosis, which we refer to as complex developmental trauma. Primarily it involves multiple or chronic exposure to one or more forms of developmentally adverse interpersonal trauma. This can include abandonment, physical or sexual assault, emotional abuse, and witnessing violence and death. As a result, many survivors may feel a sense of fear, rage, betrayal, defeat, or shame.[7]

In the early years of life, we depend on consistency and predictability to help us understand how the world works. When we do not have this, it is difficult to organize our experiences and emotions and consider future outcomes. Early on, we depend on our parents or caregivers to help us regulate our feelings and manage our stress. When our parents are unable to do this, we may find our own ways to adapt to the situation to survive. We typically see this when parents or caregivers are abusive or unavailable.

Another feature of developmental trauma disorder is persistently altered attributions and experiences. In other words, traumatized people tend to have a skewed perspective of the world. They tend to have a low view of themselves and their worth and a negative view of others. They do not trust others to protect them, and they have little, if any, belief in the protection of social service systems. They have resigned themselves to believing justice will never be served and it is inevitable that they will continue to be victimized in the future.[8]

The dysregulation and altered attributions will likely lead to functional impairments in multiple aspects of life. The concept of a committed relationship is probably unfamiliar, so dating and marriage become difficult. They may have learned some maladaptive coping mechanisms such as lying or stealing during the chronic stress of childhood, but these behaviors make it difficult to hold down a job and engage in meaningful relationships.[9]

Trauma-Informed Care

A trauma-informed counselor or ministry organization understands the impact of trauma on individuals and considers their perspectives in programming and

---

[7] See van der Kolk.

[8] See van der Kolk.

[9] See van der Kolk.

decision-making. Without a working knowledge of trauma and its impact, it is difficult for a helper to understand the recovery process.

A number of years ago, a missionary from East Asia came to speak with some women at our (Brooke) church about the work she was doing in her country. She had opened a bakery, where she employed women who were coming out of brothels. She shared the gospel with the women and equipped them with skills that would allow for them to make a living outside of the sex industry. The original plan was for a group of ladies from our church to go over and help with her work. This missionary told them not to come to her country and do this work unless they were going to do it in their own city.

From this, we formed a ministry that reaches out to the women and men in the sex industry in New Orleans, and more specifically, on Bourbon Street. A group of women from various churches in the area go into the strip clubs on Bourbon Street and build relationships with the women who work there. Much of our work involves planting the seeds of the gospel. We bring gifts, share the gospel, offer assistance, and meet needs when the opportunity arises.

Trauma-informed care is an essential part of our approach in this ministry because research indicates that those with higher ACE scores have a higher prevalence of human trafficking. Child sexual abuse was the strongest indicator of human trafficking. For girls who experienced sexual abuse, the likelihood of human trafficking was 2.52 times greater and 8.21 times greater for boys.[10]

For healing and recovery to take place, stability and a felt sense of safety must be established. There is a difference between being safe and feeling safe.[11] In some cases, we may know that a person is safe, but if she does not

---

[10] See J. A. Reid et al., "Human Trafficking of Minors and Childhood Adversity in Florida," *American Journal of Public Health* 107, no. 2 (January 2017): 306–11, https://doi.org/10.2105/AJPH.2016.303564.

[11] See Karyn Purvis, David Cross, and Wendy Lyons Sunshine, *The Connected Child: Bring Hope and Healing to Your Adoptive Family* (New York: McGraw Hill, 2007).

feel safe, healing will be difficult, if not impossible. Those who have experienced developmental trauma were often betrayed by those they should have been able to trust, which means they may be skeptical of new people and trust may take a while to build. The amygdala, the part of the brain responsible for fear and emotion, takes over when a threat, whether real or imagined, is perceived. This can send a person into survival mode, which means the part of her brain responsible for making logical decisions is rendered ineffective. Taking the time to establish a sense of safety can calm the amygdala and help the person feel safe.

We also want to foster a sense of hope. Change can never happen if there is not a sense of hope that things can be different. Without a doubt, one of the most horrific cases of trauma I (Brooke) have ever encountered was one of my first clients as a graduate student. Normally, the counseling center would not have given such an intense case to a new counseling student, but there was nothing on her intake form to indicate her level of intensity. I worked with her for a long time, and little progress was made. This client baffled me, and I sought consultation for this case multiple times.

To cope with the trauma my client had endured over the course of at least ten years, she turned to various substances. After multiple drinking and driving charges, her driver's license had been revoked, and she had nearly died of an overdose about two years before we started working together. The overdose had been a wake-up call to her, and she had been clean for the last two years. Because she didn't have a driver's license, she had to rely on family members and friends to get her to counseling.

My client presented as extremely dedicated. She was always present and on time for our sessions. On one occasion, she asked me about five months in advance if it would be fine for her to miss her appointment for a family member's graduation. On another occasion, she called when she thought she would not be able to make it to counseling because she was not going to be able to find a ride. She ended up making it, and I found out she had gotten into an argument with her driver because he had tried to cancel on bringing her. She said that counseling was too important to cancel. In many ways, this sounds like the type of client any counselor would want, but this woman was not progressing in therapy. Her disposition was still melancholic, and processing her past trauma did not seem to bring much relief.

I tried new things and spent a substantial amount of time trying to understand the lack of progress. Then we had a conversation that provided some limited insight. We were discussing an assignment she had failed to complete, and she mentioned that it was difficult to get started because she was so afraid of doing it wrong. Perfectionism can be paralyzing for many of us. In continuing to work with her, I discovered her biggest obstacle to progress. She showed that perfectionism had paralyzed her actions, and she had no hope that things could be different. Research has indicated adolescents who experience household dysfunction growing up (e.g., parental separation or divorce, domestic violence, household mental-health conditions, household problematic substance use) have a more difficult time conceptualizing the future as it relates to potential consequences and planning.[12]

Hope seems like a relatively easy thing to resolve, but my experience has been that it can be one of the greatest obstacles to healing. Hope is what allows us to conceptualize alternatives. Without hope, we do not believe things can be different. People seem to be misled into believing these women have a choice, which is not always true. In many cases, they have been forced or coerced into the sex industry.

Implications for Ministry

Unfortunately, we sometimes view the sex industry like the '90s movie *Pretty Woman*. This movie romanticized prostitution and failed to portray the darkness involved in the sex industry. I (Brooke) frequently hear people

[12] Carys Chainey, Kylie Burke, and Michele Haynes, "Does Parenting Moderate the Association between Adverse Childhood Experiences and Adolescents' Future Orientation?" *Journal of Child and Family Studies* 31 (2022): 2359–75.

ask why these men and women do not just get out. Or why they may ask for help and not follow through. Many of them have been so beaten down by life that they have no hope for their situation to improve. They have core beliefs of being unlovable and defective. As a result, they do not believe that anyone, God included, could love them or change their situation.

Making a major lifestyle change is difficult for any of us, but consider the experience of those in the sex industry. Someone who has been trafficked was never given a choice in the first place. Consider this scenario: A young lady begins working in a strip club around age twenty-one. As she is approaching her early forties, she starts thinking about making some changes in her life. With the help of a local church group, she leaves the strip club, begins counseling, and starts trying to establish a new life. She works to obtain her high school diploma, then goes for a job interview, where they ask her what she has been doing for the last twenty years. How many employers are likely to hire someone with limited work experience?

Consider the following implications for working with those who have experienced chronic childhood stress.

They Need Us to Give Voice to Their Plight

Those with chronic stress were often left without a voice. As children, they were often left in environments in which they had no control. They may have said no to abuse, and it did not matter. They may have been forced into things they did not want to do. I (Brooke) once worked with a lady who had worked as a stripper for a period of time. While she worked as a stripper, she had a stalker who continued to pursue her long after her days of working in a strip club. Over the course of a decade, he sexually assaulted her countless times. She did not report it because she didn't think anyone would believe a stripper.

Because they have had so much taken from them, it is important that we give voice. One of the most important ways we can do this is to believe them and validate their experience. They may have disclosed their abuse multiple times and were not believed, or the impact may have been minimized. I have worked with a number of clients who have been told that what happened to them is in the past and it shouldn't bother them anymore. Or their friends and loved ones may not understand the length and nature of the recovery process and all its setbacks. They may be told to forgive and forget. Forgiveness is a good thing, but pretending the abuse never happened can be harmful and unhealthy.

They Need to Be Allowed Choices

In assisting during the recovery process, it is easy to come in, take charge, and direct everything for the person, but that takes away her autonomy. Instead, help her understand all her options, and allow her to make the final decision on matters. Choices will build her autonomy and give her a voice.

They Have a Need to Be in Control

People with chronic childhood stress often have poor boundaries. In many cases, they felt that people were going to take from them anyway, so they might as well give in. They often feel in control if they are the ones giving. In the sex industry, many victims protect their real names because they are the only thing that cannot be taken from them. When a worker shares her real name, it is a huge sign of trust.

They Have a Skewed Perspective on Relationships

They may not understand a relationship with no strings attached. Because they are accustomed to someone always expecting something in return, they may be reluctant to receive help. They also have not had many healthy relationships, so they may not know how to have appropriate boundaries. They may fear abandonment. As a result, they may avoid relationships or cling to the person so fiercely that he or she feels suffocated. When walking alongside a person who has experienced ACEs, putting healthy boundaries in place can help preserve the relationship and show the person you care. We will discuss boundaries as they relate to helping relationships in more detail in chapter 29.

They Have Maladaptive Coping Mechanisms

If they grew up in poverty, stealing may have been necessary for survival. They may have been left unsupervised to care for younger siblings. Some may have been given drugs, or they may have chosen drugs to cope with what they were doing or what was being done to them. We must build their toolbox with more adaptive coping mechanisms; otherwise, they will continue to return to the maladaptive ones.

They Need Consistency

Our ministry has been going out on Bourbon Street and ministering to the women and men in the sex industry for over a decade now. Although the makeup of the group may have changed, our mission has remained the same. Consistency has allowed us to build trust over the years. One of the first times our group went out after COVID-19, we were flagged down by a person who remembered when we frequently visited his previous place of employment years before. We also had a lady who said she remembered our group praying for her sister ten years earlier.

Many of these women have never had any consistency in their lives. They may have had family members who would leave, and they were never sure when they would return. They may have had family members who were continually under the influence or suffering from an untreated mental illness and unable to care for them and their siblings. This may have led to them taking on caregiving roles at a young age. Offering a sense of stability provides a solid foundation upon which recovery can begin.

ACEs and Violence

As part of my work, I (Brooke) have had the privilege of teaching counseling classes for one of the prison extension centers at the seminary. When hearing these women and their stories, we consider the trajectories of their lives and how that led them to incarceration. Often, they relate stories of adverse childhood experiences. With an increase in the accumulation of ACEs comes an elevated risk for physical aggression in life.[13] Among a population of incarcerated women, researchers found that those with a first arrest before age eighteen, childhood victimization, and polysubstance use were more likely to perpetrate violence in adulthood.[14]

Some people experience trauma that is not visible, which can make early intervention difficult. When we are able to identify at-risk youth in our communities, we can intervene to help build resiliency from adversity. For some kids, this could include having healthy adult mentors in their lives. In some cases, it may involve ministry to the entire family.

For those involved in prison ministry, it may mean advocating for trauma-informed care within the prison and allowing those incarcerated the opportunity to process and heal from past trauma. The mental-health department of most prisons is not adequately staffed to provide long-term trauma recovery care. Sponsoring professional counselors who can conduct trauma counseling in the prison can bring hope and healing. For those who will be eligible for release, trauma recovery work can ease their reentry into society while offering them a fresh start, free from past trauma.

Conclusion

Adverse childhood experiences are more common than many of us realize. Although children can be resilient, those who have experienced chronic

---

[13] See Alan King, "The ACE Questionnaire and Lifetime Physical Aggression," *Journal of Aggression, Maltreatment, & Trauma* 30, no. 2 (2021): 243–60.

[14] See Preeta Saxena and Nena Messina, "Trajectories of Victimization to Violence among Incarcerated Women," *Health & Justice* 9, no. 18 (2021): 1–12.

childhood stress need our help and support to heal and move forward in a healthy space. When working with adults who have experienced chronic childhood stress, it is important to remember that many of their difficult, maladaptive behaviors likely come from a place of trauma. Although this does not vindicate their current and past actions, their past trauma provides a framework for us to conceptualize their current behavior. In doing so, we can look at the underlying causes of their behavior, begin to empathize with them, show compassion, and offer help.

Chapter 12

Special Considerations for Foster/Adoptive Children

James 1:27 says, "Pure and undefiled religion before God the Father is this: to look after orphans and widows in their distress and to keep oneself unstained from the world." Everyone may not be called to foster or adopt, but we may be called to care for and support those who do. There are around 443,000 children living in the US foster care system, around 125,000 of whom are eligible for adoption.[1] The children eligible for adoption could wait an average of four years for an adoptive family.[2] Assuming there are 400,000 churches in America, if one family from every third church adopted a child from foster care, all waiting children would have

[1] See "The Church Could Give Every U.S. Waiting Child a Home," Bethany .org, https://bethany.org/resources/the-church-could-give-every-u-s-waiting-child -a-home.

[2] See "U.S. Adoption & Foster Care Statistics," CCAI, https://www.ccainstitute .org/resources/fact-sheets.

a forever family. In 2018, the number of children who left foster care had been in care for an average of seventeen months.[3]

To those outside the foster care system, adoption may seem to be a fairy tale. You take a child without a family, give him or her a family, which leads to hope and a happily ever after. Although adoption is a beautiful thing, it begins from a place of brokenness. Adoption occurs when a parent is unable to care for his or her child. Generational trauma, including abuse and neglect; the loss of a parent to death; or a teenage girl who found herself in a difficult position may be at the center of adoption. To care for foster/adoptive families, the church must understand the struggles that go along with adoption and ways to overcome them.

A little over ten years ago, I (Brooke) was at a Christian counseling conference presenting on how to parent traumatized children. One question I still remember vividly came from a lady who had adopted a child at birth. She asked me what I knew about perinatal trauma. I was early on in my career, so I knew very little at the time. She told me about some of the struggles her daughter had experienced over the years. She had tried explaining to others that her daughter had been adopted and that she believed some of her issues resulted from that early trauma. People would respond by asking her how old her daughter was when she was adopted. When they found out her daughter had been adopted at birth, they were quick to place blame on the adoptive mom and how she had raised her daughter.

I now know that research has shown that prenatal events, other than drug exposure, can have long-term effects on children. Stress during pregnancy and trauma during delivery can leave a lasting impact.[4] A research study conducted after the September 11 attack on the World Trade Center

[3] See "U.S. Adoption & Foster Care Statistics."

[4] See Natalie Cook, Susan Ayers, and Antje Horsch, "Maternal Posttraumatic Stress Disorder during the Perinatal Period and Child Outcomes: A Systematic Review," *Journal of Affective Disorders* 225, no. 1 (January 2018): 18–31, https://doi.org/10.1016/j.jad.2017.07.045.

and the Pentagon assessed the cortisol levels of children whose moms were pregnant during the attacks. The study revealed that these children continued to have lower levels of cortisol after delivery. Cortisol is a hormone produced and released by our adrenal glands. Lower levels of cortisol following a trauma were associated with prior trauma exposure or the development of PTSD. Lower-than-normal cortisol levels are associated with adrenal insufficiency, which negatively impacts the body's ability to respond to stress, among other essential functions.[5] Similarly, children adopted at birth may experience long-term effects of chronic stress and trauma.

The Survival Needs of Vulnerable Children

In working with vulnerable children, we should make a distinction between being safe and feeling safe. On many occasions, we know that our children are safe, but they may not feel safe. A lack of felt safety can be at the root of what we perceive as behavioral issues. Survival needs that resulted from past trauma may fuel misbehavior.[6]

Because of previous food insecurity, they may hoard or steal food.[7] They never knew if or when they would receive food again, so they put some aside just in case. On the other end of the spectrum, I (Brooke) worked with a girl who had been adopted. Her adoptive family did not understand why she was so reluctant to eat. They wondered if she was ungrateful. Rather, she simply didn't know what to do with all the food in front of her. She had never seen that amount of food before and was overwhelmed.

Because vulnerable children have had inconsistent care from adults and caregivers, they often take on adult responsibilities in caring for themselves,

---

[5] See Rachel Yehuda and Linda M. Bierer, "Transgenerational Transmission of Cortisol and PTSD Risk," *Progress in Brain Research*, 167 (2008): 121–35, https://doi.org/10.1016/S0079-6123(07)67009-5.

[6] See Karyn Purvis and David Cross, *The Connected Child: Bring Hope and Healing to Your Adoptive Family* (New York: McGraw Hill, 2007), 36–37.

[7] Purvis and Cross, 38.

their siblings, or even their parents. This may be referred to as parentification. This is the child who, while at school, may leave a list of things for the parent to accomplish. This might also be the child who has had to take care of or clean up after a parent who has passed out drunk.

A by-product of parentification is difficulty receiving care. These kids have rarely received care and affection, so they struggle to give and receive it from others. Or the people who were supposed to care for them were the source of harm. They may be repulsed when their foster/adoptive parents express healthy affection toward them or try to help them. They have become accustomed to doing everything for themselves with no support from adults, and they often do not know how to ask for help or respond when others offer assistance.

In some cases, these kids may be completely inflexible as it relates to schedules and changes. So many things in their lives have felt out of control that they are eager to gain and maintain control in any way they can. They respond well to consistency. But when there is a change to the schedule, as there often is in life, they struggle to adapt. For many of these kids, a consistent routine is best for building felt safety. It gives them a sense of predictability and stability. Once trust has been earned, we can start to introduce changes to the schedule or environment slowly and provide them with the time and space to adapt to the changes.

I (Brooke) often tell my students that we walk through life carrying baskets. Along the way, people drop messages in these baskets. These messages may be life-giving or life-destroying. If we are not intentional about evaluating these messages for veracity, we can easily internalize the message and continue to be burdened by them as we go through life. Being abused or passed around or feeling abandoned or given away can lead to some destructive messages being dropped into the basket. Many of these kids have internalized the destructive messages and allowed them to color their view of God, themselves, and others. These kids need to know that they have value because of who they are in Christ. They also need some help in understanding they are not to blame for what happened to them.

When Typical Development Is Interrupted

A critical period of development is a time in which certain skills are acquired more efficiently. In some cases, these skills may still be learned at a later time, but it may be more difficult. For example, think about learning a second language. A child who is exposed to a second language earlier in life is better able to acquire and articulate the language than an adult who tries to learn another language. Another example might be a child with severe medical issues requiring hospitalization in the first year of life when children should be learning to sit up, crawl, and explore. The child was incapacitated during this period of development, so he was not able to master these skills in this time frame.

When a critical period of development is missed, a child could experience a developmental delay, although there are a number of reasons children are delayed in development. Developmental delays may occur when a child has been severely abused or neglected, been passed through several foster homes, experienced medical issues including hospitalization, or spent time in an institution such as an orphanage. The delays could impact motor function, speech and language, cognition, play, and social skills.

Fetal alcohol spectrum disorder (FASD) is the leading cause of neurodevelopmental disorders.[8] When limited information is available, FASD is not always easy to diagnose, although some estimates indicate that as many as 1 to 5 per 100 children may be affected,[9] with children in foster care or who were adopted domestically being at greater risk.[10] As a result, those with FASD may struggle with learning and behavior, including difficulties getting along with others; impulsivity; hyperactivity; poor coordination and balance; and memory and processing skills.

[8] See Ariel Tenenbaum, Asaf Mandel, Talia Dor, et al., "Fetal Alcohol Spectrum Disorder among Pre-adopted and Foster Children," *BMC Pediatrics* 20, no. 275 (2020), https://doi.org/10.1186/s12887-020-02164-z.

[9] See CDC, "Data and Statistics on FASDs," Fetal Alcohol Spectrum Disorders, May 15, 2024, https://www.cdc.gov/fasd/data/index.html.

[10] See Tenenbaum et al., "Fetal Alcohol Spectrum Disorder."

Interruptions during a critical period of development can also result in struggles with sensory processing. Sensory processing is the way the brain receives, organizes, and responds to sensory input. When the sensory system is not functioning well, a child may be overly sensitive to some stimuli or require more sensory input than what would achieve the same effect in another child. A child who over- or underresponds to sensory input may exhibit behavioral challenges.[11] For example, a child who is overresponsive to loud noises or bright lights may have tantrums, melt down, or run out of the room. A child who is underresponsive to sensory input may struggle with personal space because he or she craves touch and movement and may even exhibit aggressive behavior.[12] Keeping track of when a child's behavioral challenges are occurring can help us determine whether sensory processing is involved.

Developmental delays, the effects of FASD, and struggles with sensory processing can be addressed through different types of therapy. For delays in gross/fine motor skills, physical or occupational therapy can help the child get back on track developmentally. Physical therapists primarily address areas of gross motor function, including balance and coordination. They help children acquire skills needed to skip, jump rope, and ride bikes. Although there is some overlap between physical and occupational therapy, occupational therapists (OTs) typically focus more on fine motor and visual motor skills, including writing and throwing and catching a ball (hand-eye coordination). They also help children gain independence with activities of daily living, such as tying shoes, buttoning/unbuttoning shirts, and feeding. Some OTs also work with sensory processing. Sometimes sensory processing struggles are integrated, while other times they may continue into adulthood.[13] The good news is, many adults have learned adaptive ways to manage their struggles, and the rest of us are often unaware of their struggles.

---

[11] See Dayna Abraham, Claire Heffron, Pamela Braley, and Lauren Drobnjak, *Sensory Processing 101* (Coppell, TX: self-published, 2021), 5.

[12] See Abraham et al., 28.

[13] See Carol Kranowitz, *The Out-of-Sync Child: Recognizing and Coping with Sensory Processing Disorder* (New York: Penguin, 2005), 47–48.

Speech language pathologists can assist with language and articulation skills. Speech therapists, occupational therapists, and mental-health therapists may work with delays in social skills. In some cases, they offer groups for kids to practice these skills with their peers. FASD and other developmental disabilities are lifelong diagnoses, while developmental delays are not necessarily permanent. With early intervention, a child with a delay can get caught up with his or her peers and get back on track developmentally. As discussed in previous chapters, children may benefit from processing past trauma through counseling.

Special education services can provide assistance to a child with developmental delays in the school setting. Although it may not always function in this capacity, the original intention of the Individuals with Disabilities Education Act (IDEA) was for special education to be a service to children who needed it, rather than a destination. Many children with Individualized Education Plans (IEPs) have developmental trauma in their backgrounds. Encouraging trauma-informed approaches in our schools can help us address the underlying causes of these learning and behavioral struggles.

Learning Brain versus Survival Brain

Children typically do not struggle behaviorally for no reason. There will almost always be a need behind the behavior. If we want to offer a healing connection to vulnerable children, we need to learn to look under the surface at what is causing the behavior, then find a way to meet that need and help them feel safe. We want to work as detectives to discover the underlying cause.[14]

In chapter 10, we learned about the "upstairs" and "downstairs" brains. As it relates to education, we may think of the upstairs brain as the learning

---

[14] For more information on sensory processing, see Gail Belsky, "Understanding Sensory Processing Challenges in Your Child," Understood, updated December 4, 2023, https://www.understood.org/en/articles/understanding-sensory-processing-challenges.

brain and the downstairs brain as the survival brain. Both are part of the same brain, but their orientation to the environment and the manner in which they process information are different. The learning brain is curious and engaged in exploration, motivated to find a balance between novelty and familiarity. It is more comfortable with uncertainty. The survival brain seeks to anticipate, prevent, or protect against the damage caused by potential or actual dangers. It relies on automatic rapid processing while largely bypassing areas of the brain involved in more complex adaptations to the environment. When operating out of the survival brain, our ability to manage distress, along with our ability to make logical plans and judgments, is compromised. The survival brain always trumps the learning brain because it's trying to save our lives.[15]

Students will learn best when they feel safe and supported by the adults around them. Otherwise, their survival brains will take over to ensure their safety. When the survival brain takes charge, kids are likely to exhibit maladaptive behaviors as a form of self-protection. Taking time to help students feel safe and supported will allow their learning brains to take over, which will result in calm, curiosity, and an eagerness to learn.

Reflecting on Our Past

As parents, we often have the best of intentions in parenting our children. With so much research available to us today that was not available previously, we have more knowledge upon which to base our parenting strategies than our parents did. Many of us enter parenting with the desire to make more optimal decisions in caring for and relating to our children than our parents did. When we are not intentional about reflecting on our own

[15] See Julian D. Ford, "Neurobiological and Developmental Research: Clinical Implications," in *Treating Complex Traumatic Stress Disorders: An Evidence-Based Guide,* eds. Christine A. Courtois and Julian D. Ford (New York: Guilford, 2009): 31–35.

experiences as a child, we often default to parenting the way in which we were parented.

Our brains have the capacity to store memories unconsciously, which means our brains remember things that may be outside our awareness. When this happens, we can have a strong reaction to a situation without understanding why. As it relates to parenting, there may be times in which we have a strong reaction to our child's emotional response without understanding the underlying cause. This strong reaction can interfere with our ability to have a healthy connection with our children.[16]

Being able to develop a coherent narrative of our own early life experiences allows us to make connections about unresolved issues that may be triggered when we work with vulnerable children. "History is not destiny. By making sense of your own story, you can be the kind of parent you want to be—regardless of how you were parented."[17] When we make sense of our own stories, we are better able to heal and grow in such a way that we can offer more optimal parenting to our children.

In my (Brooke) Marriage and Family Issues class, we participate in an exercise that helps us make sense of our past. We reflect on the things from our families of origin (the families in which we grew up) and determine what we would like to keep and pass on, what we would like to change, and what we would like to discard. In completing the exercise, we extend grace to our families when possible. Many of them were doing the best they could with the resources available to them at the time. We also want to be mindful of any strong emotional reactions we may have to others, especially our children. These strong emotional reactions could indicate that there is still something unresolved from our own childhood that we need to address to connect more deeply with our children.

---

[16] See Dan Siegel and Mary Hartzell, *Parenting from the Inside Out* (New York: Penguin, 2003), 13–14.

[17] Dan Siegel and Tina Payne Bryson, *The Power of Showing Up: How Parental Presence Shapes Who Our Kids Become and How Their Brains Get Wired* (New York: Ballantine Books, 2020), 28.

If you have experienced any type of trauma or adverse childhood experiences as outlined in previous chapters, counseling could be beneficial in bringing healing and resolution to these past experiences. When we work on resolving our past trauma and losses, we establish a secure connection with our children and minimize interference from the past.

When a Child Comes into Care

In most cases, a series of traumatic events has brought a child into foster care. The uncertainty of coming into a new home with new people for an often unspecified period of time brings out fear, frustration, and anxiety in children. There are several things that can be done to ease the transition and help them feel safe in their new environment.

Be Sensitive When Preparing Their Space

Some of these kids are not acquainted with having a large number of toys or bright and colorful decorations and might become overstimulated. As a result, you may want to maintain a neutral color scheme for the child's room until you are able to learn more about the child's preferences. It might also be helpful to only have a few toys out, so as not to overwhelm them. Allow them to select and keep a few items that would bring them comfort and give them some options to make the space their own.

Give Them a Tour of Your House

When they first arrive at your home, show them around the house. Most important, show them their room and yours in the event that they get scared and need to know where to find you. For older children, consider providing them a list that helps them understand where certain items are kept in the house. For younger children, you might create a picture list or book that offers the same information in a way they can understand if they are unable to read. Knowing the environment will help reduce children's anxiety.

Be Mindful of Food Insecurity

Some of these children may have come from places in which they did not know when or from where their next meal was coming. They may have been left unattended, not knowing whether anyone would return with food. Some of these kids steal or hoard food in their rooms or other places. Their motivation is not deceit, but a primitive response to food insecurity.

To help with this, one option might be to leave healthy snacks on the lowest shelf in the pantry so the child can reach them at any time. For some kids, just knowing the food is there and easily accessible can alleviate their anxiety. Another option is allowing them to carry a snack in their pockets or backpacks when they go out, so they'll have the added reassurance of having access to food.

Help Them See Their Value in Your Family

Although you may not know how long they will be with you, hang up their artwork. Find ways to help them feel like they are a part of your family. You can include them on vacations and other cultural experiences. Allow them some choices about activities they might be interested in, and ask them how they would be comfortable being introduced in public. Children do not want to be introduced as "foster children."

Ways to Support Foster/Adoptive Families

Be Sensitive with Transitions

Whether you encounter the foster family through church, school, or counseling, be mindful of the difficulties involved with transitioning to a new home or church. Although the child may continue attending the same school, a new home will bring about new places and routines. Make the effort to familiarize him with the environment by taking him on a tour or allowing him to explore the new surroundings. Also, remember that these transitions may be difficult for the children already in the home. While much attention may be placed on the kids adjusting to a new home, we need to devote an appropriate level of attention to those already in the home who are trying to adjust as well.

Be Knowledgeable about the Nature of Trauma

Without prior knowledge of trauma and its impact, a child's behavioral struggles may be misunderstood. Many assume that since the child now has a safe home, he or she should be happy and have no struggles. However, many of these children have a pattern of abuse, much as we discussed in chapter 11, "Chronic Childhood Stress." As a result, a vulnerable child may not have a healthy worldview. Many foster/adoptive parents put in a substantial amount of time to build a secure attachment with their child. In the meantime, there may be quite a few struggles with establishing felt safety and a solid connection.

Consider training your church or organization in trauma-informed care. This information will help everyone involved establish a safe place for these kids while being better equipped to support and minister to the families. Without this knowledge, we may unintentionally act in a way that compromises safety and connection.

Offer Practical Help

Families often receive little notice before finding out they have a new placement. Offering to bring a meal or help in some other capacity can help them with the quick turnaround time. Many of these children may be behind in school and need extra assistance with homework. Offering to help them with homework or prepare for a test can take a load off a parent who is trying to juggle other aspects of care. Your church could host a respite night, or you could offer babysitting services to allow parents some rest.

Conclusion

The journey of foster care/adoption is not easy, but it is rewarding. Having a solid understanding of trauma and its impact will equip us to better work with vulnerable children. Establishing felt safety within our homes, churches, and schools can allow these children the freedom to learn and grow. Behavior is communication, and we are wise to consider the survival or sensory needs fueling a child's misbehavior. Then, we can meet him where he is and help him get his needs addressed.

Additional Resources

Hoffman, Kent, Glen Cooper, and Bert Powell, *Raising a Secure Child: How Circle of Security Parenting Can Help You Nurture Your Child's Attachment, Emotional Resilience, and Freedom to Explore.* New York: Guilford, 2017.

Purvis, Karyn, and David Cross. *The Connected Child: Bring Hope and Healing to Your Adoptive Family.* New York: McGraw Hill, 2007.

Siegel, Dan, and Tina Payne Bryson, *The Whole-Brain Child: Twelve Strategies to Nurture Your Child's Developing Mind.* New York: Delacorte, 2001.

———, *The Power of Showing Up: How Parental Presence Shapes Who Our Kids Become and How Their Brains Get Wired.* New York: Ballentine Books, 2020.

Part 6

Children and Adolescents

Chapter 13

Grief in Children and Adolescents

Jacob contacts you six months after losing his wife, Maria. He is concerned about his eleven-year-old son, Will, who has become quiet and withdrawn since the death of his mother. Will's grades are dropping, and one of his teachers has expressed concern. Jacob explains that his grief is so intense that he finds it difficult to speak to Will about Maria death. He asks you, "What do I do? I'm barely making it through my grief. I have no idea how to help my son with his grief."

Throughout ministry, you will encounter children who have lost loved ones to death. You can work with the adults in their lives to help support and understand the grieving process of children and adolescents. Loss is not limited to the death of a loved one. Children and adolescents may experience a variety of losses:

- moving (either themselves or a loved one, such as a friend or relative)
- divorce

- changing schools
- death of a pet
- death of a friend or classmate
- death of a parent
- death of a sibling

In this chapter, we will focus primarily on childhood grief due to the death of a loved one. The term *children* is used with the intention that the material is applicable at age-appropriate levels for those under age eighteen.

Impact of Grief

Children experience grief holistically. When working with children who have experienced various forms of grief, I (Karen) have observed the extensive emotional, physical, behavioral, cognitive, and spiritual impacts. Relationships are affected. Performance at school may change. The loss threatens their sense of safety. Yet children do not typically have the language to express their pain. We will examine some areas to watch for when ministering to or counseling grieving children.

Emotional Impact

Children and adults experience similar emotions in response to grief. Those emotions may be disbelief, denial, sadness, yearning, anger, anxiety, or guilt. However, it is important for adults not to superimpose their experience and understanding of grief on children. While children may experience similar emotions and physical symptoms as adults, children process their grief differently than adults. They tend to move in and out of emotions quickly. They may move from crying and distress to requesting to play outside. This cycling of emotion is normal for children.

Additionally, a child's silence does not mean the child is not grieving. Children may not have the words to express their sorrow, so they may need ways other than talking to express their grief (e.g., imaginative play, music, painting, drawing, physical activity).[1]

There is a broad spectrum of how children may respond to the news of losing a loved one. Some children, particularly preschoolers, may appear apathetic. You may wonder if they heard or understood the news. For example, a preschooler might ask to play with a friend after hearing the news. They may be in shock and emotionally numb, having difficulty processing the news. Other children may display an outpouring of emotion and appear inconsolable.[2] There is no right or wrong way a child "should" respond.

Physical and Behavioral Impact

Children have physical reactions to grief. Some common symptoms are stomach issues, headaches, tiredness, body aches, difficulty self-regulating, restlessness, and insomnia. Some children experience regressive behaviors such as bed-wetting, thumb-sucking, fearing the dark, clinging to an attachment figure, speaking like a younger child, using an emotionally supportive item (e.g., blanket or stuffed animal), or wanting to sleep with a parent.[3]

They may regress in their level of dependence. For example, they may require assistance getting dressed or request someone to tie their shoes when they have already mastered that skill. The regressive behaviors typically subside over time.

Children may experience sleep disturbances. They may have difficulty falling asleep or wake up at night and be unable to fall asleep again.

---

[1] See Andy McNiel and Pamela Gabbay, *Understanding and Supporting Bereaved Children: A Practical Guide for Professionals*, 1st ed. (New York: Springer, 2017), 15–16.

[2] See Atle Dyregrov, *Grief in Young Children: A Handbook for Adults* (Philadelphia: Jessica Kingsley, 2008), 17–18.

[3] See McNiel and Gabbay, *Understanding and Supporting Bereaved Children*, 17.

Nightmares are a common complaint. Sleep is particularly frightening if anyone tells them the deceased has "fallen asleep" or if the child has personified death as a monster who might take them away.

Children in emotional pain, distress, and dysregulation will communicate this through their behaviors. Those grieving may "act out" or have a "temper tantrum" to express their confusing and difficult emotions. Consider "acting out" as a form of communication, revealing that the child needs assistance regulating his or her unexpressed emotions.

Children may isolate themselves socially for a variety of reasons. They may feel their peers do not understand what they are going through. They may try to avoid personal or invasive questions about the loved one's cause of death. Crying in front of others may be a concern to some children.

Children who have lost a loved one may become socially isolated in a way that is out of their control. For example, if a parent has died, the family may relocate, thus eliminating the child's social support system at church or school.[4] If children are removed from their social circles, they may want to be near their remaining loved ones and experience separation anxiety when apart.

Cognitive Impact

One common cognitive impact of grief is difficulty concentrating, particularly at school. Grief may impact their school performance, ability to learn, and grades. Grieving children may seem "spaced out" when spoken to or forgetful beyond what is typical for a developing child.

Children may worry that another loved one will die. For the first time, they may realize they will die one day. This realization is scary, and they may need consistent reassurance from the adults in their lives. Children may develop fears of anything they perceive to be dangerous and worry when others they love are away from them.

---

[4] See Dyregrov, *Grief in Young Children*, 41–42.

Children often blame themselves for the death. This self-blame often goes unspoken but is ever present in the child's mind. For example, if she visited grandma while she had a cold and grandma died two weeks later from being "sick" with cancer, the child may believe she was the cause of grandma's death. Children may blame themselves with no apparent connection. The child may think, "Mommy died because I yelled at her (or did not clean my room)." When a child believes he or she is to blame, ask the child, "What makes you believe that?" Listen well and gently reassure the child that the death was not his or her fault.

Spiritual Impact

Children may question, "Where is God?" or "Is God really good?" or "Does God care about me?" If they realize death happens to everyone, they may begin to question, "What happens when we die?" They may ask if their loved ones are in heaven. Some may see their faith as a source of hope and their faith community as a source of support during their grief.[5]

Developmental Stages

Factors that impact grief are listed in chapter 5, and those factors may be considered when working with children. An additional consideration for children is their developmental stage. At one time, people thought infants, toddlers, and preschoolers did not experience grief.[6] This belief is incorrect. Children of all ages experience grief, but the developmental stage impacts how children understand their grief and how it is communicated.

---

[5] See McNiel and Gabbay, *Understanding and Supporting Bereaved Children*, 19–20.

[6] See Janis A. Di Ciacco, *The Colors of Grief: Understanding a Child's Journey through Loss from Birth to Adulthood* (Philadelphia: Jessica Kingsley, 2008), 57.

We will look at the primary considerations as the child develops. These are not clear-cut stages, so consider this a spectrum. Simply because a child moves from age five to six does not mean she immediately develops all the understanding of someone in that stage. Neither does it mean a younger child will not have a more advanced understanding. When working with children, provide information and answer questions based on the child's level of understanding.

Birth to Age 2

Forming a secure, healthy attachment to a primary caregiver is a critical task during this stage of development, so losing a primary caregiver during this age leaves a lasting impact on the child. Children of this age have a limited ability to understand the concept of death but will notice the person they love is not present. When children can express themselves verbally, they may ask questions about the location of the missing loved one. Even though children of this age may not fully understand what has happened, they do experience grief and feel a sense of abandonment. Children this age may not be able to verbalize the memory of this loss, but they do have a deeply imprinted felt sense of the loss.[7]

Ages 3–5

By age three, most children will ask questions about the deceased, such as when the person is returning or what happened to their loved one. Children this age do not fully grasp that death is a permanent condition that occurs to everyone. For example, they may think the person is somewhere else and could return or come back to life. They may think a person is in heaven today but could return tomorrow. Children of this age feel deep emotions but do not possess the skills to communicate what they are feeling verbally, so they may communicate with behaviors rather than words. When helping

---

[7] See Di Ciacco, 72.

grieving children of all ages, remember that they are developing their communication skills.

Ages 6–8

At this age, children begin to realize the permanence of death, but they are still concrete thinkers like younger children. As such, they may think of death as a scary monster, which can be terrifying for the child.[8] Additionally, they begin to realize death happens to everyone. This realization can be frightening and anxiety-provoking. They may be fearful that they might die and seek reassurance of their safety. Also, they may fear that others they love might die and seek reassurance of the well-being of the people they love. Children this age may ask questions about what happens when a person dies, and this can be an opportunity to share the hope of the gospel with your child.

Ages 9–12

By this age, children realize death is permanent and their loved one will not return. They realize all people will die one day, including them. If they have not already, they will begin to ask questions and seriously consider what happens after death. At this age, many children begin deciding for themselves whether or not to accept Christ, so the crisis of death may bring up additional questions or concerns.

Adolescents

Adolescents have an increasing ability for abstract thinking and reasoning. They have the understanding that death is permanent and can discuss their faith as it relates to grief. They may benefit from discussing what to expect

[8] See Di Ciacco, 102.

when grieving. Teens will vary in willingness and ability to identify, name, and share emotions.

Helping Children Process Their Grief

We will explore some suggestions for sharing news of the death with children, getting through the funeral and burial, and assisting children in processing their grief.

Sharing the News

Share in a timely manner. When sharing the news that someone has died, tell the child what happened as soon as possible. Sharing the news may be exceptionally challenging when the adult telling the child is struggling with his or her own grief. If the adult sharing the information is having difficulty communicating, consider having another trusted adult present to provide support and to continue the conversation if the adult sharing becomes emotionally dysregulated. This could be a minister, chaplain (if at the hospital), or another family member.

Be direct. You can briefly prepare the child for the bad news by saying, "I have something sad to tell you. It's about [name of deceased]."[9] Then, you can explain what happened at an age-appropriate level, clearly using the word "died." Do not use vague phrases such as "He passed away," "Grandma went to sleep," "Jesus took [or needed] her," "He lost his life," or "We lost her." Phrases such as these can be scary and confusing because they do not communicate the finality of death.

Be prepared to explain the death to the child multiple times. News of a death is shocking. Even as adults, we often have difficulty listening, processing, and accepting what is communicated. Children may take in the information in small increments, process it, and ask additional questions. Or they may need the information repeated multiple times.

---

[9] See Dyregrov, *Grief in Young Children*, 39–40.

Allow the child to ask questions. Answer age appropriately. If you do not know the answer, it is okay to tell a child, "That's a good question. I don't know. Let's talk about it."

Assure the child of your presence. After news of a death, children may become fearful of their own safety and whether or not their caregivers will be available. Assure them of your continued presence.

Listen for clues that the child may be self-blaming. Notice if the child is taking responsibility for the death. If so, allow him to explain the connections he is making, but then assure him it is not his fault.

Tell the child it is okay to feel sad. Parents can say they are sad too but should avoid the child becoming their emotional support system, as this is harmful to the child.

Avoid phrases such as "God needed him in heaven" or "Heaven needed another angel." Statements such as these are theologically problematic and confusing. Additionally, statements like these could potentially frighten children as they might think, *Oh no. What if God needs me? Am I going to die too?*

The Funeral

Prepare the child for the funeral. Describe what will happen at the funeral service. Include a visual description of what to expect, such as the flowers, the coffin, and how the loved one will be viewed in the casket (if the casket is open). Have someone go into the room first to provide the child with a better description of the deceased. For example, it can be disarming if the loved one has a different hairstyle or looks vastly different from when he or she was alive. Just as with telling the child about the death, it can be helpful to have a trusted person whom the child knows accompany the family to the viewing of the body to offer support.

Normalize emotions. Communicate that some people may be crying while others will not be crying. Assure the child it is okay to cry but it is also okay not to cry. Families may find it helpful to have a trusted friend monitor the children for signs of distress, provide additional support, or take them outside for a break as needed.

Mementos. Depending on the child's relationship to the deceased, ask her if she wants to take an item, such as a photograph, handmade item, or letter, to place in the casket. The caregivers should clearly communicate that the child will not be able to get the item back.

Prepare for the burial. If there is a graveside service, communicate what to expect. Discuss the burial and explain to the child that the loved one's body and the casket will be placed in the ground. After each phase of the funeral and burial, allow the child to ask any questions he may have.[10]

Recommendations for Helping Grieving Children

- Remember, there is no set timeline or time limit on grief and no "correct" way to grieve.
- Children may not make the connections between the loss and how they are feeling. Provide opportunities for children to name and explore their feelings.
- Consider the child's perception of what happened. You can use drawing, art, or play.
- Read age-appropriate books about grief with the child. Recommendations are provided at the end of this chapter.
- Maintain routines whenever possible. Routines provide stability and security.
- With the child's permission, tell the other adults in the child's life, especially if the loss was an immediate family member or someone the child interacted with regularly (e.g., a teacher or coach).
- Look at keepsakes and photographs. Share stories and favorite memories of the loved one. Consider making a memory box with mementos and a photo book.
- Take the child to visit the grave. If the child is visiting for the first time, prepare her for what to expect. She may want to take flowers, a drawing, or other tokens of remembrance.

---

[10] See Dyregrov, 46–50.

- Create opportunities for a child to communicate and process grief through art, play, music, journaling (for older children and teens), or other creative means.
- Be prepared to answer many different questions and repetitive ones multiple times.
- It's okay for adults to acknowledge they are sad about the loss, but avoid saying "you are making me sad" when the child wants to talk or ask questions.[11] This statement may cause children to shut down to protect the adult and is detrimental to their grieving process.
- Understand that a child's grief is cyclical. Previous thoughts, emotions, and memories will reemerge or "recycle" as they progress. As they age, they will mourn "what could have been." For example, a teenager may experience grief over the realization that the deceased parent will not be present for his high school graduation, college graduation, wedding, or the birth of his children.
- Children do not have the same concept of time and the future as adults. While adults might feel the pain will last forever, they can cognitively understand that they will eventually feel some relief and adjust to the loss with time. Children may not have this future understanding, so they may need reassurance that the feelings will not be this intense forever.[12]

Conclusion

Grief has a holistic impact on children and adolescents. Their developmental stage impacts their understanding of what has happened and their experience processing the grief. As you minister to grieving children and adolescents, consider how to respond in a developmentally appropriate way

---

[11] Elena Merenda, *Childhood Loss and Grief: Guidelines for Educators and Professionals* (Champaign, IL: Common Ground Research Networks, 2020), 18.

[12] See Merenda, 19.

that allows the child to process her grief in a supportive environment. Listen with empathy and acknowledge the pain. Provide reassurance and presence. And finally, remember that experiencing grief takes time and looks different for everyone.

Additional Resources

Rowlan, Joanna, and Thea Baker. *The Memory Box: A Book about Grief.* Minneapolis: Sparkhouse Family, 2017.

Schwiebert, Pat, and Chuck DeKlyen. *Tear Soup: A Recipe for Healing after Loss.* Vancouver: Grief Watch, 2005.

Chapter 14

Suicide in Adolescents

Jay is a fourteen-year-old boy from a close-knit family. He, his parents, and his two younger siblings have always done everything together. They have spent their weekends camping, hiking, and riding their bikes around local trails. Jay has always been polite, favored by his teachers, and an excellent student. Within the last year, Jay has been reluctant to go camping with his family. He does not talk much about school or extracurricular activities. Jay's parents are aware that adolescents often turn away from their parents some during the teen years. With the limited information offered about his day-to-day life, his parents want to ensure they are not missing warning signs of a deeper issue.

Mental-Health Struggles and Adolescence

Adolescence can be a confusing time period for both parents and their child. Between puberty and other changes taking place, parents often struggle to discern between typical teenage angst and mental-health issues. Between 2016 and 2019, the most commonly diagnosed mental disorders for those ages 3 to 17 were attention-deficit/hyperactivity disorder (ADHD), anxiety, behavioral struggles, and depression. These diagnoses are often comorbid with each other. About three of four children diagnosed with depression were also diagnosed with anxiety, and almost one in two had behavioral struggles. For those diagnosed with anxiety, about one in three also had behavioral problems and depression. For children with behavioral struggles, more than one in three also had anxiety, and one in five also had depression.[1]

Teens and Suicide

Suicide is the second-leading cause of death for youth and young adults (ages 10–24). This age group accounts for 15 percent of all suicides. The suicide rate for this age group increased more than 50 percent in 2020–2021. In 2021, there were 224,341 emergency room visits for self-harm involving youth and young adults. The rate for young girls and young women was around twice the rate for young boys and young men. The rate of emergency room visits for young girls in 2020 had almost doubled since 2001.[2]

What Are Adolescents Facing Today?

Identity Confusion

Adolescents are in a season of life in which they are trying to figure out who they are. Up until this point, much of their identity has been intertwined with their parents. This is a stage in which they are looking to their peers more and trying to establish an identity separate from their parents. As they begin the transition out of adolescence and into young adulthood, they will

---

[1] See CDC, "Data and Statistics on Children's Mental Health," Children's Mental Health, last reviewed March 8, 2023, https://www.cdc.gov/childrensmentalhealth/data.html.

[2] See CDC, "Health Disparities in Suicide," CDC Suicide Prevention, January 17, 2024, https://www.cdc.gov/suicide/disparities/index.html.

be overwhelmed with the decisions they need to make. They will need to determine the type of job they would like, how to complete the training required for the job, where they will live, along with many other choices.

Academic Pressure

Today, adolescents seemingly face more academic pressure than ever before. The amount of standardized testing has increased, and we're pushing academic exercises on children at younger and younger ages. The amount of homework places stress and strain on both adolescents and their families. For a number of reasons, many schools struggle to accommodate diverse learners, which further perpetuates their behavioral and mental-health struggles. Not too long ago, one of the counselors I (Brooke) supervise was discussing a case of an adolescent who was fighting depression and suicidal ideation. She remarked that she would love to have some candid conversations with the school system about the amount of stress they are placing on their students, as would I.

Social Pressure

We all have an innate need to belong regardless of our age or stage in life. For adolescents, this is especially true. During this stage of life, our children and teens typically do not have the maturity or social skills needed to navigate relationships effectively. As we discuss in another chapter, they may take their cues from adults, which might not always be positive.

Helping an Adolescent in Crisis

Be Authentic

Adolescents are not looking for adults who are cool or trying to act younger to fit in with the youth. Instead, they are looking for authentic adults. In other words, they want adults who will show up and be themselves. No pretending, but genuinely taking an interest in their lives.

Be Empathic

Empathy allows us to connect with the emotional experiences of another and see from his or her perspective, not ours. This can be tricky with adolescents. As adults, we may have a different perspective on their crises because we have more experience with the long game. We believe it will not matter in twenty years whether they got the dress they wanted for prom, made homecoming court or the varsity basketball team as a freshman, or got the concert tickets they intensely desired. When we're facing cancer diagnoses, mortgage payments, or increasing insurance costs, it's easy for us to trivialize their issues. However, we have to take ourselves back to their stage in life and remember how momentous these events seemed at the time.

Being Proactive

The anticipation of the adolescent years is anxiety-provoking for many parents. Some move through the adolescent years with little trouble or hardship. However, the majority experience difficulties with this developmental stage. As we have discussed previously, this is a period of time in which young people are trying to determine who they are, along with navigating the pressures placed on them. Parents are often curious about the best way to prepare for these years.

Although we never know what these years will bring, we can have a few things in place in the event the adolescent needs extra help during this time. One thing is to be familiar with your family's history of mental illness. Parents sometimes have difficulty determining if what their teen is experiencing is related to hormonal changes and the struggles of adolescence or if it is related to the onset of mental illness. Our family history can provide clues, although this information on its own will not be a sufficient determinant.

Parents should also be familiar with the symptoms of common mental illnesses that affect teens. These could include depression, anxiety, and attention-deficit/hyperactivity disorder (ADHD). When parents are familiar with these symptoms, it can help them to better explain and discuss with medical professionals what they are observing in their teens.[3] Depending on the area in which one lives, appropriate resources such as counselors and psychiatrists may be scarce. Taking the time to familiarize yourself with the professionals in your area can help you prepare in case your child needs extra help during this stage of life.

A number of parents have been caught off guard by the cost of services and the type of insurance coverage available for mental-health services. Taking the time to explore insurance coverage for counseling and other specialist services can help parents prepare to set aside additional finances in the event that they need them. If they end up not needing the additional money, they can always use it for other purposes.[4]

Warning Signs

Think back to Jay, whom we discussed at the beginning of this chapter. His parents want to be proactive in making sure they are not missing warning signs of a problem. Let's look at some things they should consider.

Lack of Connection

We all know the adolescent years can be difficult. With teens going through many changes, they begin to relate differently to their parents. As a result, many parents struggle with discerning between behavior that is typical of the teenage years and warning signs to be heeded. One warning sign that should be heeded is isolation. During these years, adolescents may begin to turn away from their parents and lean more on their peers. If they are isolating themselves from everyone, we should be concerned.

[3] More information on the symptoms of mental illness is provided in the appendix.

[4] See David Walsh, *Why Do They Act That Way?: A Survival Guide to the Adolescent Brain for You and Your Teen* (New York: Atria Paperback, 2014), 238–43.

Attention-Seeking Behavior

When adolescents engage in attention-seeking behavior, they could be asking for help but are unsure of how to reach out to someone. When we see attention-seeking behavior, it is easy to become emotionally reactive and possibly punitive. Instead, we should try to look for the longing behind their striving. In some cases, they may feel ignored or overlooked, especially if another family member is struggling and requiring additional attention. It's also possible they are struggling academically or in their relationships with their peers. They may be unsure who they can turn to who would understand, or they may be ashamed to ask for help. As we know, even adults often struggle with asking for help, so of course teens are likely to have even more difficulty reaching out.

Substance Use

Many adolescents experiment with alcohol or other drugs, but this behavior can indicate that they are facing challenges. There is a brain-based logic behind the legal drinking age of twenty-one. The adolescent brain undergoes intense growth and development, which makes it oversensitive to damage from substances, such as alcohol. This means alcohol does more damage to teens than it does to adults, and it often takes smaller doses to do the damage. At the same time, the teen's brain may be underresponsive to warning signs. Adults are often warned that they have consumed too much alcohol when they experience motor problems, such as stumbling or slurring words or tiredness. The undersensitivity of an adolescent's brain to alcohol's warning signs means teens can become dangerously drunk more easily than adults.[5]

A Note about Antidepressants

Many professionals are divided on the use of antidepressants with children and adolescents due to concerns that they increase suicidal ideation.

[5] See Walsh, 155–58.

Previously, the US Food and Drug Administration (FDA) issued a black box warning for antidepressant use in those under the age of eighteen. The health authorities in other countries responded similarly and, in some cases, more strongly than the US. Each adolescent is unique, and different treatment options or a combination of interventions may be needed for each one. However, most professionals believe other treatment options should be considered before antidepressants are prescribed because of the possibility of increased suicidal thoughts or actions. If you are working with an adolescent who might benefit from antidepressants, make sure to do your research and consult with medical professionals first.[6]

When a Friend Commits Suicide

Following the suicide of a friend or family member, teens who are already struggling may see their friend's suicide as a solution to their suffering. To mitigate suicide contagion following a teen suicide, we should be mindful of how the situation is handled. Having conversations with teens about options available to them if they are in a time of crisis helps them understand they can make a different choice than their friends. Providing the numbers of crisis lines and having counselors available prevents additional suicides.

In being true to our human nature, a teen's suicide will likely invite gossip, rumors, and judgment. When a young person dies by suicide, we are in a state of shock. We desperately desire to understand the situation to prevent future suicides, but we are also racked with guilt about whether we could have prevented the current tragedy. In our attempt to manage this anxiety, we try to determine what precipitated the suicide. In most cases, we will never know why. The only person who can definitively answer why is no longer with us. Rumors are likely to bring further pain and harm to

---

[6] See Jacqueline Sparks and Barry Duncan, "Outside the Black Box: Re-assessing Pediatric Antidepressant Prescription," *Journal of the Canadian Academy of Child & Adolescent Psychiatry* 22, no. 3 (August 2013): 240–46.

family and friends. Instead, we should focus on helping those who are grieving and respecting their privacy.

Adolescents may feel responsible for not being there for their friend or not realizing the depth of his or her struggle. The important thing to remember is that some who die by suicide never show outward signs that they are struggling. We never know the depths of struggle another person is suffering, so it's important to always extend compassion. However, when a person is not showing visible signs of struggle, we cannot hold ourselves responsible for not acting.

Promoting Positive Mental Health

The adolescent years can be turbulent, but the good news is, there are things we can do to build resiliency.

Emotion-Coaching

Emotion-coaching is the process by which parents help their children label their emotions and find healthy ways of coping with their feelings. Teens are often navigating changing situations and confusing emotions. They may need help sorting through their feelings by learning to name and label them. We also want to help them look beneath the surface of their feelings to understand what is driving their current moods and behaviors.[7]

For example, when teens yell "I hate you!" to their parents, what are they trying to communicate? This could vary depending on the situation. If the parents are helping them prepare for a difficult test at school, they may lash out because they are frustrated with difficulty grasping the concepts. When working on college applications, they may lash out because they are afraid of the next chapter of life. Although they may not vocalize it, they may be insecure about their ability to live and work independently. This works both

[7] See John Gottman, *Raising an Emotionally Intelligent Child: The Heart of Parenting* (New York: Simon and Schuster, 1997), 21–24.

ways. Parents may notice themselves becoming emotionally reactive as these milestones are approaching. They may be upset about the prospect of their child leaving home or afraid of what he or she is dealing with at school or with friends. All of us can become reactive as the result of fears, frustrations, and insecurities. As adults, we want to model for teens the appropriate ways to understand and regulate these feelings.

Developing Skills and Talents

To help in their search for identity during this stage of life, you might encourage teens to try different activities and skills. They could try sports, art, or music. These activities can provide a sense of accomplishment and help with their sense of self. These opportunities can also extend beyond finding a talent and can include the opportunity to develop skills. Allowing the opportunity to experiment with various skills can help them determine a direction following high school. Many college students change their majors, some more than once. And many adults make changes in their career paths. Teens do not need to know exactly what they want to do and be when they become adults, but trying different things can help them develop a sense of self. When they have opportunities to develop their identities, they can develop a deeper sense of belonging, rather than trying to change who they are to fit in.[8]

Mentoring

Chap Clark proposed the five-to-one adult/student ratio. He believes every teen needs at least five adults who will say, "I'm going to love that kid until they are fully walking as an adult member of this congregation." Because youth may turn away from adults and toward their peers, we're often inclined to leave them alone. However, many of them want and, most importantly, need to have healthy relationships with adults in their lives. They just may

---

[8] For more information on belonging versus fitting in, see chapter 16.

not always know how to initiate them. The problem is, adults are not always sure what to do either.[9] We need to encourage the adults in our churches to be genuine and authentic in their attempts to connect with teens. They want adults who are taking a genuine interest in their lives. They are not looking for adults who act like teenagers or pretend to like music and other things just to fit in with the young kids. Instead, they are looking for adults who are comfortable being themselves, even if they're older.

The idea of five adults investing in each teen at church can be overwhelming. After all, many of us are short on volunteers in the first place. However, we are not implying that each adult should spend a structured hour per week with the teen. Instead, we are talking about being involved in his or her life. This might include going to basketball games or awards ceremonies, sponsoring a mission trip, or simply inviting a teen to join us and our families for activities. I (Brooke) am one of the first to assume that teens and unmarried adults would not want to join my family in some of our activities, especially when they involve small children. However, many young people actually enjoy the option of being a part of someone's family and getting to know them in real life. It may not be anything other than an evening walk around the block.

Conclusion

The adolescent years can be unnerving for both teens and their parents. Being intentional about building resiliency can help the adolescent weather the storms that may come not only in this developmental stage, but in the years beyond adolescence. In addition to building protective factors with their teens, parents can also familiarize themselves with the symptoms of mental disorders common to teens, along with the risk factors for suicidal ideation. Being familiar with both the warning signs and the mental-health

---

[9] See Chap Clark, "In Spite of How They Act . . . Teenagers Don't Want to Be Left Alone," *Decision*, August 17, 2004, https://decisionmagazine.com/in-spite-of-how-they-act.

resources available in their communities can help them prepare in the event they need to access services.

Additional Resources

Fuller Youth Institute: https://fulleryouthinstitute.org

This website offers a wide range of helpful resources for parents, youth leaders, and other ministry professionals.

Siegel, Daniel J., and Tina Payne Bryson. *The Power of Showing Up: How Parental Presence Shapes Who Our Kids Become and How Their Brains Get Wired.* New York: Ballantine Books, 2020.

This book talks about how we can show up for our kids in a way that will help them feel safe and secure.

Walsh, David. *Why Do They Act That Way?: A Survival Guide to the Adolescent Brain for You and Your Teen.* New York: Atria, 2014.

This book helps explain the changes taking place in the brain during adolescence and helps parents understand and navigate this developmental stage.

Chapter 15

Trauma in Children and Adolescents

Trauma in children and adolescents is prevalent. The Substance Abuse and Mental Health Services Administration (SAMHSA) reports that more than two-thirds of children will experience at least one traumatic event by age sixteen.[1] These traumatic events may include any or all of the following:

- exposure to school, community, or domestic violence
- physical, psychological, or sexual abuse
- neglect
- bullying
- natural or human-made disasters
- medical trauma
- traumatic loss

[1] See "Understanding Child Trauma," SAMHSA, last updated May 28, 2024, https://www.samhsa.gov/child-trauma/understanding-child-trauma.

When working with children exposed to traumatic events, there are some unique considerations due to their developing brains. We will build on the concepts presented in previous chapters and include some additional implications for working with trauma in children and adolescents.

The Developing Brain

In chapter 10, we explored the concept of the "upstairs" and "downstairs" brain. The "downstairs" brain is well-developed at birth, but the "upstairs" brain is not fully developed until the midtwenties, so minors cannot be expected to exhibit the same abilities to regulate as those whose brains are fully mature.

In addition, the developmental stage of minors makes it easier for them to get "trapped" in the "downstairs" brain and have difficulty getting to the "upstairs" brain.[2] Siegel and Bryson liken it to having a staircase between the upstairs brain with a safety gate locked at the bottom, keeping the child from accessing his or her "upstairs." The younger the child, the greater the difficulty because the brain circuitry for communication is still developing. Later in this chapter, we will explore how you can help unlock this gate by how you respond and provide support for the dysregulated child.

In addition to recognizing that the brain is not fully developed and can be easily trapped "downstairs," various factors impact a child's response to a traumatic event. Consider the child or adolescent holistically when you are responding, asking questions such as these:

- Does the child have a history of previous trauma?
- What are the family dynamics in the home?

[2] See Daniel J. Siegel and Tina Payne Bryson, *The Whole-Brain Child: 12 Revolutionary Strategies to Nurture Your Child's Developing Mind* (New York: Delacorte, 2011), 37–61.

- Does the child have a safe and secure connection with the primary caregivers? If not, are there other adults with whom the child is securely connected?
- What other caregivers spend a lot of time with the child? What are those relationships like?
- What is the minor's support system other than family (e.g., school, church, friends, extended family)?
- Are there any medical conditions (e.g., diabetes, asthma)?
- Are there any preexisting mental-health concerns or developmental disorders (e.g., anxiety, depression, developmental delays, autism spectrum disorder, attention-deficit/hyperactivity disorder, sensory processing issues)?

These additional considerations may impact how the minor experiences the traumatic event and how he or she responds and can influence the development of trauma symptoms.

Communication

Children and adolescents often do not have the vocabulary or communication skills to express what they think and feel in response to a traumatic event. They also may not have the vocabulary to tell an adult what happened to them. Crisis and trauma experiences are exhausting and dysregulating, so exhibiting an understanding and calm response provides a safe environment for the child to process the experience.

Observe the child's behavior and interactions with others. He or she may express emotional dysregulation in "acting out" or "withdrawal" behaviors. In other words, the child may be in a "fight, flight, freeze," lower/limbic brain response. The behavior is a stress response and communicates critical information about the child's well-being. Consider the behavior an adaptive response. The child is using this behavior to help tolerate or regulate overwhelming emotions and bodily sensations in the attempt to experience a sense of safety. Instead of immediately trying to shut down the behavior, become curious instead. Think of behavior as communication. Ask yourself, "What information is this behavior providing about the child/adolescent?"

When emotionally dysregulated behavior occurs, the adult needs to remain calm and avoid top-down approaches such as lecturing or trying to help the child "think" himself out of the behavior. When a child reacts in the limbic brain, logic and reasoning are shut down. A top-down approach will not work when a bottom-up approach is needed. Instead, the caregiver should engage in connection and regulation (bottom-up) activities with the child (discussed in the following two sections).

Delahooke describes the problem with misinterpreting challenging behaviors: "When we fail to recognize that many behaviors represent the body's response to stress, not intentional misbehavior, we expend effort on techniques designed to help children logically connect their thoughts, emotions, and behaviors when they simply can't . . . yet."[3] Let's explore how we can respond with a bottom-up approach that moves the child toward connecting her thoughts and emotions.

Recommendations for Response

Imagine a child or adolescent coming to your office the week after a traumatic event. Working with children is a team effort. Caregivers, ministers, mental-health providers, and the child's support system all play a role in well-being and recovery. As such, involve the support system to the extent possible. For example, you might contact the child's teachers and coaches and inform them of what is happening and what self-regulation strategies are helpful to the child. Involve them in monitoring the child for signs of needing additional support.

We will review some recommendations for responding to children impacted by trauma. You can use the acronym SCAN to assist you in

---

[3] Mona Delahooke, *Beyond Behaviors: Using Brain Science and Compassion to Solve Children's Behavioral Challenges* (Eau Claire, WI: PESI, 2019), 11.

remembering the main points: safety, connection, activities, and notice. Teach these skills to the child's caregivers.

S = Safety

Establish safety and security. Consider physical, emotional, and relational safety. Think about the child's relationships in the various places of engagement. Ask yourself, how can we make this child or adolescent feel as safe and secure as possible? As previously noted, involve other adults (such as coaches and teachers), so they also can be aware of the child's increased need to feel safe and secure.

Provide for any physical needs. In the case of the fire discussed in the previous chapter, the Smith family lost all their possessions and needed immediate physical assistance. Consider food and drink intake. Appetite may be impacted, so provide opportunities for small, healthy meals. Monitor how the child sleeps and notice how changes in the sleeping environment may impact sleep. The child may benefit from using a sound machine or weighted blanket. Did the child lose a special "lovey" he slept with at night?

Consider other environmental factors. For example, avoid playing the news nonstop in the background, particularly if the crisis is on the news. Decide how you will communicate news about what is happening at an age-appropriate level. You can check in with the child about what information she heard secondhand at school or on social media.

Provide emotional safety and security. Feeling safe in relationships is critical for children and adolescents. The calmness and emotional regulation of the caregiver provides emotional safety for the child. If the child's caregiver struggles to self-regulate, the child will be impacted. In this case, provide opportunities for the caregiver to receive professional counseling services to gain coping and self-regulation skills. Many parents and caregivers will forgo personal counseling and obtain counseling for the child, but it is important that caregivers are provided the opportunity.

Caregivers might consider the following questions to determine if they are also struggling with emotional dysregulation:

- What are your nonverbal cues, such as your tone of voice, when you speak to the child?
- What nonverbal cues does the child notice when you talk to others or spend time together?
- What level of stress might the child sense from you?

Suppose the caregiver is activated in the "downstairs" brain and unable to regulate. In that case, it will be more difficult for the caregiver to assist the minor in opening the gate to the "upstairs" brain. If this is happening, one of the best things the caregiver can do for the child is to seek help to process the trauma and develop self-regulation skills.

In addition to practicing self-regulation skills, the caregiver should avoid "parentifying" the child. After a crisis, parentifying a child may look like seeking emotional support from the child or oversharing difficult emotions. It is okay for the caregiver to say, "I'm sad too." But keep it minimal, and do not overshare. Providing the caregiver a place to process these emotions is helpful to both the adult and the child.

Emotional safety is a felt sense. As such, it is possible to be safe physically but not feel safe. This sense is how the child or adolescent actually feels, not how the responding adult thinks the child should feel. Let's explore how connection can assist in providing emotional safety.

C = Connection

Connection is critical for children. When we connect, we build bonds of secure attachment. Karyn Purvis describes attachment as the "affectionate bond between a caregiver and a youngster."[4] We communicate to the child that we will respond to his needs. The child will not be abandoned and alone; instead, he will receive love and care. Through this affectionate bond

[4] Karyn Purvis and Lisa Qualls, *The Connected Parent: Real-Life Strategies for Building Trust and Attachment* (Eugene: Harvest House, 2020), 35.

of attachment, children learn they are valued, they have a voice, and their needs are important.[5]

As you connect with the child, observe whether she is in the "upstairs" or "downstairs" brain and communicate accordingly. Siegel and Bryson note, "When a child is upset, logic often won't work until we have responded to the right brain's emotional needs. We call this emotional connection 'attunement,' which is how we connect deeply with another person and allow them to 'feel felt.'"[6]

Attunement that assists in regulating and calming the child's nervous system is called "co-regulation." When co-regulating, we connect to the child's right (emotional) brain. As discussed previously, children do not have the capacity to regulate their own emotions due to their developmental state, so the process of co-regulation is critical for children who have experienced trauma.

Delahooke emphasizes the importance of human connection in calming a dysregulated child: "Emotional co-regulation comes first, and this is how emotional self-regulation is developed."[7] The process of co-regulation is healthy and developmentally appropriate. The process of co-regulation requires the caregiver to explore his or her own emotional state (as we discussed previously) to provide the calm connection necessary to assist the minor in regulation.

Through a safe, secure, and connected relationship, caregivers can attune to the child's needs and assist in regulating the child's nervous system. You can help unlock the gate to the upstairs brain through your communication and connection. You can help him "feel felt," providing emotional safety.

As you connect, provide opportunities for the child or adolescent to discuss what happened. You can tell him you are available to talk whenever he is ready, letting him share as much as he is comfortable. Here are some tips for providing safe opportunities to talk:

---

[5] See Purvis and Qualls, 39.

[6] Siegel and Bryson, *The Whole-Brain Child*, 24.

[7] Delahooke, *Beyond Behaviors*, 154.

- Avoid peppering the child with a barrage of questions, particularly yes or no questions, leaving him feeling interrogated rather than connected. For example, instead of saying, "Did you have a good day?" you could say, "What was the best part of your day? What was the hardest part of your day?"
- Allow him to open up at his own pace in response to occasional open-ended prompts, such as:
  - "Do you have any questions about what happened?"
  - "What happened was really scary. Sometimes, I think about it when I am trying to do something else. Does that ever happen to you?"
- Look for natural opportunities for discussion, such as driving somewhere in the car together, preparing food, or playing a game.
- Normalize that what he is feeling is a natural response.
- Listen more than you talk.
- Avoid distractions, such as looking at your cell phone.

Remember: as you communicate, the foremost goal is to convey a safe connection.

A = Activities

A few activities may be helpful to a minor experiencing a crisis. First, caregivers should maintain a routine if at all possible. A predictable schedule is helpful when life may feel out of control. If the schedule needs to be changed, provide the child with advance notice and understand that this change may be difficult even if the child did not previously feel challenged by change.

Secondly, allow the child or teen opportunities for relaxation and fun activities with peers and adult caregivers. When caregivers join in play, whether shooting hoops or engaging in a board game, they can bond with the child or adolescent and open opportunities to engage in conversation. During this time, set aside the cell phone and other distractions to fully engage with the minor.

Finally, teach and practice coping skills and self-regulation strategies. Teach and practice self-regulation skills when a child is *not* experiencing dysregulation or when minor distress occurs in preparation for more significant dysregulation. Some ideas are listed below:

- Breathing exercises
  - Belly breaths: Breathe in and blow up an imaginary balloon in your stomach, hold for a few seconds, and then slowly release the air from the "balloon" while allowing your body to relax with the exhale.
  - Starfish breathing: Hold one hand up in the air, spreading fingers into a "starfish" position. Using your index finger on the opposite hand, slowly trace up and down each "starfish" finger. Inhale as you trace up each finger. Pause briefly at the top. Then, exhale as you trace down each finger. You will do this with all five fingers. Continue as needed.
- 54321: Using your senses, name and describe:
  - 5 things you can see (e.g., a black and white kitten, a blue blanket)
  - 4 things you can touch (e.g., soft, fuzzy fur)
  - 3 things you can hear (e.g., a cat's purring)
  - 2 things you can smell (e.g., peppermint)
  - 1 thing you can taste (e.g., minty gum)
- Play a game of naming five things in various categories.
  - 5 types of animals (or a specific animal, such as dog breeds)
  - 5 flavors of ice cream
  - 5 pizza toppings

  You can take turns calling out a category.
- Drinking ice-cold water
- Journaling or drawing
- Naming or drawing the child's emotion(s)
- Blowing bubbles with a bubble wand
- Taking a walk outside

- Rocking
- Hand massage with scented lotion
- Saying a positive statement or a comforting scripture

Teach the child to "check in" with himself and identify emotions throughout the day. Emotion charts and wheels are readily available through a quick internet search, and these can be posted in the home or school notebook.

N = Notice

The final recommendation is to notice changes in the minor's behavior, demeanor, and interactions. If you see an increase in any of the following behaviors, provide referrals for counseling so a professional can evaluate the minor's well-being.

- withdrawing from people or previously enjoyed activities
- bursts of anger
- feeling fearful and anxious
- intrusive memories about the event
- nightmares
- difficulty falling asleep or staying asleep
- fear of being alone
- hypervigilance for danger (increased startle response)
- avoidance of discussing what happened or being near reminders of the event
- blaming themselves for what happened
- difficulty focusing
- physical complaints (e.g., stomachache, headache, tightness in chest)
- difficulty eating
- reliving the event in their minds
- regressive behaviors (e.g., bed-wetting, thumb-sucking)

Tips for Responding to an Emotionally Dysregulated Child

If a child is currently experiencing emotional dysregulation, let's review some tips for responding:

- Establish a calm presence by regulating yourself.
- Provide safety. What is needed to establish physical and emotional safety for the child?
- Meet the child where she is, whether the "upstairs" or "downstairs" brain. If the minor senses a threat, she may be in fight, flight, or freeze.
- Connect to the right (emotional) brain by validating her emotions or providing an opportunity to name her emotion(s). By naming the emotion, we begin to bring back "online" the "upstairs" brain. Siegel and Bryson note that "merely assigning a name or label to what we feel literally calms down the activity of the emotional circuitry in the right hemisphere."[8] If the child cannot name the experience, try drawing it.
- In naming the emotion, help her use the phrase "I feel [angry, scared, sad]" instead of "I am [angry, scared, sad]." The emotion reflects her current, temporary state of mind, not a personal trait. In other words, the emotion is *not who they are* but reflects *what they are experiencing*. Siegel and Bryson describe the potential danger in using "I am" language when naming emotion: "The danger is that the temporary state of mind can be perceived as a permanent part of themselves. The state comes to be seen as a trait that defines who they are."[9]
- Make eye contact and get on her level, such as sitting on the floor or kneeling.

---

[8] Siegel and Bryson, *The Whole-Brain Child*, 29.

[9] Siegel and Bryson, 97.

- Avoid using too many words or questions.
- If possible, help the child recognize when she is responding from the "downstairs" brain.
- Be aware of the child's physical need for comfort. Is a hug needed? Or does she prefer physical space?
- Is the child hungry, thirsty, or tired?
- Do a calming, regulating activity such as those listed in this chapter. If the child or teen is verbally communicating with you, consider asking what would be most helpful to her at this moment.

Conclusion

In this chapter, we reviewed special considerations when addressing trauma in children and adolescents. We overviewed the impact of the developing brain and how to communicate in a developmentally appropriate way. Recommendations for ministering and responding were provided using the SCAN acronym: safety, connection, activities, and notice. Finally, we summarized tips for responding to an emotionally dysregulated child. There is hope for children who have suffered trauma to heal within the safe haven of healthy relationships.

Additional Resources

Delahooke, Mona. *Beyond Behaviors: Using Brain Science and Compassion to Solve Children's Behavioral Challenges.* Eau Claire, WI: PESI, 2019.

Purvis, Karyn and Lisa Qualls. *The Connected Parent: Real-Life Strategies for Building Trust and Attachment.* Eugene, OR: Harvest House, 2020.

Siegel, Daniel J., and Tina Payne Bryson. *The Whole-Brain Child: 12 Revolutionary Strategies to Nurture Your Child's Developing Mind.* New York: Delacorte, 2011.

Chapter 16

Bullying

Nearly 20 percent of students report being bullied during the school year.[1] Bullying can occur in a wide range of places, often where supervision is lacking, including church. It frequently occurs when there is an imbalance of power. This could include a difference in age, social status, or abilities. Bullying often results in diminished self-esteem, an increase in depression and anxiety, and in some cases, suicide.[2]

Types of Bullying

There are four types of bullying: verbal, social, physical, and cyber. Verbal abuse covers a wide range of name-calling, inappropriate remarks, threats, and insults that diminish another person's self-worth. Social bullying involves relational aggression in the form of spreading false rumors, humiliation,

[1] See "Bullying," Megan Meier Foundation, https://www.meganmeierfoundation.org/bullying.

[2] See "Effects of Bullying," stopbullying.gov, https://www.stopbullying.gov/bullying/effects.

and turning others in the group against the person or excluding them from activities. Physical bullying involves acts of violence and aggression, such as hurting another person or destroying his belongings. Cyberbullying takes place online and resembles verbal and social bullying. Deception can also be a part of cyberbullying when someone impersonates another person. This deception can be to further rumors and gossip or to ostracize a member of a social group.

Signs of Bullying

It would be nice if our kids could come home and tell us everything that went wrong during their day. Unfortunately, that's not how it typically occurs. I (Brooke) continually ask my son how his day was, and I get an "I can't remember" or something generic, such as "It was great." In the absence of verbal communication, you are often looking for indications of what's taking place outside the home. When bullying occurs, there may be physical evidence, such as cuts or bruises along with damaged and lost possessions. Similar to the signs of depression, a student may feign illness, eat too much or too little, or lose interest in activities. They may be fearful of school or church, experience a decline in academic performance, or have a sudden loss of friends or avoidance of social situations.[3]

Causes of Bullying

Social status is often at the root of bullying. Those who bully may be trying to maintain or elevate their social status or prove their loyalty to the group. For some, an element of control is present in determining whom their peers should or should not befriend.

Perhaps these students are in schools or churches in which bullying is facilitated by adults. Adults may not intend to set up an environment in which bullying takes place, but it may happen nonetheless. Some schools

[3] See "Bullying," Megan Meier Foundation.

attempt to incentivize academics or other things. In doing so, they may inadvertently set the stage for bullying. For example, let's say a school gives reading achievement shirts to students who make a certain score on a standardized test. Then, they allow these students to wear these shirts on designated days. There is a continual reminder throughout the day, the various times they are worn, of the discrepancies between the star readers and the struggling readers. In some cases, these reading achievers may make fun of the ones who are struggling. In contrast, those who feel shame for their reading struggles may bully the high achievers to cope with their own sense of inadequacy. Those with learning disabilities may be giving their best effort, yet still falling short. We need to find ways to celebrate the hard work students are putting in without ostracizing either group.

Some of those who bully have a history of adverse childhood experiences. They may come from homes where violence is used or have low parental involvement and support. In some cases, they themselves may have been bullied, which is considered an adverse childhood experience.[4] They may be insecure or have low emotional intelligence, meaning they do not have a clear understanding of their own feelings or the feelings of others.[5]

Why Bystanders Do or Do Not Intervene

As parents, we are always hoping and praying our children will have at least one friend in their classes each school year and a teacher who is looking out for them. Our hope is that someone will stand up for them in the event that they are treated unfairly or bullied. Although having an advocate in a friend or teacher may increase the likelihood of our child having someone stand with them during adversity, this may not always be the case. When kids are bullied, bystanders may not always intervene. In cases where peers choose not to intervene, this often occurs because they fear retaliation and that the

---

[4] For more information on adverse childhood experiences (ACEs), see chapter 11.

[5] See "Why Some Youth Bully," Stop Bullying, https://www.stopbullying.gov/bullying/why-some-youth-bully.

bullying will be directed toward them. They may be concerned about losing their social status. In some cases, they may genuinely desire to help but are unsure how to intervene or address the situation.[6]

When bystanders choose to intervene, they may be friends with the target of the bullying or see the person as innocent and undeserving. They may also have empathy for the person and believe teachers or adults will address the situation appropriately.[7] As a parent, it can be easy to think about the short-term benefits of social status, especially if we were left out of the "cool kid group" at school growing up. If our children are part of the "in crowd," we may be so relieved that our children are not the ones being bullied that we forget about those who are targets. If we stop to think about the long-term implications of bullying and social status, most of us would agree that we want our children to be the ones with friends with whom they are able to find a sense of belonging without compromising who they are. We would probably also agree that we want our children to develop empathy and find the courage to stand up for their friends.

Belonging versus Fitting In

As adolescents, many of us engaged in behaviors outside our values and belief systems because we were so desperate to fit in. Making the necessary changes to fit in didn't always bring the sense of belonging we were longing for. This may come down to the difference between fitting in and belonging. Brené Brown distinguishes between the two: "Fitting in is about assessing a situation and becoming who you need to be in order to be accepted. Belonging doesn't require us to change who we are; it requires us to be who we are."[8] Belonging is what many of us are after, but we settle for fitting in.

---

[6] See "Bystander Fact Sheet," stopbullying.gov, August 2018, https://www.stopbullying.gov/sites/default/files/2018-08/Bystander-Factsheet.pdf.

[7] See Bystander "Fact Sheet."

[8] Brené Brown, *Daring Greatly: How the Courage to Be Vulnerable Transforms the Way We Live, Love, Parent, and Lead* (New York: Penguin, 2012), 231–32.

What are we willing to do to fit in? A popular phrase I heard growing up was "If all your friends jumped off a cliff, would you jump as well?" Our brains are not fully developed until our mid-twenties, which means adolescents do not have the capacity to weigh and understand the long-term implications of their actions, at least not in the same way adults can. This means they are only thinking about how fitting in will benefit them in the present. The long-term implications of fitting in, such as compromising their integrity or values, is lost on them. I recently read an article about a teenager who had been involved in a carjacking in our area. The quote from his mother was "He just wanted to fit in."[9] If someone is willing to carjack to fit in, jumping off a cliff is not outside the realm of possibility.

Frequently, we see gossip as a conduit of connection. Gossip is one of the quickest ways to connect for both teens and adults. Although gossip may hot-wire connection,[10] it does not bring the deep sense of connection and belonging many of us desire. If gossip is the foundation of our instant connection with another person, it won't be long before we struggle to trust this person with our own personal information. After all, the relationship began by discussing someone else's misfortune; what's to stop her from discussing our personal issues with another? If we're guarded with the person because we do not trust her, then we'll settle for fitting in, rather than belonging.

Recently, I (Brooke) stumbled across an article about some kids being excluded on their overnight camp trip. The most concerning part of this article is that a mom was the one doing the excluding. Somehow the mom had gotten access to the camp bus and designated a section for her daughter's chosen group. Then, she proceeded to wait until all of the "chosen

---

[9] Mike Perlstein, "Arrested 16-Year-Old Explains Why Teens Are Committing Violent Crime," 4WWL, February 16, 2022, https://www.wwltv.com/article/news/investigations/mike-perlstein/one-wrong-turn-teen-explains-how-he-ended-up-in-a-stolen-car-with-drugs/289-17596f08-c241-437c-bf83-3411a950e240.

[10] See Brené Brown, *Braving the Wilderness: The Quest for True Belonging and the Courage to Stand Alone* (New York: Ebury, 2017), 135–36.

ones" were present to take their reserved spots, while telling others the seats were saved.[11]

One of the reasons the article caught my attention is because it used the term *social engineering*. After reading the article, I found the term *social engineering* both intriguing and appropriate. If you were to do a Google search of the term, you would likely find sites related to information security. In that context, social engineering refers to deception and manipulation tactics that result in people giving up confidential security information such as passwords, bank information, or social security numbers. For our purposes, social engineering involves two parts: (1) an entity or individual assessing relationships within a social structure such as a culture, organization, or church and (2) using the information gathered to manipulate alliances and messaging to wield power and gain influence. It follows that once the power is gained, the person or entity will attempt to maintain its status at all costs.

One of the struggles in addressing a parent's behavior in a situation such as this is that parents are so thrilled that their child is part of the "in crowd" that they do not want to stand up for the kids who are excluded. Many of us remember the pains of childhood and adolescence and what it felt like to be left out or picked last at PE. These wounds run so deep in us, even as adults, that we cannot fathom the possibility of our children experiencing something similar. However, if we do not deal with our own issues with belonging, we will raise up a new generation of kids engaging in exclusion rather than showing kindness and acceptance to others.

A great example of social engineering comes from the 2004 movie *Mean Girls*. In this movie, Cady is returning to America from being overseas with her family. Through a series of events, she decides to infiltrate a clique with some of the school's most popular and influential girls. She schemes her way into becoming the queen bee of the group by finding ways to exclude

---

[11] See Lisa Barr, "Being Left Out Hurts: Moms, Stop 'Social Engineering,'" Today.com, November 4, 2015, https://community.today.com/parentingteam/post/being-left-out-hurts-lets-stop-social-engineering-now.

one of the other girls, so that the excluded one feels the rest of the group has formed an alliance against her. She also spreads gossip through a "Burn Book" created by the group, containing terrible rumors and secrets about students and faculty at the school.

Later on, the contents of this book are released all over school, resulting in chaos and strife. At this time, Cady is forced to confront who she has become. Once a kindhearted person, she has taken part in spreading rumors and secrets about people she cared about, which proved to be costly for all involved. She has plotted so that some members of the clique felt excluded, which is how she felt at the beginning of the movie. She went from being a straight-A student to failing math, and she did all these things so she could fit in. She lost the two friends who had accepted her and befriended her when the popular girls did not. These friends were a group in which she belonged without having to change who she was to be accepted. They were fine with her being herself.

In chapter 12, we mentioned the baskets of messages we carry through life. The messages dropped in these baskets heavily influence our belief systems, which impact how we live. As adults, we should evaluate these messages against the truth of God's Word. Otherwise, we may inadvertently pass on unhealthy messages to our children.

Consider some of the messages our children may be learning from us when we engage in social engineering. The first message is *People could never accept or like you as you are. You must find a way to conform.* Psalm 139 talks about how we are fearfully and wonderfully made, while Ephesians 2:10 says we are God's workmanship, created for a purpose that God planned for us in advance. We lose ourselves and the uniqueness that God created in us when we change ourselves to fit in with others.

In my (Brooke) Social Problems class, my students complete several reflection exercises, one of which is about someone they know who has experienced oppression. A few years ago, I had a student write about her brother, who was being made fun of for the shoes he wore to school. It got to the point where his mom went out and bought him a new pair of shoes similar to what the other kids were wearing so the teasing would cease. At the end of this story, the student remarked that she thought her mom may have missed a valuable opportunity.

I didn't like being made fun of for what I wore in school, and I do not want to see my child go through the same thing. I can easily see myself in this mom. My immediate impulse would be to buy the shoes the other kids are wearing to stop the teasing, but that wouldn't be a brave response. Belonging requires courage to show up and let ourselves be seen. In this case, a courageous response might involve having a discussion with my child about how he feels about the shoes. We might also discuss the implications of making changes to ourselves or our appearance simply to appease a group of people. At this moment, we can adjust our focus to the long-term implications of fitting in.

Another message we may inadvertently teach our children is *It does not matter how other people feel or are treated. As long as we are part of the "cool group," nothing and no one else matters.* Going back to the reflection exercise on oppression in my class, many students share about someone they know who was being bullied or mistreated in some way. Oftentimes, they also share about how they wish they would have intervened on behalf of those being mistreated. Many of us might feel the same. Earlier in this book, we discussed empathy. We encourage our children to take the perspective of another person and consider his or her feelings.

A third unintended message is *We should fear those who are different from us.* One of my newfound favorite books that I (Brooke) read with my son is *Aaron Slater, Illustrator* by Andrea Beaty. This book is about a little boy who aspires to be a writer, but struggles with reading because of his dyslexia. As it turns out, he is an incredibly gifted artist, and he uses his gifts to paint pictures for stories. Sometimes we focus so intently on the struggles of others that we miss their giftedness.

One of my students has shared about her sister, who is on the autism spectrum. Some of the other students cheer for her sister, who is on the dance team, but not because they are supportive. Instead, they cheer for her while she is performing, or tell her how well she did, then turn around, laugh, and make fun of her behind her back. Her sister believes these girls have finally accepted her since they were being nice. She does not realize they are making fun of her. These girls have gotten into trouble multiple times, but there has never been a behavioral change. My student made an astute observation when she said the only way they would change their behavior is if they had a change of heart. She went on to say, "They crave fitting in so badly that they would isolate those who are different from themselves and put them down just so they can feel some sense of worth."

In chapter 21, we consider the work of Bruce Perry with a boy adopted from Russia, who struggled with a wide range of delays from his early years in an orphanage. Perry took the time to help that first-grade class understand the child's experience. Once the children had a better understanding of his struggles, they were better equipped to be a friend and help him. Perhaps we should spend more time helping our children understand people who are different from us.

Belonging is the more difficult path and it requires intense courage, so why choose it when it would be easier to fit in? My response is: If God created each of us for a distinct purpose, will we ever be able to fulfill that purpose if we are spending our energy trying to change who we are just to fit in? Continuing to fit in does not bring the sense of belonging we are after, especially when we compromise our values and belief systems to do so. Fitting in also means we spend our time being someone we weren't created to be in the first place, missing the calling God has placed on our lives.

When the "Cool Kids" Come to Church

We want our churches to be safe places where all feel welcome. As such, we want to ensure they are free from cliques and social engineering. The adult leaders in children's or youth ministries should be intentional in their efforts to make sure everyone feels included. Often, our tendencies are to invest in the students who are less challenging or demanding. Maybe they are cool or popular. As a result, we have children with multiple adults investing in them, while we have kids on the fringes with no adult support. When serving youth or children, look for kids who are being left out or who do not have an adult investing in them.

Oftentimes, children and teenagers follow the lead of the adults. If the adults are being inclusive of everyone, young people are likely to follow. We should engage in conversations with the kids about the importance of including others, going deeper than telling them to be inclusive. Demonstrate and discuss belonging and empathy. More information on this is discussed in the next section.

Dealing with the Effects of Bullying

Modeling

One of the first things to consider is what the parents, teachers, and church leaders are modeling for their children. Are adults modeling inclusion for students and engaging with people who are different from them? As we will discuss in chapter 21, kids typically see differences between themselves and other children, but they do not usually evaluate them on their own. Rather, they take their cues from adults. If they notice their teachers treating a child differently, they are likely to follow suit. If their parents discourage them from playing with certain kids because of their differences—whether race, social status, or disability—they receive the message that some kids may not be worth their time.

Next, how do they see the adults in their lives treating others? Do their parents make fun of other kids in their classes or gossip about their adult friends? When the teenager with different interests leaves the youth group on Wednesday night, do the youth leaders make jokes about her when she's not around? What we model for our children will carry a deeper impression than what we tell them.

Empathy

Kids and teenagers need to understand that their actions influence other people. To do this, we must first help them recognize and communicate emotion.[12] As discussed earlier, we may not know what it is to be in the exact same situation as another person, but we have likely experienced similar emotions. When we connect with the emotional experience of another, we are able to see their situation from his or her perspective rather than ours. Connecting can help us understand how our actions may have harmed another person. Or we recognize the importance of supporting others when they are bullied.

We want to help those who perpetuate bullying to consider the perspective of the person they have hurt. Although the people bullying may not easily identify with those they are putting down, they may have had some similar life experiences. Helping them remember their experiences and emotional reactions in past situations can allow them to connect with the person they hurt. The hope is that they would gain a deeper understanding of the impact of their actions on others and make some healthy changes to their behavior.

Courage

Previously, we talked about how it takes courage to belong. We want to encourage our children to become people of integrity, which is difficult to have when we abandon friends who are being bullied. We want them to have the courage to stand up for their friends and those who are being mistreated. Often, kids do not intervene because they are not sure what to do. We need to equip our children with ways to support those who are being bullied. It could be something as simple as inviting their friend to sit with them at lunch or walking away from a bully together.

---

[12] See Theresa Wiseman, "A Concept Analysis of Empathy," *Journal of Advanced Nursing* 23, no. 6 (June 1996): 1162–67, https://doi.org/10.1046/j.1365-2648.1996.12213.x.

Restorative Conversations

Although it may not be appropriate in all situations, have a restorative conversation between the person who was hurt and the offending adolescent after conversing with each party. This conversation is designed to allow the victim to share how the offender's words or actions have hurt him. In turn, the offender is given the opportunity to take responsibility for his actions, make amends, and seek forgiveness.

To determine if a restorative conversation would be helpful, consider the following questions:

- Does the offender seem remorseful?
- Does the offender understand the impact of his or her actions on the other person?
- How much of the hurt has the victim processed? How emotionally reactive is he or she?
- Has the victim considered the impact of the bullying on him- or herself?
- Has the victim started the process of forgiveness?

If the offender seems ambivalent about the impact of his or her actions on the other person, then a restorative conversation is likely to cause more harm than good. While we expect the victim to experience some intense emotions as a result of what has happened, if the victim is so reactive that he is unable to listen and receive from the offender, the timing for the conversation may not be the best.

Forgiveness is a process. The deeper the hurt, the longer it may take. We want to make sure the victim has taken the time to begin the process of forgiving and healing. Part of forgiveness is considering the impact of the other person's action on you and choosing to forgive. Choosing to forgive does not minimize the hurt or impact of the other person's actions on us, nor does it absolve him or her of consequences. Instead, forgiveness is an opportunity to release our hurt, anger, and bitterness and create space for love and compassion.

Help for the Bullying Victim

Helping those who have been bullied is a difficult process. In some cases, victims may have waited before disclosing to anyone out of fear or shame. They may blame themselves. We should help them to build their sense of self-worth and encourage them to build a support system of friends who will walk with them. We also want to give them space to process their feelings in a healthy way. We should discuss the dangers of revenge and retaliation and emphasize the personal benefits of forgiveness.

When the Offender Seems Ambivalent

There may be times when, despite our best attempts, the adolescent who has engaged in bullying seems apathetic about the impact of his actions on others. In these cases, there is likely a deeper issue involved, and we want to encourage him to seek counseling. This apathy could stem from a number of factors. He may have been the victim of bullying or some other type of early childhood adversity. Addressing the root cause of bullying will result in a healthier and more productive long-term outcome than punitive measures.

Conclusion

Bullying begins with the brokenness of one person and can result in the brokenness of another person. Both the offender and the offended can experience long-term negative effects. We want to take steps to get to the root of bullying behavior. Otherwise, we leave both people broken. We must be intentional about establishing safe and inclusive environments in our homes, schools, churches, and communities.

Additional Resources

Dewdney, Anna. *Llama Llama and the Bully Goat.* New York: Viking Books for Young Readers, 2013.

This is a great book for children ages 4–8, explaining what bullying is and how to handle it if it happens.

Saeed, Aisha. *The Together Tree.* New York: Salaam Reads, 2023.

Intended for children ages 4–8, this book gives an example of bullying and bystander intervention. The author realized that many children desire to intervene when a friend or classmate is struggling to fit in or being bullied but do not know how. She wrote this book to help children understand that being with their friends can be one of the best ways to intervene.

Part 7
Couples and Families

Chapter 17

Divorce

Marriage is intended to be a reflection of the relationship between Christ and the church. Inherent sinfulness and the nature of this fallen world results in conflict and marital discord. When marital conflict is persisting and intense, some couples think divorce may be the best option to shield their children from the chronic stress and strife in the home. However, marital conflict can have adverse effects on the children, whether their parents are married, separated, or divorced. Kids fare best when their parents have a healthy relationship. This does not mean the parents' relationship is free from conflict; rather, those parents have found healthy ways to address and resolve disagreements.

Though God's original design for marriage was meant to be permanent, life's various challenges and our own imperfections can impact the duration of marriage. As such, divorce happens and can cause devastating and long-lasting effects for all involved. Divorce is one of ten adverse childhood experiences (ACEs) that can potentially influence long-term mental and physical health outcomes. Research has shown that those who experienced parental separation or divorce in childhood, along with those who reported lack of support from a trusted adult, perceived their childhood to be difficult and had a negative quality of life in adulthood.[1] The unfortunate reality of parental separation and divorce is that parents are often caught up in their own struggles, which can result in being unavailable for their children.

John Gottman's research on marital conflict and divorce revealed that emotion coaching can help buffer the effects of divorce on children. Emotion coaching is the practice of helping children recognize, understand, express, and manage their emotions. The first step is to help children understand what they are feeling by helping them label their emotions. Then, we need to teach them how to handle their emotions in a healthy manner.[2]

Marital Conflict and Children

Communicate When Conflicts Are Resolved

Kids rely on their parents as a safe haven, which offers them a sense of security in life. Although conflict in any marriage is inevitable, kids can become rattled when their parents argue. Letting children know the conflict has been resolved can relieve some of the distress they experience. Conflict resolution demonstrates a few things to the children. First, it brings them comfort because the conflict has been resolved. Kids are able to rest in the safety of their parents when they feel a sense of stability. Parents should acknowledge the disagreement and communicate with the children that the conflict has been resolved. When kids see their parents walk away from a conflict with no clear path of resolution, they are more likely to continue feeling uneasy.[3]

Second, repair attempts model appropriate ways to resolve arguments. A repair attempt is a gesture intended to diffuse a disagreement and prevent

---

[1] See John–Kåre Vederhus, Siri Håvås Haugland, and Christine Timko, "A Mediational Analysis of Adverse Experiences in Childhood and Quality of Life in Adulthood," *International Journal of Methods in Psychiatric Research* 31, no. 1 (2022), https://doi.org/10.1002/mpr.1904.

[2] See John Gottman, *Raising an Emotionally Intelligent Child: The Heart of Parenting* (New York: Simon & Schuster, 1997), 25, 75.

[3] See Gottman, 158.

the conflict from escalating.[4] A repair attempt could include an apology, validating the other's feelings, empathy, and humor, when appropriate. This modeling allows children to learn appropriate ways to restore connection when it has been broken.

I (Brooke) have worked with a number of premarital couples over the years. On the premarital assessment I use, several of them scored extremely high on the idealism scale. This scale measures the degree to which couples view their relationship through rose-colored glasses. Many of these couples make remarks such as "I never heard my parents fight growing up. They had a great marriage." Or, "We have never once had an argument, and I don't anticipate we ever will." In some cases, I have also heard the opposite: "My parents would constantly argue in our presence, and it was unnerving for us." Modeling appropriate ways to resolve conflict can demonstrate to our children healthy ways to engage in relationships. Rather than painting the picture of a perfect marriage or leaving conflicts unresolved, we can show our kids appropriate ways to manage and resolve conflict in relationships.

Be Mindful of the Impact of Conflict on the Children

Kids should not be allowed to insert themselves as mediators. This may be an attempt to maintain control in a situation that is out of control, or it might be a sign that the level of conflict is too high. When we notice children inserting themselves into their parents' conflict, we want to encourage the parents to practice techniques, such as repair attempts, to de-escalate the conflict. We also want to encourage them to check in with their children about how they are feeling. For some parents, this can be an eye-opening experience, when they realize the degree to which their conflict is impacting their children. Parents should also offer reassurance that this conflict is between the parents and they will work it out on their own. We should communicate clearly to the child that it is not his or her responsibility to resolve the disagreement.[5]

---

[4] The concept of repair attempts originated from John Gottman.

[5] See Gottman, *Raising an Emotionally Intelligent Child*, 157.

Dealing with Divorce

Parents Must Communicate Clearly with Their Children

Parents should communicate to their children in clear terms that they are getting a divorce, and why. They do not need to share specific details or place blame with one parent, but they do need to make it clear that the issues were between the parents and not the kids. I once had a teen client who told me she and her brother fought over why their parents divorced. The brother blamed the sister because of her struggles in school, and she blamed her brother because he was always in trouble. They thought that if they had not caused so much trouble, their parents might still be together.

Unfortunately, a couple divorcing, especially in the church, invites gossip. Parents should let their children know that if someone makes inappropriate comments or asks difficult questions about the situation, then they are always available to talk about it.

Couples also want to avoid using vague language to describe the divorce. In some cases, parents may think they are helping their children by not using the word *divorce*. Instead, they may say that mom and dad have decided to live apart or separate for a while. However, since children do not want their parents to get divorced, they long for them to reunite. When their parents use terms such as *live apart* or *separate*, this leaves children in a place of uncertainty while they hope for a favorable outcome. Though it may be difficult, parents should make their intentions to divorce clear.

There may be situations in which the parents are separating while they are trying to work things out. If this is the case, they need to be intentional about keeping the children informed about their current state. If the parents reach a point at which they realize their relationship will not be reconciled, they need to communicate this to the children. I have heard from many children whose parents had been separated that they were holding out hope for their parents to get back together only to find out, without warning, that their parents had finalized their divorce. There was no conversation leading up to it, and they were caught off guard.

Children May Not Move On as Quickly as Their Parents

Sometimes, children are still reeling from the shock of their parents' divorce when one of the parents begins to date again. They see the impact of dating on the parent who is still struggling to heal and recover from the divorce. To them, it seems that if the parent who is dating had really cared about the other, then he or she would not have moved on so quickly. When one or both of the parents is ready to begin dating, it might be helpful to have a conversation with the children. This conversation could allow them to ask questions and process any feelings they have about the situation.

Children Should Not Be the Messengers for Their Parents

Parents should not pass messages through their kids. For example, "Tell your dad I still don't have his child support check. I'll have to notify my attorney if he cannot get the money to me." This kind of message is alarming to kids and is likely to bring a negative reaction when delivered. These are issues the parents should work out themselves. Children should not be asked to keep secrets. When one parent asks them to keep a secret from the other, children struggle with feeling as though they are betraying the other parent by withholding information. All of these scenarios place unnecessary stress on children when the situation is already difficult.

Parents Should Not Speak Negatively about Each Other

When speaking about an ex-spouse, parents should remember that this person is still the child's parent and that it grieves children to hear derogatory remarks about him or her. Parents who continually speak negatively about their ex-spouses are likely to alienate their children. Kids grow weary of feeling as though they are caught in the middle.

Children Should Not Be Used as Pawns in Marital Conflict

Unfortunately, there are some situations in which parents use their children to retaliate against an ex-spouse. This could include withholding information about the child's schedule so the other parent is unaware of recitals or games they might want to attend. One parent might schedule an important event during the other parent's visitation. Or he might drop the kids off late or arrive early to get them, infringing on the other parent's visitation time. Engaging in these types of behaviors may result in long-term damage to the relationships between the child and both parents.

Children Need a Network of Emotional Support

During a divorce, the parents will be working through their own healing, which may not leave much emotional bandwidth to ensure the children's emotional needs are being met. As a result, the parents are wise to establish and maintain a solid support system for their children. This support network could include children and youth leaders from church, along with other extended family members and friends. A solid group of healthy adults who are willing to spend quality time with the children and invest in them while they are struggling to make sense of their family life can provide a buffer against the negative impact of divorce. Parents also want to make sure they give extra attention to their children's friends and activities during this time to ensure the kids are coping in a healthy manner.[6]

Parents Need to Remain Emotionally Available to the Children

Although a support network can provide benefits to the children during this difficult time, parents also need to find a way to remain emotionally available to the children.[7] This means parents need their own support system to help them so they are able to help their children through this time. In the

---

[6] See Gottman, 159.

[7] See Gottman, 161–62.

same way that parents need time to grieve and heal, children will as well. Finding a counselor to help them process their feelings is often beneficial.

Being emotionally available to the children is not just a short-term issue in the midst of a divorce; it's also the most optimal long-term trajectory. Following divorce, research has shown that children's relationships with one or both parents suffered.[8] Adult children of divorce often have a distant relationship with one or both parents as well. Although it is significantly more challenging with shared custody, parents need to make sure they remain available and offer support to the children.

Healing from Divorce

Grieve

From the outside, it may seem as though couples would be relieved when the divorce is finalized. Although this may be the case for some, for many divorce is still a loss. A majority of us enter marriage with the idea of forever. We make plans and dreams for the future. When the divorce is finalized, a wave of grief can wash over a person and provide a stark realization that the future he or she thought was secure has been shattered. For others, grief may come from hurt or betrayal that took place in the marriage.

Sometimes, people are so busy establishing a new routine and adjusting to their new normal that they do not take the time to process what has happened. Unresolved grief can sneak up on a person when he or she least expects it. We should facilitate recognizing and grieving losses that have occurred as a result of the divorce. Unresolved grief could lead to self-destructive choices in the future.

---

[8] See N. Zill, D. R. Morrison, and M. J. Coiro, "Long-Term Effects of Parental Divorce on Parent-Child Relationships, Adjustment, and Achievement in Young Adulthood," *Journal of Family Psychology* 7, no. 1 (1993): 91–103, https://doi.org/10.1037/0893-3200.7.1.91.

Take Time to Heal

In our society, there is a tendency to rush things, especially the healing process. When dealing with divorce, it's important to take your time. Avoiding the grieving process could cause us to rush into a relationship before being ready, which could be detrimental to your own healing and your children's. In some cases, the loneliness is overwhelming or the single-parent life is hard, and you long for companionship. Others may be rushing you by trying to find people for you to date.

The time it takes to heal from a divorce will vary from person to person and may depend on the circumstances involved. Some say you should not begin dating again for at least a year and a half, while others say five. I do not believe there is a specific time frame that is applicable to everyone. Instead, each person needs to consider his or her own healing process. Here are some questions to consider:

- How have I grown since my divorce?
- Have I extended forgiveness to people involved in issues from my previous marriage?
- In what ways do I think I am equipped to enter into another relationship?
- What have I learned that will make me a better partner coming into the relationship?
- How are my children doing? In other words, what kind of impact do I think dating will have on my children at this time? How can I prepare them for this?

Work Together in Co-Parenting

Following divorce, children often do the best when parents work together collaboratively. This could mean negotiating visitation times. As when married, working together to be on the same team in parenting decisions is important. When kids receive conflicting information about participation in certain activities or other major decisions, one parent may be outed as the "bad" parent because he or she said no. Taking the time to discuss these things together can provide a unified front that will serve both the parents and kids well.

A Word to the Church

When a couple decides to separate or divorce, it is a tumultuous time for all involved. As with any crisis, the church should be a refuge for the family during this time. That means care and concern should be the top priority, rather than gossip and rumors. Fishing for information from children is never appropriate. When a divorce takes place, we often default to caring for the parents. Many churches and counseling centers have offered some type of support group for parents going through a divorce, but we often overlook the children who are also impacted.

The parents are working through their own grief and trying to navigate life on their own. As such, they may struggle with how to best support their children during this time. Surrounding them with a community that will express care and love to them during this recovery process is crucial for ensuring that everyone is supported.

Conclusion

Regardless of marital status, conflict in a family can have a negative impact on children. Parents can ameliorate the effects of conflict by working together. They can be intentional about communicating with children regarding the nature of the conflict and its resolution. Parents can also take measures to ensure that children are not feeling caught in the middle of their parents' disagreements. When all else fails and the divorce is finalized, each member of the family should take time to grieve and recover.

Chapter 18

Domestic Violence

We acknowledge both men and women can have lived experiences with domestic violence. In this chapter, for the sake of readability, we work from the perspective of the female's experience with domestic violence. This in no way is an intention to minimize a man's experience with domestic violence. Many of the principles discussed in this chapter can be applied to the lived experiences of either males or females.

About one in three women and one in four men report having experienced severe physical violence from a partner in their lifetimes. One in fifteen children is exposed to intimate partner violence each year, with 90 percent of these children bearing witness to the abuse. Research has suggested a relationship between intimate partner violence and depression, suicidal behavior, and a range of other health issues, including an increased risk of addiction.[1]

---

[1] See "National Statistics," National Coalition against Domestic Violence, https://ncadv.org/statistics.

Domestic violence is not limited to physical violence. It can also include sexual abuse, emotional or psychological abuse, spiritual abuse, economic abuse, or technological abuse. Even when you're married, consent should always be given before any form of sexual relations takes place; otherwise, it's sexual abuse. Emotional abuse occurs when one partner belittles or offers continual criticism to the other, resulting in a diminished sense of self-worth. Threatening the spouse and/or those closest to her, along with forced isolation from friends and family and destruction of her property, are forms of psychological abuse.[2] Another form of abuse is spiritual abuse. Although it may overlap with other forms of abuse, spiritual abuse distinguishes itself by the use of Scripture or other religious teachings. A husband may twist Scripture to control or manipulate his wife.[3]

Economic and technological forms of abuse are terms that may not be widely used or understood. Economic abuse is when one spouse restricts the use of financial resources to which the other spouse is entitled. This could include putting her on a tight budget while he spends frivolously. Economic abuse can also include ruining the other spouse's credit, along with preventing or impeding her input in making financial decisions. Technological abuse is an act or pattern of behavior intended to cause harm to another. This can include using tracking devices to know the spouse's location with the intention of stalking or harassing her or monitoring her activity on apps and the Internet with the intention to extort or exploit her.[4]

Relationship Dynamics

People who abuse their partners may be heavily involved in the church or may be considered a respectable member of the community. Their positions

---

[2] See "Domestic Violence," U.S. Department of Justice, Office on Violence against Women, https://www.justice.gov/ovw/domestic-violence.

[3] See Karen Roudkovski, *Understanding Spiritual Abuse: What It Is and How to Respond* (Brentwood, TN: B&H Academic, 2024), 33–35.

[4] See "Domestic Violence," U.S. Department of Justice, Office on Violence against Women.

in both the church and community, combined with their charisma, make it difficult to believe the stories coming from their wives or children about the abuse occurring at home. This often leaves women trapped and isolated in an abusive relationship with no clear path to freedom. In one case, the husband had abused both his wife and his children repeatedly over the course of several years, and was arrested. When he appeared in court, he had over thirty character witnesses, including a pastoral counselor. This was both devastating and intimidating for the wife and children.

Why They Stay

People often question why women stay with abusive husbands. There are several reasons. One reason is related to threats she may have received. Her husband may have threatened to physically harm her, the children, pets, or anyone who would attempt to help her. When children are involved, she may be concerned about him having unsupervised custody. In some cases, the husband is a prominent member of the church or community. Because of his reputation and standing, he assures her that no one would believe her. Depending on the situation, it might be a risk for anyone to take a stand against him.

A second reason is the husband has controlled many aspects of her life, including her social life. She has been progressively isolated from her friends and family members. As a result, she may not have a strong support system. A strong support network is instrumental in leaving an abusive relationship. Along with having control of her social life, the husband has likely maintained control of the finances, meaning she has no access to money to support her or the children.

Another reason she stays is she has not had any autonomy to make decisions during the duration of her marriage. Deferring to others for decisions has become normal to her. If she has struggled with depression, which research indicates is likely,[5] she may not have the capacity to follow through

[5] See "National Statistics," National Coalition against Domestic Violence.

with a safety plan or the emotional resources needed to take action. It is also plausible that her self-esteem has been depleted. She may have been led to believe everything is her fault, and that if she were a better wife, their marriage would not be so troubled. It's difficult to find the confidence needed to take action when you have been fed lies about your worth and competence.

The fourth reason a person may stay in an abusive marriage is she fears the repercussions of divorce on her Christian belief system. In some cases, a pastor or lay leader may have advised her to stay to protect the institution of marriage. In other cases, she may be operating from a set of rigid beliefs that have been ingrained in her throughout the years from the doctrinal tenets of her church denomination. This belief system will be discussed later in this chapter.

One last reason she may choose to stay is her husband always promises to change. If she is a Christian, she believes in forgiveness and extending grace to others. However, she may have a mistaken understanding about what forgiveness or grace looks like in an abusive situation. Years ago, Lenore Walker described this experience in a cycle theory of abuse:

> Stage 1, Tension building: Minor incidents may occur. The spouse may believe she can control the situation. She may avoid the offending spouse or comply with his demands. She sees it as her responsibility to manage his anger. When small incidents occur, she may believe it was her fault his anger escalated.
>
> Stage 2, Incident: Here, a major attack occurs, which does not undermine the minor incidents from the first phase. The minor incidents are just as sinful. During this phase, the offending spouse is often triggered by an external episode or an internal state and discharges an uncontrollable response. Both spouses recognize the abusive behavior is out of control.
>
> Stage 3, Calm: The offending spouse recognizes that he has crossed a line and seeks to reconcile. He begs for forgiveness and offers assurances that it will never happen again. He may also believe that

she learned her lesson. With her compliance, he reasons that he will not be tempted to cross the line again. One major problem with this is the emphasis is on her to manage his anger, with him taking no responsibility for his internal state or external actions.[6]

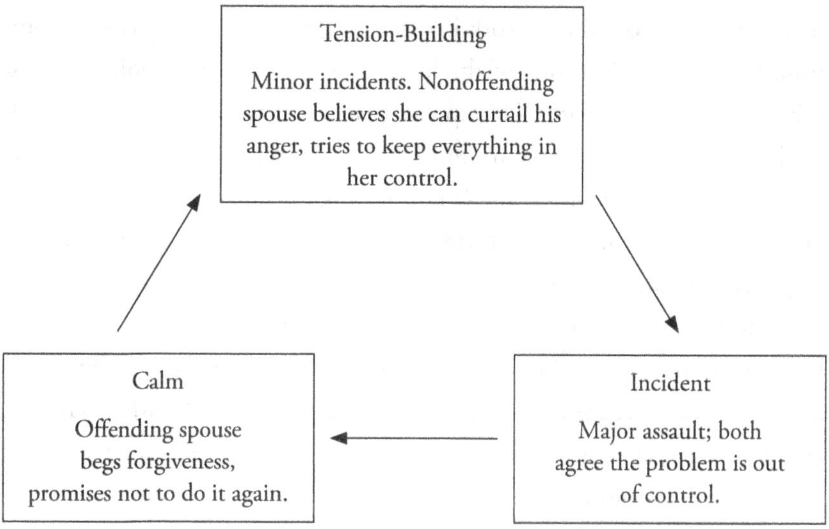

Walker's cycle theory of abuse has undergone several iterations over the years. Some have criticized the theory because of its lack of universal application. Domestic violence may follow this cycle, but each relationship will differ in how violence is expressed. However, this cycle may offer insight as to why women may stay in an abusive relationship. Later in this chapter, we'll discuss appropriate boundaries, along with looking for the fruit of repentance.

Reactive Abuse versus Controlling Abuse

When working with couples in high conflict, a counselor needs to distinguish between reactive abuse and controlling abuse. Reactive abuse occurs when the stress of life has become too much and overwhelmed a person's

---

[6] This cycle theory of abuse was adapted from Lenore E. Walker, *The Battered Woman* (New York: Harper & Row, 1980), chap. 3 (55–69).

capacity to cope. He is not managing his stress or anger in a constructive way. As a result, when provoked, an explosion occurs. In reactive abuse, as the name implies, a person reacts without any thought about the most productive way to navigate the conflict.[7]

During reactive abuse, for example, a spouse is overwhelmed by the demands placed on him at work in a struggling economy. He comes home from work to find out one of the kids got in trouble at school, while the other one is failing math. This spouse just wants to check out for a little while to escape the turmoil around him. Then, the other spouse explodes because he has checked out and is not helping her. Things may get thrown, or names may be called. This form of abuse is destructive, but the underlying issues are different from controlling abuse.

On the outside, controlling abuse may look the same as reactive abuse, but the root cause is different. Controlling abuse limits, or eliminates, an individual's freedom to make her own choices. In a healthy marriage, couples work together to negotiate differences and work toward a solution, making compromises when needed. Controlling abuse occurs when one spouse believes the other spouse should not be allowed to make her own decisions. The controlling spouse may react with threats or force to get the other to comply with his choices or way of doing things. He does not take the other spouse's desires into account. The decision is solely his.[8]

To be clear, neither form of abuse is appropriate. However, being able to distinguish between the two impacts how the counselor approaches the issue. If a counselor mistakes controlling abuse for reactive abuse, she may encourage the wife to be more sensitive to her husband's needs when the issue runs much deeper. While we should all be attentive to the needs of our spouses, we want to be careful that we are not placing responsibility on either spouse to manage the other's emotional state.[9]

---

[7] See Leslie Vernick, *The Emotionally Destructive Marriage: How to Find Your Voice and Reclaim Your Hope* (New York: Waterbrook, 2013), 39–44.

[8] See Vernick, 39–44.

[9] See Vernick, 39–44.

Boundaries

In any marriage, we cannot change our spouses; we can only change ourselves. This is especially true in abusive relationships. We may not be able to control how our spouses treat us, but we do have a decision to make about our response to destructive and abusive behaviors. Ultimately, a wife is not responsible for her spouse's behavior, which he has free will to exercise. Rather, she is responsible to her spouse to set appropriate boundaries that will not enable abusive behavior.

When we are not treated well or we are tolerating destructive behavior toward ourselves without addressing it, we can become resentful. This can lead to us lashing out at others, including our friends, children, and spouse. It's safe to say that when our way of addressing any form of behavior is to belittle, criticize, or shame, we are more likely to invite defensiveness and further perpetuate the very behaviors we are trying to eliminate. Instead, when we become secure enough to set boundaries and refuse to tolerate destructive behavior, we can set boundaries and hold fast.[10]

Setting boundaries involves a refusal to let one's spouse exhibit abusive or destructive behavior toward her. According to Dr. John Townsend, protective boundaries "are designed to 'guard your heart' (Proverbs 4:23), and your life, from danger or trouble."[11] Protective boundaries should be stated as "If ______, then ________" statements.[12]

Some examples:

> "If you are under the influence of alcohol or drugs, then you will not be allowed to stay at the house. I will call your brother to come get you."
>
> "If you yell and call me names, then I will leave the house."

---

[10] See Vernick, 134–35.

[11] John Townsend, *Beyond Boundaries: Learning to Trust Again in Relationships* (Grand Rapids: Zondervan, 2011), 39.

[12] Townsend, 39.

A solid boundary by the person being abused requires both commitment and follow-through. Work with the client in advance to be decisive and steadfast in holding her boundaries.

Many of these women have likely been told they should not set boundaries. Instead, they should just suffer for Christ. However, Christ is not honored in a marriage in which abuse is taking place. God is not glorified when we continually allow someone to sin against us with no consequences. "Sacrificing yourself by allowing someone to sin against you to keep peace in your marriage is never a wise choice—not for you, not for your husband, not for your marriage. God calls us to be biblical peacemakers, not peacekeepers or peace fakers."[13]

What Submission Is and What It Is Not

In the introduction to this chapter, we mentioned spiritual abuse as a form of abuse in which Scripture may be taken out of context to manipulate a spouse into compliance. One of the ways in which spiritual abuse can present itself involves misunderstandings about biblical submission. Let's consider what biblical submission is and what it is not.

Biblical submission is:

Service: Jesus modeled submission for us during his time on earth. He took on the nature of a servant, washing his disciples' feet (John 13:14–15). In the same way, both husband and wife should seek to serve each other and their family.

Devotion: Jesus sees people as they are and how they could be. As a result, he asks us to submit to his will because he knows what's best for us. The path he places us on may not be the one we would have chosen, but it is ultimately for our best and to bring him glory. In the same way, submission in marriage should be about the husband and wife operating in the best interests of each other (Philippians

[13] Vernick, *The Emotionally Destructive Marriage*, 104.

2:3–4; Ephesians 5:21). The intention is never harmful. Instead, his intention is to place our families on a path that will be best for us and to build God's kingdom.

Biblical submission is not:

Misuse of Power and Authority: Scripture never describes biblical submission as "entitlement to do what you want, demanding that others do what you want, or permission to get your own way."[14]

Force: Jesus submitted fully to God's plan; however, he was given a choice in submission. Submission should always be a choice. It should never be coerced. In a healthy marriage, couples should discuss differences, try to understand the other's perspective, and work together to resolve conflicts.

The Sanctity of Marriage

Have we considered how we have protected the image of marriage while disregarding the inner reality? We want to honor God with our marriages, but is God always honored by what is taking place behind closed doors? Is God honored when one spouse abuses another spouse or when pornography is being viewed? Or when one spouse demeans and belittles the other to the point that she believes she is worthless?[15]

Many of those who have experienced violence at the hands of their spouses have been advised by pastors, church leaders, and even some counselors to stay because God hates divorce. Malachi spoke of Judah's marital unfaithfulness and how God did not respect or welcome their offerings. In Malachi 2:14–16, he said,

---

[14] Vernick, 96.

[15] See Diane Langberg, *Redeeming Power: Understanding Authority and Abuse in the Church* (Grand Rapids: Baker, 2020), 94–95.

> Because even though the LORD has been a witness between you and the wife of your youth, you have acted treacherously against her. She was your marriage partner and your wife by covenant. Didn't God make them one and give them a portion of spirit? What is the one seeking? Godly offspring. So watch yourselves carefully, so that no one acts treacherously against the wife of his youth. "If he hates and divorces his wife," says the LORD God of Israel, "he covers his garment with injustice," says the LORD of Armies. Therefore, watch yourselves carefully, and do not act treacherously.

Divorce was not part of God's original design for marriage, but neither was any form of abuse. God emphatically expressed that he does not respect the offering of a husband who acts treacherously toward his wife. In many cases, the sanctity of marriage was compromised long before one spouse filed for divorce.

Taking Action

Documentation

Although it may be concerning, it is important for the person with lived experience to document the abuse she has suffered. Documentation can take the form of pictures, detailed logs, or phone or credit card bills.[16] There are several reasons for this. First, some perpetrators are living a double life. They present differently to their church, community, or place of employment than they do at home. As a result, some have a difficult time believing a particular person is capable of abuse. Evidence makes it difficult to stay in a place of disbelief. In some cases, documentation may bring self-awareness to the one perpetrating abuse.

It's important to consider the motive behind documentation. It's true that 1 Corinthians 13 says that love keeps no record of wrongs, and keeping

[16] See Vernick, *The Emotionally Destructive Marriage*, 122–24.

such a record solely for the purpose of bringing up again and again a matter that has already been settled should not be the goal in documentation. However, offering clear, concrete examples of abusive behavior makes the abuse more difficult to dismiss. These examples might include names the husband is calling his wife or threatening messages she has received. Being able to provide details of the abuse may help those involved to understand the depth of the situation.

Unfortunately, many women endure years of abuse that wear on them. By the time women begin to reach out for help, they are often in a place of despair, and their emotional well-being is extremely low.[17] As a result, these women may come asking for help in anguish. No one presents well when coming from deep desperation. If those close to the family were unaware all this was taking place, it will likely come as a shock to them, and they may even be in denial for a period of time. The shock combined with the intense emotions of the woman may make it difficult for friends and family to believe her, which makes them slow to take action, if they act at all. Being able to present evidence can help mitigate these issues.

Safety Plan

If a woman is concerned for her own safety and that of her children, she needs to work with a counselor to establish a safety plan. If her only banking account is a joint account with her husband, she may want to consider opening her own account or getting a credit card in her name. Unfortunately, there have been situations in which women have tried to leave, but their husbands canceled their debit cards or put a hold on other funds. They were unable to take care of themselves and were forced to return to an unsafe situation.

A safety plan should include a bag packed with important documents (children's birth certificates, account records, etc.) in the event that a situation escalates quickly and she needs to be able to leave immediately. She

[17] See Vernick, 125.

should develop a contingency plan for places she can stay. Depending on the circumstances, family members or friends may be a good option, but she may also want to check with local women's and children's shelters. A solid shelter will have staff members who are well-trained and equipped to manage these types of crises, and the location will be private to keep the women and children safe.

While establishing a safety plan, the person may also want to schedule a brief consultation with an attorney. At this stage the purpose of this consultation is to protect her from legal issues. When kids are involved, a safety plan may involve taking the kids and leaving the home. However, depending on where they take the kids and the circumstances under which they are taken, this can invite legal trouble. Legal consultation can assist the person in establishing a safety plan that protects her and the children without inviting legal issues.[18]

Confrontation

In preparing to confront her spouse, a wife should consider the words of Matthew 18:15–17: "If your brother sins against you, go tell him his fault, between you and him alone. If he listens to you, you have won your brother. But if he won't listen, take one or two others with you, so that by the testimony of two or three witnesses every fact may be established. If he doesn't pay attention to them, tell the church. If he doesn't pay attention even to the church, let him be like a Gentile and a tax collector to you."

Before we break this passage down, let's discuss some stipulations in choosing to confront her spouse alone. If the person and/or her children are in any type of physical danger, or physical abuse has occurred, she should not confront her spouse alone. In the event of physical danger, she should follow steps outlined in this chapter. We recommend that a professional counselor with experience in this area be involved, outlining a safety plan and making decisions about confrontation.

---

[18] See Vernick, 126–27.

Once the person has established a solid safety plan, along with documentation of what has been happening, she may be ready to confront her spouse. One option is to schedule the meeting in a public place. If they both arrive separately, this will allow the opportunity for her to leave on her own if needed, and it will decrease the likelihood that an angry outburst will occur. Another option is to have a support team of people who are aware of the situation and are willing to call and check in every thirty minutes if they do not hear from her.[19]

In any relationship, there are things we can find fault with. When preparing to discuss these issues with her spouse, she should "emphasize the pattern over the event. Events cannot be changed; patterns can."[20] Encourage her to consider the things she cannot continue to allow in their relationship. Is it a spouse who engages in extramarital affairs, struggles with sexual addiction, or is prone to subjecting her or the kids to angry outbursts that leave them all in fear? These are the things that need to be confronted directly with a clear boundary drawn.[21]

The Story of Jane

Her husband had a persistent drug addiction. Apparently, he was good at his job. So anytime he was caught under the influence at work, his boss would have him attend a rehab program, but never fired him. They would spend a substantial amount of money on rehab, but he never seemed motivated to change. Things continued to escalate until Christmas one year. Jane and the kids woke up on Christmas morning to find all the presents gone. During the night, the husband had taken the presents and sold them to buy drugs. Jane should confront this behavior and set a clear boundary. In this case, she might explain to him that he is not allowed back in the

---

[19] See Vernick, 121–24.

[20] Brad Hamrick, *Self-Centered Spouse: Help for Chronically Broken Marriages* (Phillipsburg, NJ: P&R, 2014), 29.

[21] See Vernick, *The Emotionally Destructive Marriage*, 127–28.

house until he is clean and has a solid recovery plan involving a professional counselor. Or, she and the kids might stay somewhere else until these things are in place.

When one must confront an abusive spouse, it is best to be empathic and compassionate, taking note of the good things seen in him. If the spouse comes at him with condemnation and angry reprimands, he is likely to become defensive, which may escalate the situation. He will likely be surprised if she chooses to approach him with a tender heart. She might say something such as "We always dreamed of the day when we would become parents, and I know you love being a dad. However, I am concerned that your angry outbursts are frightening the children, and they are losing their desire to have a relationship with you."[22]

A conversation with a softened start-up is more likely to invite reflection from the person on the other end of the confrontation.[23] This reflection could lead to a change in heart and a desire for repentance. If not, or if he responds in an inappropriate or unsafe way, it may be time for her to take someone with her. She may wish to bring a friend, a church member, or a pastor. Bringing witnesses follows the biblical mandate for restoring those who have fallen away, and it helps the spouse to understand the seriousness of his sin and the consequences that will follow.

When Kids Are Involved

The children are another reason we should encourage boundaries to be in place so as to prevent any abuse from continuing. Children are often the ones most impacted by domestic violence. In addition to the typical effects of trauma and family instability, many of them may grow up believing violence is normal, which leads them into an abusive relationship, thus perpetuating the cycle of abuse. Or they themselves may become abusers.

---

[22] Vernick, 142–43, 145.

[23] The "softened start-up intervention" originated from the work of John Gottman.

Guidance to Helpers

Avoid Shame

Whenever we shame others, we typically perpetuate the behavior we are trying to stop, so we want to avoid shame. Instead, we want to bring about conviction. Shame is synonymous with condemnation. When a person believes he is hopeless and cannot change, he usually does not exercise effort and remains stuck in his sin. According to Robert McGee, God's answer to shame is regeneration. "Our sins have been forgiven, and we now have tremendous capabilities for growth and change because we are new people with the Spirit of God living in us. Yes, when we sin we will experience its destructive effects and the Father's discipline, but our sin will never change the truth of who we are in Christ."[24]

Understand the Risks

Our ultimate desire is that all involved are safe. However, there may be safety issues in telling women to leave without a plan. Calling the police or leaving abruptly can potentially escalate the abusive behavior. As a result, we need to make sure any plans to leave or to involve law enforcement have a well-thought-out safety plan in place.

Be Conscious of Becoming a Benevolent Rescuer

Because we genuinely care for those we are helping, we want to see them safe and thriving. We think if they would just listen to us, we could make their situation better. After all, we want the best for them. The problem is she has free will to make her own decisions. She is probably accustomed to her spouse telling her what to do, and she will easily defer to us. Being able to help her effectively long-term involves helping her to find her voice, make

[24] Robert McGee, *The Search for Significance: Seeing Your True Worth through God's Eyes* (Nashville: W Publishing, 2003), 108.

her own decisions, and take ownership of them. In other words, our role is to empower her, not to decide for her.[25]

Conclusion

Multiple safety issues are involved when we choose to address domestic violence. Before taking any action, we want to make sure a solid safety plan and support system are in place for the family. When abuse and other sinful behavior have pervaded the relationship, the sanctity of marriage has already been compromised. We must remember that God is just as displeased with the sins that lead to divorce as he is with divorce. Likewise, encouraging a person to remain in a dangerous situation to protect the institution of marriage was not God's intent.

Additional Resources

Cloud, Henry, and John Townsend. *Boundaries: When to Say Yes, How to Say No to Take Control of Your Life.* Grand Rapids: Zondervan, 2017.

Hamrick, Brad. *Self-Centered Spouse: Help for Chronically Broken Marriages.* Phillipsburg, NJ: P&R, 2014.

Vernick, Leslie. *The Emotionally Destructive Marriage: How to Find Your Voice and Reclaim Your Hope.* New York: Waterbrook, 2013.

[25] See Vernick, *The Emotionally Destructive Marriage*, 218.

Chapter 19

Infidelity

You can feel the tension when Tom and Carissa arrive in your office. As they share their story, you immediately realize the situation's complexity. Carissa shares how she picked up Tom's phone one evening and saw a series of text messages. She shares the devastation of realizing Tom was engaging in infidelity with a coworker for the previous six months. After Tom confessed to the behavior, Carissa requested he move out of the couple's home. Tom moved in with his parents and suggested the couple begin counseling. Deeply hurt, angry, and feeling the trauma of the infidelity, Carissa told Tom she needed some time and was not ready to see someone about their relationship. But, still needing support, she began to rely emotionally on a friend at work whom she knew had divorced the previous year after his wife's infidelity. Within a month, the pair became emotionally entangled. One evening, the relationship progressed to physical involvement. Carissa experienced immediate regret and realized she wanted to see if her marriage could work. She contacted Tom to accept his offer to begin marriage counseling. The evening before their appointment, she told him of her infidelity. Tom was shaken, angry, and consumed with guilt. Now what? How do you unravel the complexities for the couple to begin healing their relationship?

When Vows Are Broken

Infidelity occurs when a spouse breaks the commitment to maintain certain emotional and physical boundaries. Secrets are formed and maintained. Infidelity shatters trust. Prevalence rates for the occurrence of infidelity in the form of extramarital sex range from 11 to 25 percent.[1] But infidelity need not include the physical act of sex to be considered a breaking of the marriage vows. Any relationship crossing the boundaries of the couple's commitment to each other is a form of infidelity, including emotional affairs and pornography use. With the prevalence of social media usage, crossing the boundaries of emotional intimacy on social media platforms is a rising concern.[2]

Infidelity does not only affect the couple. It impacts the family and social circle surrounding the couple. Children are affected and potentially feel caught in a contentious relationship between their parents. The affair may impact parents, in-laws, grandparents, and the extended family. Friendships are impacted. Churches are impacted.

Types of Infidelity

Dave Carder has decades of experience specializing in the recovery and prevention of infidelity. Based on his experience, Carder identified five types of "emotional and sexual betrayal."[3]

---

[1] See Benjamin Warach and Lawrence Josephs, "The Aftershocks of Infidelity: A Review of Infidelity-Based Attachment Trauma," *Sexual and Relationship Therapy* 36, no. 1 (February 2021): 69, https://doi.org/10.1080/14681994.2019.1577961.

[2] See Irum Saeed Abbasi and Nawal G. Alghamdi, "When Flirting Turns into Infidelity: The Facebook Dilemma," *American Journal of Family Therapy* 45, no. 1 (February 1, 2017): 1–14, https://doi.org/10.1080/01926187.2016.1277804.

[3] See David Carder, *Anatomy of an Affair: How Affairs, Attractions, and Addictions Develop, and How to Guard Your Marriage Against Them* (Chicago: Moody, 2017), 13–31.

The "One-Night Stand"[4]

The one-night stand is a single sexual experience and is typically an unplanned event. The two individuals usually did not previously know each other. For example, it may occur during a business trip. Carder notes that the individuals do not seek emotional closeness, nor do they seek to continue the relationship.

The "Entangled Affair"[5]

This type of infidelity develops over time and involves a powerful emotional connection. The emotional connection typically precedes the sexual component of the relationship. The relationship may last for months or years, creating a vast amount of entanglement. As such, disentanglement from this type of infidelity may be challenging and involve complex feelings of grief and loss from all parties involved.

At times, the term *emotional affair* is used to describe an infidelity that has not crossed the boundary of sexual activity. An emotional affair might involve sharing intimate details about one's life or struggles in his or her marriage. Sharing secrets often fuels a friendship or a deep sense of connection. In these cases, there is the question of how to distinguish between friendship and infidelity. Glass and Staeheli describe emotional affairs as characterized by three components: "secrecy, emotional intimacy, and sexual chemistry."[6] Keeping secrets and hiding an intimate, emotional connection combined with sexual chemistry rob the marital relationship of intimacy and connection. Emotional infidelity can quickly escalate into physical infidelity.

---

[4] Carder, 17–20.

[5] Carder, 20–23.

[6] Shirley P. Glass, with Jean Coppock Staeheli, *Not "Just Friends": Rebuilding Trust and Recovering Your Sanity after Infidelity* (New York: Free Press, 2003), 31.

The "Sexual Addiction"[7]

The "sexual addiction" infidelity involves compulsive sexual behavior. The unfaithful partner may have a pornography addiction or multiple sexual partners over a period of time. The infidelity is focused on sex and does not involve an emotional relationship with the sexual partner. A unique component of recovery from this type of infidelity is that the spouse with the addiction needs to achieve sobriety and participate in long-term recovery.

The "Add-On Affair"[8]

According to Carder, the add-on infidelity begins with a platonic friendship based on a common interest and is typically contained to the shared experience. These experiences may range from a hobby, work project, sport, or shared ministry. The relationship is primarily confined to times when the couple is together for the shared interest. But the relationship breaks the boundaries of a platonic friendship by eventually expanding to sexual activity. Carder describes the sexual activity of this type of infidelity as "infrequent and dissatisfying to one partner, but is provided out of obligation or for the purpose of maintaining the friendship."[9]

The "Reconnection"[10]

This type of affair involves reconnecting with an "old flame" from one's younger years. In the age of social media, this reconnection is relatively easy and may begin with a simple curiosity about how the person is doing. Yet Carder describes the danger of this type of relationship and the potential for rapid development because, for most people, this was potentially the spouse's first sexual experience, which was "fueled by hormones and sexual

[7] Carder, *Anatomy of an Affair*, 23–25.
[8] Carder, 25–27.
[9] Carder, 25.
[10] Carder, 27–28.

attraction." The relationship involved "freedom with little or no responsibility," and both participants have memories filled with "nostalgia that only intensifies infatuation."[11] This highly charged nostalgic memory may be romanticized as an escape from reality, and emotional and physical intimacy may quickly be rekindled. Infidelity expert Shirley Glass emphasizes, "If friendships and collegial relationships can become overheated, former lovers are positively flammable."[12]

Ministering in the Aftermath

A couple who has experienced infidelity by one or both partners will experience challenges in recovery. When responding in the aftermath of infidelity, keep the following in mind:

Initial Discovery and Shock

Discovering infidelity is a life-altering moment, a nightmare that shakes the very core of a person. The initial shock is emotionally dysregulating, overwhelming, and devastating. Over the days, weeks, and months to follow, one might expect to feel grief, rage, anxiety, panic, humiliation, and fear. It is common for the betrayed partner to experience obsessive and intrusive thoughts about the infidelity.

The Importance of Validating the Grief and Trauma

Waves of grief will sweep over the couple. The betrayed spouse may mourn past experiences after realizing the infidelity was occurring during that time. The previous Christmas or last family vacation may be painfully clouded

---

[11] Carder, 27.

[12] Shirley Glass, with Jean Coppock Staeheli, *Not "Just Friends": Rebuilding Trust and Recovering Your Sanity after Infidelity*, 3rd ed. (New York: Atria, 2003), 34.

when the spouse realizes things were not as they seemed. The couple's dreams for the future are irrevocably altered.

Acknowledge that this is a painful and traumatic experience. Infidelity in marriage is a form of interpersonal trauma where someone who was considered safe and secure violated that trust.[13] The betrayed partner's response can be similar to individuals who experience other forms of trauma. Some even display symptoms of PTSD. Recognizing these intense symptoms as a trauma response can be validating for the spouse who was betrayed.[14] In a study conducted by Lonergan et al., participants reported feeling "clarity, validation, and relief" when they were "exposed to external sources (e.g., books and interviews by psychologists and researchers) that used a trauma and PTSD framework to explain the effects of betrayal."[15] The impact is felt interpersonally, emotionally, cognitively, behaviorally, and physically.[16]

The traumatized spouse may have difficulty stopping obsessive thoughts and questions about the infidelity. Unwanted, unexpected, and intrusive thoughts may invade the mind without notice. Triggers may occur that remind the spouse of what happened. For example, if the infidelity occurred on a business trip, the spouse may feel triggered by the spouse being away for business. If the infidelity was discovered through a text message, the sound of an incoming text may trigger a response.

The Need to Establish Safety

The first step is to establish safety. If the infidelity has not already ended, the unfaithful spouse needs to end the relationship immediately and cease contact with the partner with whom the affair was committed. Boundaries

---

[13] See Michelle Lonergan et al., "Is Romantic Partner Betrayal a Form of Traumatic Experience? A Qualitative Study," *Stress and Health: Journal of the International Society for the Investigation of Stress* 37, no. 1 (February 2021): 19, https://doi.org/10.1002/smi.2968.

[14] See Lonergan et al., 29.

[15] Lonergan et al., 19.

[16] See Warach and Josephs, "The Aftershocks of Infidelity," 73.

for accountability need to be established. For example, unfaithful spouses may need to provide proof of their whereabouts and whom they spend time with when away from home. The partners need to have a medical check-up to be tested for sexually transmitted infections. Additionally, using the information provided in chapter 8, assess whether either partner is having suicidal ideation and respond appropriately.

Immediate Decisions

Decisions will be made in the immediate aftermath of the discovery. The couple will decide whether or not they will remain in the same home or separate with an agreed-upon purpose, such as a cooling-off period or seeking counseling. The wronged partner needs to consider whether separation will increase concerns about trust.[17]

It is common for the betrayed spouse to ask many questions about the details related to the affair, but the individual should be encouraged to carefully consider the impact of this knowledge on one's well-being. Knowing details of the sexual relationship may cause further harm, leaving images in one's mind that cannot be erased. Keeping a journal of the questions may be helpful, knowing that these questions can be asked as they feel ready to hear the response. It's often best to share broad information without specific details.

The Process Will Not Be Linear

In this book, we have discussed how healing from other forms of grief and trauma does not take a linear path. Recovery from infidelity is also a nonlinear path. New discoveries, for example, may return the couple to a previous stage. Or fresh waves of grief may occur on anniversaries. These anniversaries may have formerly held positive memories, such as a first date. Or the anniversaries may be traumatic memories, such as the discovery of the affair.

---

[17] Glass and Staeheli, *Not "Just Friends,"* 130–31.

A Referral May Be Necessary

Working effectively with infidelity requires expertise and training, so referrals to a professional marriage therapist with experience in this area are highly recommended. Without thoroughly addressing the issue, the couple may find themselves years later realizing the amount of unresolved resentment and hurt still festering. Like an invasive cancer, this damage can be challenging to treat and potentially fatal to the relationship.

Underlying Complexities

A critical reason for engaging a professional in healing is that complex circumstances and histories impact a marital relationship. Individual, marital, historical, and cultural factors contribute to the underlying issues involved in infidelity. These are just a few issues that should be considered in therapy.

- Individual factors:
  - What personal needs does each spouse have?
  - Are there personal disappointments that do not involve the spouse (e.g., unrealized professional goals, unmet hopes or dreams that one had for their life)?
  - Is there a history of other trauma (including betrayal by those they trusted)?
  - What were the relational and communication patterns in the family of origin?
- Relationship factors:
  - What are the communication patterns in the relationship?
  - What are the expectations and needs within the relationship? How are those needs communicated? These should be realistic, and we should not expect a marriage partner to meet all the needs of the other.
  - Is the unfaithful spouse genuinely remorseful? Is he or she taking responsibility for his or her actions?

— What concrete steps need to be taken to rebuild trust? What level of accountability works best for the couple?

Forgiveness Cannot Be Rushed

The couple must identify the areas of hurt and harm that need to be addressed when considering forgiveness. By naming each hurt, we realize the seriousness of the actions. Each hurt needs to be named and grieved. Each hurt needs an apology and request for forgiveness rather than a blanket apology.

Unfortunately, much of the forgiveness burden is often placed on the one granting forgiveness rather than the one receiving forgiveness. To work through the complexities of forgiveness, the unfaithful spouse needs to recognize the losses and wrongs committed, take responsibility for his or her actions, show empathy and a desire for emotional connection, and offer a genuine apology for each wrong committed.

Forgiveness does not equate to the immediate granting of trust. When a spouse chooses to forgive, he or she should not be expected to grant immediate restoration of the relationship, nor does this mean the relationship will look the same as before. Trust is earned over time. The offending spouse needs to establish and maintain boundaries that will assist in rebuilding trust. The person who was wronged will need to identify what he or she needs to begin the process of rebuilding trust. Without the unfaithful spouse taking responsibility for the wrongs committed, reconciliation cannot occur.

Rebuilding

As time passes, the initial shock and wave of intense emotions will begin to stabilize. The couple begins to make decisions about the future of their relationship. If they have been working on the relationship, they may assess whether progress is being made and both partners are committed to repair and restoration. They will consider whether trust is slowly being rebuilt. If not, they may consider what adjustments could be made to improve the situation.

Is Healing Possible?

Infidelity has a devastating impact on marriage. Promises are broken. Trust is shattered. Lives are turned upside down. Infidelity tarnishes the precious memories of the past and steals from the hopes and dreams for the future. Decisions are difficult to make when under stress, yet after an infidelity, some immediate and long-term decisions will be determined over the days, weeks, and months to come. For some couples, infidelity is the end of the relationship. Some stay together out of sheer determination and commitment but do not work through the hurt and underlying issues, allowing resentment to fester over the years. Others build a post-infidelity relationship that flourishes.

Infidelity expert Shirley Glass states, "It's hard to believe that a marriage can be better after an affair, but it's true—if you learn how to handle the nightmarish days after discovery, the traumatic reactions of the betrayed spouse, the revelation of details when the story is told, and the period of construction when the marriage is rebuilt, brick by brick."[18] Even for those unable to stay in the relationship, she notes, "The road to recovery can be a stimulus for growth whether you travel it with your partner or if you make your way alone."[19] In sum, yes. Healing is possible. There is hope after infidelity.

Additional Resources

Carder, David. *Anatomy of an Affair: How Affairs, Attractions, and Addictions Develop, and How to Guard Your Marriage Against Them.* Chicago: Moody, 2017.

[18] Glass and Staeheli, 12.

[19] Glass and Staeheli, 12.

Chapter 20

Financial Crises

Lucas has a good job, a home, and a car. He had one month of savings put away for emergencies. Last month, he was hospitalized with pneumonia and unable to work while recovering. He depleted his savings, yet medical bills are pouring in. How will he pay his family's regular expenses and the piles of medical bills?

After her husband's death, Mia became a single mom of two teenage children. Several months ago, she was laid off from her job. She could not find a job in her field of experience, so she took another job that paid poorly but at least allowed her to pay some of her bills. Christmas is almost here. How will she provide gifts for her daughters when she cannot make ends meet?

Naomi left an abusive relationship one month ago. She has no recent job history and three children, ages six and under, to support. How will she find help for the impact of the abuse on the lives of her and her children? Where will she find employment with her limited work experience? And if she does, how will she afford childcare?

Samuel, a former accountant, once had a career and a wife. After his beloved wife died of cancer, he became addicted to alcohol. He was fired from his job for going to work while intoxicated. The drinking continued until he lost everything. He is living on the streets, his life in danger due to the addiction.

The focus of this chapter is responding to individuals who are in financial crisis within your community. For the purpose of this chapter, a financial crisis is defined as the inability to provide for one's basic needs: food, shelter, medication, health care, or other necessities. The term *financial benevolence* refers to financial and financial-related assistance.

Financial Strain in the United States

A 2022 survey conducted by Pew Research reflects the financial strain and stress parents faced during the previous year:[1]

- 25% reported a time when they could not afford food, mortgage, or rent.
- 24% reported difficulty affording health care.
- 20% could not afford childcare.
- 19% were worried about loss of wages if they had to take a day off to care for a child.

A study of emergency savings and financial security conducted by the Consumer Financial Protection Bureau's Office of Research revealed more concerning data about the state of finances for some Americans:[2]

[1] See Dana Braga, "One-in-Four U.S. Parents Say They've Struggled to Afford Food or Housing in the Past Year," Pew Research Center, December 7, 2022, https://pewrsr.ch/3UCzzjd.

[2] See "Emergency Savings and Financial Security: Insights from the Making Ends Meet Survey and Consumer Credit Panel," Consumer Financial Protection Bureau, https://files.consumerfinance.gov/f/documents/cfpb_mem_emergency-savings-financial-security_report_2022-3.pdf.

- 24% reported no savings for emergencies. Of those with no savings, there are additional concerns:
  - — 40% reported having sixty days or more of delinquent debt.
  - — 35% reported at least one overdraft during the previous twelve months.
  - — 55% reported no available credit.
  - — 68% reported that finances often or always control their lives.
- 39% reported less than one month of savings. These individuals report additional concerns as follows:
  - — 19% reported having sixty days or more of delinquent debt.
  - — 19% reported at least one overdraft during the previous twelve months.
  - — 24% reported no available credit.
  - — 35% reported that finances often or always control their lives.

Biblical Foundations for Benevolence

Caring for those in need is a theme seen throughout Scripture. We see instructions to help those in need in the Old Testament (Deuteronomy 15:1–11; Psalms 41:1; 82:3–4; Proverbs 14:21, 31; Isaiah 58:10), the New Testament and ministry of the early church (Acts 6:1–7; James 1:27; 2:14–17), and the teachings of Christ (Mark 10:21–22; Luke 14:12–14). There is a biblical mandate to help those in need.

Through caring for those in need, we demonstrate Christ's love. Consider the following passage in 1 John: "If anyone has this world's goods and sees a fellow believer in need but withholds compassion from him—how does God's love reside in him? Little children, let us not love in word or speech, but in action and in truth" (3:17–18).

When ministering to others, we show the love of Christ. Additionally, whenever possible, we need to offer benevolence within our relationships with others. Consider Isaiah 58:10: "If you offer yourself to the hungry, and satisfy the afflicted one, then your light will shine in the darkness, and your night will be like noonday."

Notice the phrase "offer yourself," which may also be translated "spend yourselves" (NIV) or "pour yourself out" (ESV). As you read the practical suggestions in this chapter, identify what it might look like to "offer yourself" to others in a relationship that surpasses simply providing financial assistance. What does it look like to "pour yourself out"? How might your assistance be different if you "spend yourself"?

Corbett and Fikkert emphasize that the phrase "spend yourself" in this passage "often involves more than giving a handout to a poor person, a handout that may very well do more harm than good."[3] They emphasize, "Until we embrace our mutual brokenness, our work with low-income people is likely to do far more harm than good."[4] We are all created in God's image, yet we all experience brokenness or "poverty" in some form. For some, it is material poverty.

Benevolence should be conducted in a spirit of humility and grace rather than a sense of pride and superiority.

Identifying the Underlying Causes of the Financial Crisis

Identifying the underlying cause of the presenting financial crisis can provide insight into how we may provide assistance beyond the initial crisis response. Keep in mind that, like any crisis, financial crises are complex. As such, there may be multiple underlying causes. Here are a few of them:

Disaster

Financial crises may result from a human-made disaster or a natural one, such as a tornado, hurricane, flood, or fire. These families typically need

---

[3] Steve Corbett and Brian Fikkert, *When Helping Hurts: How to Alleviate Poverty without Hurting the Poor . . . and Yourself* (Chicago: Moody, 2012), 53.

[4] Corbett and Fikkert, 61.

immediate assistance with basic needs, referrals to disaster assistance provided by the government or other agencies, and long-term support as they rebuild their lives. Also, consider whether the event caused a job loss. For example, after Hurricane Katrina devastated the city of New Orleans, businesses were disrupted, and many lost their jobs. Homes were destroyed, vehicles were flooded, and many people lost most, if not all, of their possessions.

Health Crisis

An unexpected health crisis can lead to significant expenses and the inability to work. Approximately four in ten adults report having medical or dental debt. Medical debt is higher among the noninsured, but the insured also struggle with outstanding medical bills. Individuals with medical debt report reducing the purchase of basic necessities, depleting their savings, accruing additional debt, delaying payment of other bills, and working increased hours or multiple jobs to pay down the debt.[5] Medical bills have been cited as the most common cause for debt collection. Medical-related issues, such as medical debt or the inability to work due to health issues, are common causes of bankruptcy.[6]

Divorce

After divorce, the family's resources that once supported one household now have to be divided among two households. Combine this with the monetary

---

[5] See "KFF's Kaiser Health News and NPR Launch Diagnosis: Debt, a Yearlong Reporting Partnership Exploring the Scale, Impact, and Causes of the Health Care Debt Crisis in America," *KFF* (blog), June 16, 2022, https://www.kff.org/health-costs/press-release/kffs-kaiser-health-news-and-npr-launch-diagnosis-debt-a-yearlong-reporting-partnership-exploring-the-scale-impact-and-causes-of-the-health-care-debt-crisis-in-america.

[6] See David U. Himmelstein et al., "Medical Bankruptcy: Still Common Despite the Affordable Care Act," *American Journal of Public Health* 109, no. 3 (March 2019): 431–33, https://doi.org/10.2105/AJPH.2018.304901.

cost of the divorce itself, and financial difficulties may arise. If only one spouse worked, the other spouse may be jobless, have no recent work history, or be underemployed and potentially without health insurance.

Death

A death in the family can become a financial crisis. If there was a medical crisis or long-term illness before the death, there may be medical debt. After the death of an income earner, the family's income is reduced by at least half. This reduction in household income impacts families of all ages, including older adults. If the deceased did not have life insurance, the family may struggle to pay for the funeral and burial expenses. Moving forward, the surviving wage earner, who is dealing with grief, may not earn enough to provide for the family, which can cause a great deal of stress.

Job Loss

A person may become suddenly unemployed or experience a demotion or other job change that reduces income. The job loss may come with a loss of health insurance. A medical crisis or unexpected expense during this time can be financially devastating.

Insufficient Income

Combine insufficient income with rising costs, and a family barely covering their expenses may become unable to do so. A rise in gas and food prices can be devastating to a family. In some areas of the country, mortgage and rent prices exceed what is realistic for a low-income family to afford.

Financial-Management Issues

Financial-management issues may be a contributing factor, such as when a family purchases items above their means. There may be a history of overspending or accruing consumer debt. At times, a family may purchase a home beyond what they can comfortably afford, leading to financial stress and strain.

Trauma

Survivors of trauma may include individuals who fled an abusive marriage, adult survivors of childhood abuse, survivors of assault, military veterans, accident survivors, or survivors of any other event in which an individual was abused and/or feared for his or her safety. We discussed the impact of trauma in part 5. The impact is pervasive and can potentially affect a person's ability to maintain adequate employment. In many cases of trauma, additional medical and mental-health support is needed, which can be expensive.

Financial Stress and Mental Health

Research indicates financial stress is a predictor for poor mental health. For example, in one study investigating the experience of college students, financial stress predicted anxiety, depression, and alcohol dependence. These findings were consistent with previous research. Moreover, this research indicates that financial stress and mental-health issues could develop into a "vicious cycle" in which one exacerbates the other.[7] Mental-health issues are a cause of absenteeism at work, and for some their condition deteriorates to the point they can no longer work.

Responding to Those in Financial Crisis

Use the following techniques when engaging the person who presents with a financial crisis:

---

[7] See Thomas Richardson et al., "A Longitudinal Study of Financial Difficulties and Mental Health in a National Sample of British Undergraduate Students," *Community Mental Health Journal* 53, no. 3 (April 2017): 344–52, https://doi.org/10.1007/s10597-016-0052-0.

Engage with Humility and Respect

Avoid having a sense of pride or superiority. Instead, engage those you are serving with humility and respect. A financial crisis can happen to anyone. Moreover, everyone has areas of struggle. In exploring how the church can engage with poverty alleviation efforts, authors Corbett and Fikkert state:

> One of the biggest problems in many poverty-alleviation efforts is that their design and implementation exacerbates the poverty of being the economically rich—their god-complex—and the poverty of being of the economically poor—their feelings of inferiority and shame. The way that we act toward the economically poor often communicates—albeit unintentionally—that we are superior and they are inferior. In the process we hurt the poor and ourselves.[8]

Establish Safety

Ask yourself, is there any part of this situation that needs immediate attention to maintain the safety of the family? For example, is it the middle of winter and the electricity was disconnected? Does the family need groceries?

Connect with Resources

Connect the individual or family with community resources (such as food banks, utility assistance, government programs) that provide both short-term and long-term assistance.

Determine the Need: Short-Term Relief versus Development

Consider the question, Is this financial crisis a onetime event or an ongoing problem for the individual or family? If a onetime event, short-term assistance may be sufficient. For example, when a family experiences a medical

---

[8] Corbett and Fikkert, *When Helping Hurts*, 62.

crisis that depletes their resources, relief for immediate needs may be provided. For those who have a history of financial struggle, it may be appropriate to provide opportunities for development, such as mental-health counseling, financial counseling, career counseling, or other assistance meant to have a transformative impact.

Corbett and Fikkert emphasize the distinction between relief and development. They state, "Relief doesn't ask people to take actions to improve their situation; development does. Relief is done *to* people or *for* people; development is done *with* people."[9] Development respects the dignity and value of an individual and provides hope that the person can move toward financial stability.

Be cautious about adopting a one-size-fits-all mentality for development. Instead, consider an individual's background. There is a difference between a history of poor financial management and poverty. Poverty is a multifaceted and challenging circumstance that includes many complex barriers to overcome.

Assist with a Job Search

If the individual desires employment but is unemployed or underemployed, be intentional about assisting him or her with a job search. This assistance may include networking in the community, hosting a job fair, developing a résumé, or providing career counseling. Career counseling may be provided to assist individuals in discovering potential jobs that not only provide financially but also match the skills and interests of the job seeker.

Help in Obtaining Financial Counseling

Provide opportunities for the person to meet with someone who has expertise in finances and can provide assistance with analyzing expenditures,

[9] Steve Corbett and Brian Fikkert, *Helping without Hurting in Church Benevolence* (Chicago: Moody, 2015), 27.

budgeting, financial problem-solving, planning for debt payoff, and other financial-related tasks. These meetings can be formally scheduled over a set period of time based on the needs of the individual seeking assistance.

Support the Person's Mental Health

Explore how the person's mental health can be supported. Mental health can be an overlooked area during a financial crisis. Many counselors accept insurance, but if a person is struggling financially, the co-pay may be unmanageable. Some may not have insurance at all. If they are stuck in a cycle of mental-health issues contributing to difficulty maintaining a job, mental-health treatment may be a pathway toward financial stability. I (Karen) have worked with numerous individuals whose mental-health diagnoses impacted their ability to work. And with treatment, the individuals were able to find a job and maintain employment.

Policies and Procedures for Financial Benevolence Ministries

Perhaps the most helpful suggestion for responding to financial crises is proactively planning. This plan can be written in the financial benevolence ministry's policies and procedures manual. When you have a plan, the individuals responsible for aid distribution will have guidelines to follow. Also, having a plan allows for good stewardship of resources.

Consider the following components when developing a written benevolence policy. Consultation with a CPA or tax attorney is recommended to ensure that the church follows all legal guidelines and documentation as required by the IRS.

Purpose of the Financial Benevolence Ministry

- What is the biblical foundation of the church's benevolence ministry?
- What is the purpose of the financial benevolence ministry?

Financial Benevolence Committee

- How will the church establish and maintain a committee or board to oversee the benevolence funds?
- What are the committee guidelines for membership, frequency of meetings, and procedure of emergency meetings? How will the committee handle special called meetings to approve larger amounts of funds?
- How will members be trained?

Eligibility Criteria

- Clearly list the criteria for providing assistance. What types of aid will be provided? Which needs qualify and which do not? For example, the church may include assistance with housing, food, and medical needs, but what about assistance for car payments or school tuition?
- How will needs be determined?
- Will funds be available to the entire community or limited to church members?
- If funds are available to the community at large, will there be any geographical boundaries to the assistance?
- Will there be a quarterly, biannual, or annual limit for each household applying for assistance?

Application Process

- What is the process of applying for assistance?
- How can the process be expedited for financial crises/emergencies?
- Will individuals be referred to community resources? If so, will they be encouraged to use the community resources first (e.g., a food bank, utility assistance programs)?
- If you are using community resources, the church needs to have a community resource book that is updated regularly. Who will be in charge of developing and maintaining the resource book?

- Include an application request form to apply for assistance. Include the following information (and any other information the church deems appropriate):
  - — Name, address, and phone number of applicant
  - — Amount requested
  - — Reason for request
  - — Eligibility criteria
  - — Amount provided
  - — Dates of application, approval, and disbursement of funds
  - — How the funds were disbursed and to whom
  - — Recipient's relationship to the church and church leaders/ board members
  - — Who approved the request
  - — Employment information and income (optional)
  - — Will any documentation be required with the application (e.g., submission of the cutoff notice for electricity)?

Procedures

- Where will the applications be stored? They need to be kept secure and confidential. Who has access to the applications?
- Who can approve assistance? Will there be levels of approval? For example, will expenses under $100 require the approval of only one or two members, while larger expenses require the approval of the entire board? If the board only meets quarterly, how will emergency approvals be conducted?
- Will payments be made directly to the landlord, electric company, and so forth? Some churches only allow for third-party payments to be made. If your church only does third-party payments, how will you handle requests for food assistance or miscellaneous needs?
- Maintain documentation of all assistance provided. Keep written records with receipts.

- How will the church report to the congregation to maintain financial transparency while upholding confidentiality?
- Where will the policy be posted?

Future Development

- Will the church request a visit with the applicant to assess long-term security goals?
- Will the church recommend and provide financial-counseling opportunities? If so, how many sessions? Are there community opportunities to receive free financial counseling?
- Will a financial class be required for those requesting assistance or for those requesting assistance more than once? If so, who has the expertise to teach this class?

Conclusion

Financial crises are prevalent in society. Many families are one accident, job loss, or illness away from a financial crisis. Others face ongoing poverty. This chapter reviewed possible underlying causes for financial crises and some recommendations for responding to a financial crisis. Finally, we overviewed some considerations for developing policies and procedures for financial crisis response.

Additional Resources

Corbett, Steve, and Brian Fikkert. *Helping without Hurting in Church Benevolence.* Chicago: Moody, 2015.

———. *When Helping Hurts: How to Alleviate Poverty without Hurting the Poor . . . and Yourself.* Chicago: Moody, 2012.

Chapter 21

Parenting Children with Developmental Disabilities

The stigma against people with disabilities dates back to Scripture. In John 9, Jesus passed by a man who was born blind from birth. "His disciples asked him, 'Rabbi, who sinned, this man or his parents, that he was born blind?' 'Neither this man nor his parents sinned,' Jesus answered. 'This came about so that God's works might be displayed in him'" (vv. 2–3). Today, we have a similar mentality. We walk past a child or an adult with a disability and feel either pity or relief that we are not in his situation. Many times, we are missing an opportunity to learn about another person.

Some disabilities are recognized easily, while others may not be as readily apparent. Developmental disabilities are a group of conditions due to either a physical, learning, language, or behavioral impairment impacting about one in six children in the US.[1] *Neurodivergent* is a term used frequently

[1] See "Developmental Disability Basics," Centers for Disease Control and Prevention, https://www.cdc.gov/child-development/about/developmental-disability-basics.html.

to refer to individuals with differences in how their brains function and process information. *Neurotypical* refers to individuals whose brains function and have capacity similar to most people. *Neurodiversity* means our brains all function differently and have a degree of individuality. As you can imagine, we have neurodiversity in our world regardless of diagnoses.[2] Some of the more common developmental disabilities are autism spectrum disorder (ASD), attention-deficit/hyperactivity disorder (ADHD), cerebral palsy (CP), intellectual disability (ID), and various types of learning disorders (dyslexia, dyscalculia, dysgraphia).

Disability is the largest minority group in the US. It affects approximately 61 million or nearly 26 percent of people in the US living in communities.[3] Some are able to blend in with society, while others struggle to function in a world that does not fit them. They are often misunderstood, misjudged, and underestimated. However, they can be some of the most creative and brilliant among us. Their abilities may go unnoticed and unappreciated, and they often struggle to find their place in church.

A Day in the Life

Consider the following case study:

Charlie is a seven-year-old boy with a developmental disability. Due to his disability, he has multiple appointments throughout the week. He sees an occupational therapist twice a week, a speech therapist three times a week, and a physical therapist. Between homework and Charlie's various appointments throughout the week, there is no time left for extracurricular activities. His parents see other families attending their child's basketball or soccer games, and they long for their child to be included.

---

[2] See Louise Gooding, *Wonderfully Wired Brains: An Introduction to the World of Neurodiversity* (New York: DK, 2023), 26–27, 257–58.

[3] See "Disability Inclusion," Centers for Disease Control and Prevention, https://www.cdc.gov/ncbddd/disabilityandhealth/disability-inclusion.html.

Parenting a child with a disability is challenging, to say the least. Many of these parents blame themselves. They wonder if something they did caused this. In some cases, parents suspect something is not quite right with their child at an early age, but professionals may miss the diagnosis. The parents' concerns may be dismissed with comments such as "He'll grow out of it" or "She's just a late bloomer." Then, some parents regret not advocating harder for their child or not getting their child in for a specific service sooner. With such a wide range of services available, it's nearly impossible for any parent to be aware of and knowledgeable about them all. Oftentimes, services such as occupational therapy, speech, and applied behavioral analysis have long waitlists. Finding a provider who has the needed qualifications and works well with their child can take many months.

Due to their disabilities, these children may experience an array of social and behavioral difficulties, resulting from struggles with sensory processing, communication, or impulsivity. As a result, many of these families report being asked to leave places because of their child's behavior, which is disheartening, to say the least. These parents are exhausted and sense those around them questioning their parenting abilities when they are doing the best they can.

The parents are always waiting for the other shoe to drop. They're on the edge of their seats during Bible study, waiting for a text from the children's leaders. A phone call from the school typically does not bring good news: the parents have been called and asked to pick up their kids. Their child has been asked to leave a school because she's too far behind. When mom and dad try to set their child up for success in school, they hear things such as "If I put him in her class, she'll quit," or "He's not going to be able to do this."

They want their child to feel included and to be able to participate in activities just like their peers. However, much of their free time is spent running from appointment to appointment while juggling the challenges of school. When they are able to squeeze in extracurricular activities, they struggle to find activities at which their child will be welcomed and included. Those who lead these activities are often uninformed about effective inclusion strategies.

These families are often on autopilot. In their mundane exhaustion, they may be unaware that their experience is different from that of other families, so it does not always occur to them to ask for help. When you live in a situation day in and day out, it becomes normal to you, even if it is unhealthy, dysfunctional, or exhausting.

Impact on Marriage and Social Relationships

Having a child with a developmental disability can place a strain on the marriage. Depending on the nature of their disability, many of these kids may not sleep well, meaning the parents do not sleep well. While continually sleep-deprived, they hold down jobs while getting the child to multiple appointments and dealing with the financial strain of the expenses involved in the care of their child. With so much time and energy centered around their child, parents have few opportunities to build relationships with other adults, meaning they live in isolation.

Research related to the impact of disabilities on the family is somewhat inconsistent. One parent may process his or her experience in a different manner than the other. However, what we do know is that parents in these situations take one of two paths. The first is to turn toward each other, find a way to work together, and support each other throughout the process. The other is to turn away from each other. Each parent may isolate him- or herself in coping with the situation and shut the other one out. One or both of the parents may find maladaptive ways to numb their feelings, such as addiction or other unhealthy behaviors. They may feel anger or guilt toward themselves or each other for not preventing the situation or identifying a diagnosis sooner. The parents may struggle to get on the same page about which treatment or educational options to pursue.

For some families, additional stress is added when their extended family members or friends are not accepting of their children. Other families may desire to be helpful and accepting, but they are uninformed. One of the primary ways to buffer the effects of stress on families of children with developmental disabilities is to have a solid support network with extended family, friends, and their local church or community who understand the nature of the disability or are willing to learn.

These families often avoid activities at which they might connect with other families because the environment might be overwhelming or difficult for their child. For a child who is easily overstimulated, this may mean no loud or crowded places such as Disney World, the trampoline park, or the fall festival at school. When a child struggles with gross and fine motor skills and coordination, the family may avoid swim parties and bike-a-thons. The other kids are solid swimmers, so their parents get to mingle by the pool. However, the parents of the weaker swimmer have to get in to supervise their child. Kids with sensory struggles may find riding a bicycle difficult because of their vestibular system. Again, other parents are watching their children ride around the neighborhood, while these parents have a child who is terrified of riding.

If all this is not enough, the parents' stress levels are further exacerbated by the judgment they feel coming from others. When their child melts down in a public place, they feel the stares from others. They may have even overheard remarks from others about how they needed to get their child under control. In some cases, they are not invited to some functions out of fear of the child's behavior. In other cases, they stay home to avoid the condemning stares and remarks from others, furthering the family's social isolation.

The chronic stress, lack of social support, and stigma take a toll on the family's mental health. Many of these parents experience depression and anxiety, which makes it more difficult to follow their child's care plan. With so much focus on their child, they often do not take the time needed to address their own physical and mental-health needs.

Disability in the Church

In many cases, the church has not been a safe place for families with disabilities. Some churches are reluctant to accommodate the current families they have out of concern they may attract more families with disabilities, causing a strain on the current children's workers. Quite possibly, this comes from a place of being unaware or uninformed, or it can be indicative of a bigger problem. Other churches say they do not have families with disabilities; otherwise, they would accommodate them. In response to that statement, the question might be, "What are you doing to make your church an environment that will communicate to these families that you desire to serve them?" This leads to a discussion of what families with disabilities typically look for in a church home.

Empathy

These families are looking for people who are willing to enter their perspective and connect with their emotional experience. They want people who see their struggles and look for ways to support them.

Judgment-Free Zone

These families are likely accustomed to attracting attention because of a behavioral issue that their child exhibits. They need people who understand the underlying causes of the behavioral struggle and work with them, rather than people passing judgment on them for their child's struggles.

Sensory-Friendly Environment

Many of these children may become overwhelmed by sensory stimuli, which can result in meltdowns, running away, or other behavioral struggles. Offering a quiet space, soothing colors, reduced fluorescent lighting, and headphones can help mitigate overstimulation. When possible, a sensory room that allows children a safe place to calm down can be helpful. Although it might not be feasible for one church, several churches could work together to host a sensory-friendly vacation Bible school.

Mental Health and Disability

There is a significant need for mental-health practitioners who can address the mental-health needs of those with developmental disabilities. The average mental-health practitioner did not receive extensive training related to developmental disabilities, which means they are unsure as to how to best assist them. Many families have grown frustrated with seeking mental-health services only to realize the practitioner does not understand the needs of their family. We need more mental-health professionals who are willing to develop expertise in working with those who may have both disabilities and mental-health concerns.

Because of the communication barriers and reliance on caregivers, many children and adults with developmental disabilities are at an increased risk of abuse. Although they only make up a small portion of the population, disabled people were the victims of 26 percent of nonfatal violent crimes from 2017 to 2019. They are the victims of violence at almost four times the rate of those without disabilities.[4] As a result, they need a place to process trauma with experienced practitioners. In some cases, the church may want to consider covering the costs of their counseling fees. Insurance coverage for mental-health services is often less than ideal. Many of these families may be on Medicaid, which is not widely accepted by mental-health providers.

As previously mentioned, we want to address the mental-health needs of parents and caregivers. There may be other family members, such as siblings, who are feeling the strain as well. Parents of children with developmental disabilities often carry an intense measure of guilt over divided attention with nondisabled siblings.

The Power of Understanding and Inclusion

In Bruce Perry's book *The Boy Who Was Raised as a Dog*, he shares about his work with a family who adopted a boy from Russia. Spending the first three years of his life in an orphanage, where little care and attention were given, had left him with several developmental deficits. Academically, he was doing

---

[4] See Kiara Alfonseca, "Crime against Disabled People Is Rising and Advocates Say More Needs to Be Done," ABC News, November 21, 2021, https://abcnews.go.com/US/crime-disabled-people-rising-advocates/story?id=81210410.

well, but he was behind socially. It was difficult for the other children in his class to understand some of his immature behaviors. His parents struggled with whether to hold him back in school or keep him moving forward.

Perry had the idea of addressing the child's first-grade class. As best he could, he explained the nature of brain development and the impact of this child's early life experiences. After Perry's talk, this class embraced the child. He ended up with many friends, and over time, he was able to catch up developmentally at all levels.

Perry summarizes his approach to this situation:

> Children, just like us as adults, react badly to the unknown, to the strange and unfamiliar, especially when they themselves are trying to adjust to a new situation like the start of a school year. Although their social hierarchies aren't always so easy to influence, most bullying and social rejection begins with the fear of the unfamiliar, and adults have more influence over the process than they may believe. When children understand why someone behaves oddly, they are willing to extend more grace, usually. And the younger the children are, the more easily they are influenced by both obvious and subtle cues of rejection and acceptance from adults. These cues often set the tone for the children's status systems, and teachers and parents can either minimize bullying or unfortunately, maximize it, by either strongly discouraging or tolerating the scapegoating of those who are "different."[5]

Kids see differences. They notice one of their classmates does not speak as clearly as others. They'll notice a child in a wheelchair. On their own, kids do not typically make evaluations about the differences. Instead, they follow the cues of adults. If adults include the child the same as they do the others, then the children are likely to follow. If the children notice the adults treating the other child differently, then they are likely to do so as well.

---

[5] Bruce Perry, *The Boy Who Was Raised as a Dog: And Other Stories from a Child Psychiatrist's Notebook* (New York: Basic Books, 2017), 257–58.

Inclusion occurs when we ensure that everyone has access to "the same opportunities to participate in every aspect of life to the best of their abilities and desires."[6] The beauty of inclusion is that we are all enriched by the perspectives and experiences of others. People with developmental disabilities often see the world in a different manner. When we exclude them, we are missing an opportunity to see the world through another perspective.

Ways to Encourage Inclusion

Be Sensitive

Parents of misbehaving children have likely received many phone calls from schools and other youth-serving organizations regarding their children's behavior. Because of these past experiences, many of these parents live in a constant state of fear. They are anxious about the next phone call, which is important to keep in mind when we need to address behavioral issues or other concerns. We want to communicate that we value their children's engagement and participation and that we are willing to work with them.

If a child is struggling, remember that behavior is communication. A child is not misbehaving for no reason. Misbehavior may result from an unmet need, a frustration, a lack of felt safety, or overstimulation. When children do not communicate well or their speech is not easily understood, they can become frustrated. Begin by meeting physiological needs. Allow kids access to a snack and some form of hydration every few hours. Research has shown that dehydration can increase aggressive behavior and compromise cognitive processing.[7] Listen patiently to the child and watch for nonverbal cues to intervene before a situation escalates.

---

[6] "Disability Inclusion," Centers for Disease Control and Prevention, https://www.cdc.gov/ncbddd/disabilityandhealth/disability-inclusion.html.

[7] See Karyn Purvis et al., "Trust-Based Relational Intervention (TBRI): A Systemic Approach to Complex Developmental Trauma," *Child & Youth Services* 34 (2013): 365–67.

Maybe the environment is too loud, too crowded, or too bright. Allowing kids to participate in a sensory activity every few hours can also help them with self-regulation. A sensory activity might include jumping on the trampoline, playing with Play-Doh, or climbing through a tunnel. You can also work in these activities naturally throughout the day by asking a child to hold the door for the entire class. The heavy work from holding the door can help with sensory regulation.[8]

Kids may become frustrated when tasks are too difficult for them, especially if it comes easily to their peers. Their frustration and, in some cases, embarrassment may lead to acting out. When this happens, we may be quick to attack the behavior rather than consider the underlying cause. For example, kids who struggle with fine motor skills or sensory processing may find art projects frustrating and be reluctant to participate.

There are things we know to be true, but we may not always feel them. For example, in times of crisis, we may know that God is good, but we do not feel it. In the same way, our kids may find themselves in situations where they do not feel safe. We know they are safe, but they are uneasy. A change in a schedule, service provider, teacher, or environment can cause a child to feel unsafe. When felt safety is not present, kids may act out. They may engage in avoidant behaviors such as not participating with the rest of their group, or they may run out of a room.

One of the things we can do to encourage felt safety is to help build familiarity. When going to a new place, whether school, the doctor, or Bible study, it's helpful to prepare them. When possible, make an early visit to meet the new teacher or staff and explain to the child how things will work. Establishing a consistent routine can encourage a sense of security by knowing what comes next. Ensuring that the personnel working with your child are aware of helpful ways to engage, encourage, and redirect your child is helpful as well.[9]

---

[8] See Purvis et al., 365, 367.

[9] See Purvis et al., 363–64.

Do Not Diagnose

Over the years, I have noticed teachers and children's workers prematurely placing labels on children. This is inappropriate for many reasons. One, most of the time neither the teachers nor the children's workers have the knowledge or experience to diagnose. For example, autism is a diagnosis that gets thrown around frequently. People seem to think that if they have encountered one child with autism, then they are qualified to recognize and diagnose. Autism is a complicated spectrum disorder that can look different in every child. No two children with an autism diagnosis are the same. It is unlikely any good will come from labeling a child, and it may bring harm to both the parents and the child.

Second, if we have seen a child function in one setting (e.g., church or school), then we know how he or she functions in that one setting. Without observing the child in other settings and situations, the information we have is limited and insufficient for diagnosing. A comprehensive approach, along with professional training, is needed to diagnose effectively.

Lastly, kids grow and develop at different rates. Due to a variety of circumstances, some kids may have a late start with speech, reading, motor skills, and social skills. Some kids may be ahead in some areas, while others may lag behind. In many cases, this evens out in childhood. Just because a kid is behind in some areas does not mean we jump to a diagnosis. This is why we prefer the term "typical child development" rather than "normal child development." After all, are any of us normal?

Instead of diagnosing, children's leaders should defer to the parents. One option might be to have parents complete an informational form about their child that is available to the workers. This form may include information related to any accommodations the child may need, along with other information the workers should know, such as a child's favorite activities or items. If a worker needs to address a concern with a parent, he or she should describe the behavior to the parent and ask for collaboration.

For example, let's say a worker is concerned about a child who does not engage with the workers or other children. He always plays by himself, never talking to anyone, not even the workers. The children's worker could say something like this to the parent: "We've noticed your child tends to keep to himself. He doesn't seem interested in playing with the other children. He doesn't engage with us much either. Do you have any suggestions for how we could help him feel more included in our class, or ways to help him feel comfortable participating with us?"

Do Not Equate Pity with Kindness

People with disabilities do not want to be pitied. Pity is "the near enemy of compassion."[10] When we pity others, we view ourselves as superior. We emotionally distance ourselves from them and avoid connecting with them. In other words, we spend our time feeling sorry for them rather than connecting with them. Compassion recognizes that, in our shared humanity, we are all vulnerable.[11] Those with disabilities do not want us to feel sorry for them, and parents do not want others to see their children as a burden. Instead, they are looking for acceptance. "Nowhere is wisdom more necessary than in the guidance of charitable impulses. Meaning well is only half our duty; thinking right is the other, and equally important, half."[12]

Help Cultivate Community

These families do not need to walk alone. We need to come alongside them and offer support with no strings attached. I met a family who had a son with a disability so significant they did not have the capacity for any other outside activities. They struggled with the idea of reaching out to their local church for help because they knew they would not be able to reciprocate in

---

[10] Brené Brown, *Atlas of the Heart: Mapping Meaningful Connection and the Language of Human Experience* (New York: Random House, 2021), 120.

[11] See Brown, 116–17, 120.

[12] Samuel Gridley Howe, 1868, at the dedication in Batavia, New York, of an institution to serve people with disabilities, https://health.alaska.gov/gcdse/pages/history/html_content_main.aspx.

that season of life. Giving without the expectation of return is important. Practically speaking, we can offer meals, house cleaning, and respite services to the family.

Find Ways to Give Value

Think about what you value most in life. It might be your children, your spouse, your job, ministry opportunities, or something else. Now, imagine what it would be like to have these things taken from you. You would be lonely without your spouse, kids, and friends. You would lose a sense of purpose without your job, your church, or community involvement.

If we are not intentional, this could be the life of a person with disabilities. We segregate them from the rest of us and do not allow them to participate in a meaningful way in our churches and communities. Look for a way to involve them that will add value to their experience. Encourage them to pursue their interests just as you would any other child. You might encourage them to take music lessons. Some music therapists offer adapted lessons for various types of instruments.

Find a way for them to serve at church. Maybe they can help with packing backpacks for the homeless ministry. Some of them may love to cook or have an interest in learning. They can help with large meals prepared at the church or meals delivered to church members recovering from sickness. The important thing is encouraging them to build their skills and use their gifts. In the same way many of us derive a sense of joy and satisfaction from serving others, those with disabilities long to do the same.

Listen More Carefully

With many developmental disabilities, there are limitations in communication, which make connection more difficult. For kids, their behavior is communication, and we should look for the underlying cause perpetuating a specific behavior. For adults, we may need to learn to listen at a deeper level. Consider the following advice:

> The practice of listening to people with an intellectual disability can be far more challenging if they have limitations in their capacities to communicate or articulate what they are experiencing—if they cannot talk. But then this brings up another dimension of listening. Listening is not just with our ears but with our eyes and with our hearts, attending to body language (theirs and ours!!). And additionally, we need to consider people's backgrounds, the context of the behavior, and a deeper sense of curiosity as to WHO they are as individuals—their dreams, aspirations, and needs, what is important to them. Am I someone supporting them in those directions or am I an obstacle?[13]

A wholehearted approach to listening will allow us to hear things that may not be communicated through spoken language.

Conclusion

Our churches should be a safe and welcoming place for the families of those with developmental disabilities. Many of them are not involved in church because they struggle to find a place where they and their needs are understood. The parents, other family members, and the neurodivergent individuals often have unmet mental-health needs due to lack of providers with knowledge about disabilities. We also need mental-health professionals who are willing to receive additional training and specialization to serve these families well.

Additional Resources

Leadership Education in Neurodevelopmental and Other Related Disabilities (LEND)

---

[13] David Yeiter, *Lessons in Listening* (Ontario, CA: Inclusion Press, 2022), 12.

This program provides long-term, graduate-level interdisciplinary training as well as interdisciplinary services and care. The purpose of the LEND training program is to improve the health of infants, children, and adolescents with disabilities. It accomplishes this by preparing trainees from diverse professional disciplines to assume leadership roles in their respective fields and by ensuring high levels of interdisciplinary clinical competence. For more information, visit: https://www.aucd.org/template/page.cfm?id=473.

Partners in Policymaking

Partners in Policymaking is a national leadership training program for people with developmental disabilities and parents of young children with developmental disabilities. It provides the most current knowledge about disability issues and develops the competencies necessary for effective advocacy to influence public policy at all levels of government. For more information, visit your state's Partners in Policymaking website.

Yeiter, David. *Lessons in Listening.* Ontario, CA: Inclusion, 2022.
Free download at https://inclusion.com/product/lessons-in-listening/.

Books for Children

Beaty, Andrea, and David Roberts. *Aaron Slater, Illustrator.* New York: Abrams Books, 2021.

This book is about a boy with dyslexia who struggles to read but is able to use his artistic abilities to tell a story. It is printed with a dyslexia-friendly font.

Gooding, Louise, and Ruth Burrows. *Wonderfully Wired Brains: An Introduction to the World of Neurodiversity.* New York: DK Children, 2023.

This book serves as a reference guide for a wide range of developmental disabilities and is on a second- to fourth-grade reading level.

Hammond, Tiffany. *A Day with No Words.* New Egypt, NJ: Wheat Penny Press, 2023.

This is a book for children ages 4–8 about a child with autism who uses a communication device.

Windness, Kaz. *Bitsy Bat School Star.* New York: Simon & Schuster, 2023.

This book, for children ages 5–8, is about a bat on the autism spectrum who struggles to fit in at school.

Chapter 22

Caring for Aging Parents

Helping others correlates with life satisfaction, overall well-being, and increased longevity. However, chronic stress and lack of time for oneself can negate the benefits. As a result, caregivers often experience a decrease in life satisfaction, burnout, mental-health issues, and health complications.[1] We will explore the unique challenges of caregiving and provide suggestions for how to support caregivers. With support, caregivers can enjoy the sense of purpose in their caregiving role.

The "Sandwich Generation"

The "sandwich generation" refers to adults who have aging parents while still having children in their home.[2] Approximately 23 percent of adults in

[1] See Ann Kaiser Stearns and J. Raymond DePaulo, *Redefining Aging: A Caregiver's Guide to Living Your Best Life* (Baltimore: Johns Hopkins University Press, 2017), 4.

[2] The term "sandwich generation" was coined by social worker Dorothy Miller. See Dorothy A. Miller, "The 'Sandwich' Generation: Adult Children of the Aging," *Social Work* 26, no. 5 (September 1981): 419–23.

the United States have at least one child under the age of eighteen (or an adult child whom they are financially supporting) and at least one parent over the age of sixty-five. For individuals in their forties, the percentage jumps to 54 percent.[3] Almost one-fourth of individuals in this sandwich generation are caring for at least one parent over age sixty-five and for at least one child under eighteen.[4] The majority of these caregivers are female.

Approximately 12 percent of parents in the United States are engaged in unpaid "multigenerational caregiving" for more than two and a half hours daily. That is, they provide care for children under eighteen in their homes and for an adult in need. The adult may be a parent, relative, or unrelated adult. Of those engaging in multigenerational caregiving, 72 percent are employed. Caregiving parents who are not employed spend approximately one and a half additional hours on caregiving.[5] Due to adults living longer and the increase of adult children moving back home or living at home longer, we will likely see an increase in the number of caregivers and years spent providing care.

The Smorgasbord of Sandwiches

Paninis. Club sandwiches. Open-face sandwiches. These are a few terms used to describe various situations caregivers might encounter. Journalist and sandwich generation advocate Carol Abaya describes three categories of the sandwich generation: traditional, club, and open-faced. The *traditional sandwich* is adults in their forties or fifties sandwiched between their parents

---

[3] See Juliana Menasce Horowitz, "More than Half of Americans in Their 40s Are 'Sandwiched' between an Aging Parent and Their Own Children," *Pew Research Center* (blog), April 8, 2022, https://pewrsr.ch/3vazMQa.

[4] See Kara Gavin, "'Sandwich Generation' Study Shows Challenges of Caring for Both Kids and Aging Parents," Michigan Medicine, December 8, 2022, https://www.michiganmedicine.org/health-lab/sandwich-generation-study-shows-challenges-caring-both-kids-and-aging-parents.

[5] See Gretchen Livingston, "More than One-in-Ten U.S. Parents Are Also Caring for an Adult," *Pew Research Center* (blog), November 29, 2018, https://pewrsr.ch/2FOqmDe.

and children.[6] The *club sandwich* refers to adult caregivers who have multigenerational family commitments. The different generations may include adult children, grandchildren, parents, and grandparents, with any or all individuals potentially needing assistance. The *open-faced sandwich* refers to those providing unpaid caregiving for their aging family members.[7]

Another group facing caregiving stress is those who are taking care of their adult children or grandchildren. Abramson refers to this group as the "panini generation" to describe the situation when the older generation are the caregivers instead of the ones receiving the care.[8] They may care for spouses, adult children, grandchildren, or siblings. This population includes those caring for adult children who are unable to live on their own due to disabilities, mental illness, or other situations. Additionally, this group includes those who are custodians of their grandchildren due to death, imprisonment, substance use, mental illness, or any other reason their adult children are not the primary caregivers for their own children.

The panini generation faces challenges related to their aging process, such as decreased energy or health concerns. They face decisions about what will happen to those in their care should they become unable to continue providing care. The financial burden may lead to these previously retired individuals needing to return to the workforce.[9] Research indicates that caring for one's grandchildren impacts the caregiver differently than caring for the older generation. Luna et al. state, "Although caring for older relatives is related to family conflicts and worse health, conversely, caring for grandchildren is related to slightly better health."[10] As such, do not assume caregiving

[6] See Sharon Oliver, "'Sandwich Generation' of Caregivers Is Caught in the Middle," *Fifty Plus Advocate*, June 27, 2023, https://www.fiftyplusadvocate.com/2023/06/27/260037-sandwich-generation-of-caregivers-is-caught-in-the-middle.

[7] See Tobi A. Abramson, "Older Adults: The 'Panini Sandwich' Generation," *Clinical Gerontologist: The Journal of Aging and Mental Health* 38, no. 4 (August 2015): 253, https://doi.org/10.1080/07317115.2015.1032466.

[8] See Abramson, 251–67.

[9] See Abramson.

[10] Sara Luna, Francisco Rivera, and Pilar Ramos, "Dual Caregiving by Grandmothers with Older Relatives: Personal Factors Influencing Health and

will have an overall negative toll. As we will explore later, caregiving has benefits despite its unique stressors.

Tasks Performed by Caregivers

Three categories of tasks are provided by caregivers: instrumental activities of daily living (IADLs), activities of daily living (ADLs), and medical/nursing tasks. IADLs include transportation, housework, preparing meals, shopping, finances, administering medication, and arranging additional caregiving. In a study conducted by the National Alliance for Caregiving (NAC) in partnership with Caring Across Generations, the most commonly reported IADLs are transportation (80 percent), housework (76 percent), and preparing meals (62 percent). ADLs include personal care and mobility tasks, such as moving from one place to another, getting dressed, toileting, bathing, and eating. Medical/nursing tasks that caregivers most often do are injections, tube feeding, colostomy care, and catheter care.[11]

Unique Needs and Challenges

Caregivers experience unique needs and challenges due to the stress and complexity of the caregiving role. Consider the following as you minister to caregivers.

Impact on Relationships

Each individual in a family system has needs, and the family has to distribute its resources to meet those needs to maintain individual and family

---

Stress," *Journal of Health Psychology* 26, no. 11 (September 2021): 1882, https://doi.org/10.1177/1359105319893112.

[11] See Rosemary Ziemba, "Family Health and Care of Older Adults: Universal Solutions to Unique Caregiving Challenges," *Michigan Family Review* 20, no. 1 (January 2016): 15–25, https://doi.org/10.3998/mfr.4919087.0020.104.

well-being.[12] When one person in the system is expending an increased amount of time and energy caregiving, this impacts the entire family system, disrupting and challenging the status quo and distribution of resources. The family must readjust in areas such as time spent together, assignment of tasks, distribution of resources, and parenting responsibilities.

Marriage is impacted. The time limitations of caring for two generations of dependents impact the time the couple spends together. Even if the caregiver carves out time, he or she may feel so mentally and emotionally exhausted that little is left to give. The couple's future plans and dreams may be set aside.[13]

Preexisting relational conflict and dysfunctional patterns can be exacerbated by the stress. For example, a couple who struggles with communication may find the need for increased planning and sharing of needs to be challenging. Spirituality and religious involvement can have a positive impact, but a reduction in marital satisfaction has been reported among those who do not have effective coping strategies.[14] The negative impact can be mediated by healthy coping strategies, such as accepting help or improving their communication patterns.

The relationship with one's children may be impacted. Once again, time and exhaustion may impact opportunities for engagement and connection, leading to feelings of guilt for the caregiving parent. There can be unspoken resentment from the spouse of the primary caregiver because of additional parenting responsibilities.

Caregiving can impact friendships outside the family. There is barely enough time and energy for the immediate family needs, so time with friends may be postponed indefinitely, leading to feelings of isolation and loneliness.

---

[12] See Ziemba, 18.

[13] See Jennie S. Murphy et al., "Caring for Aging Parents: The Influence of Family Coping, Spirituality/Religiosity, and Hope on the Marital Satisfaction of Family Caregivers," *American Journal of Family Therapy* 43, no. 3 (May 2015): 244, https://doi.org/10.1080/01926187.2015.1034636.

[14] See Murphy et al., 244.

Medical Stressors

Activities of daily living do not require specialized training. However, medical tasks such as tube feeding or colostomy care require training and skill. Learning these new tasks can be stressful and intimidating for caregivers, particularly those with no history of medical training. Addressing mental health or cognitive decline may also demand skills that require additional training. As such, caregivers may experience stress due to the lack of knowledge about specialized caregiving tasks.

Another medical-related stressor is the challenge of communicating with medical professionals. Even if appropriate documents are signed to allow the caregiver access, speaking to the doctor can be challenging if the caregiver cannot be present at every appointment and throughout hospital stays.

Caregivers should be encouraged to keep a notebook with the contact information of all doctors and medical professionals, in addition to an updated list of medication names and dosages. In this notebook, the caregiver should also log all medical appointments, emergency room or urgent care visits, and interactions (such as phone calls) with medical professionals. This notebook assists the caregiver in remembering complex medical history and also helps other caregivers who step in to help.

Negotiating Expectations[15]

The expectations of the caregiver and the individual receiving care may vary. For example, the caregiver may have limited time to drive the dependent to a medical appointment. The individual receiving care may not recognize the limitations due to the caregiver's other responsibilities and personal needs. These expectations extend to a variety of daily tasks and availability. As such, expectations must be discussed and clarified to reduce potential conflict and stress.

---

[15] See Alana M. Boyczuk and Paula C. Fletcher, "The Ebbs and Flows: Stresses of Sandwich Generation Caregivers," *Journal of Adult Development* 23, no. 1 (March 2016): 57, https://doi.org/10.1007/s10804-015-9221-6.

Role Reversals

Role reversals are challenging to navigate in caring for aging parents. These aging parents were once the caregivers for those now caring for them. As such, the dependent adults may be hesitant to take advice or help from the caregivers. This role reversal can result in frustration, stress, and conflict.

Dealing with Changes in Temperament

If the one receiving care experiences cognitive decline from dementia or brain injury, the individual's temperament may change. The individual may become combative, have difficulty with self-control, be unable to communicate effectively, and have reduced empathy. Some may become withdrawn and show little to no emotion. Changes in disposition have an emotional and mental toll on the caregiver. A previously cheerful, compassionate mother may become combative and withdrawn. The caregiver mourns the loss of her mother's encouraging personality.

Facing the Unknown

The unpredictable nature of caring for someone in declining health can make it challenging to maintain a predictable routine. The entire family system needs to remain flexible. For example, suppose a caregiving mother planned to transport the children to basketball practice but was called to the hospital after her father's medical event. In that case, she will need to find the child a ride to practice, or the child may miss practice. The stress of juggling schedule changes such as this can take a mental toll on the caregiver.

The "Trickle-Down" Effect[16]

The "trickle-down" effect refers to the stress placed on the spouse of the caregiver (and potentially on other family members). Time relegated to

---

[16] See Boyczuk and Fletcher, 56–57.

caregiving decreases the amount of time the caregiver can spend on the division of labor in the home. This labor may include shuttling children to sports, helping children with homework, preparing meals, cleaning, home maintenance, or caring for pets.[17] The trickle-down may also happen when acute crises occur, requiring a rapid readjustment of schedule and responsibilities.

Financial Stress

Approximately one in five caregivers reports financial stress.[18] Financial stress results from a variety of factors. Caregivers may have to take unpaid time off to attend medical appointments or assist with emergencies. In addition to absenteeism, there is the issue of "presenteeism" when the caregiver is physically at work but mentally preoccupied, potentially impacting job performance.[19] Some caregivers may resign from their jobs or switch to part-time hours to provide care. Or caregivers may provide financial assistance to those in their care.

Decisions about Long-Term Care

Short-term caregiving is stressful, but the limited time frame improves the manageability. However, caregiving is often long-term and requires decisions about long-term care. The decision to place a loved one in a long-term care facility can be heart-wrenching. In familial cultures where importance is placed on the family providing long-term care, this decision can be particularly challenging when the caregiver is no longer physically or

---

[17] See Boyczuk and Fletcher, 56–57.

[18] See "New Research Shines a Light on a Forgotten Generation—GenX Caregivers 'Sandwiched' between Kids and Parents," PRWeb, November 26, 2019, https://www.prweb.com/releases/new_research_shines_a_light_on_a_forgotten_generation_genx_caregivers_sandwiched_between_kids_and_parents/prweb16746134.htm.

[19] See Ann O'Sullivan, "Pulled from All Sides: The Sandwich Generation at Work," *Work* 50, no. 3 (March 2015): 2, https://doi.org/10.3233/WOR-141959.

emotionally able or does not have the skilled care abilities the individual in decline may require.

Feelings of Grief and Loss

The caregiver, family, and individual being cared for may all experience feelings of grief. The aging individual may grieve the loss of independence, health, relationships they can no longer maintain, and activities they can no longer engage in. For all, there may be anticipatory grief of future loss of ability or life itself.

Challenges with Life Balance

Caregivers face the challenge of balancing their work and family life responsibilities while also trying to maintain their personal well-being. Unfortunately, due to time constraints, caregiving can limit time spent engaging in their personal well-being. The stress of caregiving can take its toll on the physical, mental, and relational health of the caregiver.

The caregiver may have unrealistic expectations of how much they can accomplish due to the additional time caregiving requires. The caregiver may experience feelings of guilt when there is not enough time for everything he or she believes is essential. The caregiver may feel resentful toward the person in their care, which can lead to additional guilt for feeling this way.

Caregiver Stress and Burnout

Approximately one-third of caregivers experience emotional stress. Approximately one in five reports physical stress.[20] The emotional aspect of caregiving can be the most difficult. In one recent study, the emotional stress of trying to balance work and caregiving responsibilities was reported as the

[20] See O'Sullivan.

greatest challenge.[21] Caregivers experience a risk of anxiety and depression. Lei et al. identified that caregivers are often exhausted, have more responsibilities than they can handle, lack time for themselves, and struggle with the changing needs of those in their care.[22]

In a 2021 study exploring the impact of COVID-19, 85 percent of adults who were both caretaking and parenting reported adverse mental-health symptoms, and approximately 50 percent reported experiencing suicidal ideation in the month before the survey. This rate was eight times higher than adults who were not parents or caregivers.[23]

Caregivers face dealing with their own emotions related to the health decline of their loved one in addition to being the primary emotional support for the person in their care. Caregivers may not have the time or financial means to seek emotional support through counseling services or support groups. The high rate of stress can lead to burnout for the caregiver.

Benefits of Caregiving

Caregiving is challenging, but there are benefits. In a 2023 study, Lei et al. identified four caregiving "gains." These gains are increased confidence in

[21] See Elizabeth Harrington and Bill McInturff, "Working While Caring: A National Survey of Caregiver Stress in the U.S. Workforce," Rosalynn Carter Institute for Caregivers, September 28, 2021, https://rosalynncarter.org/wp-content/uploads/2021/09/210140-RCI-National-Surveys-Executive-Summary-Update-9.22.21.pdf.

[22] See Lianlian Lei, Amanda N. Leggett, and Donovan T. Maust, "A National Profile of Sandwich Generation Caregivers Providing Care to Both Older Adults and Children," *Journal of the American Geriatrics Society* 71, no. 3 (March 2023): 801, https://doi.org/10.1111/jgs.18138.

[23] See Mark É. Czeisler et al., "Mental Health among Parents of Children Aged <18 Years and Unpaid Caregivers of Adults During the COVID-19 Pandemic—United States, December 2020 and February–March 2021," *Morbidity and Mortality Weekly Report* 70, no. 24 (2021): 882, https://doi.org/10.15585/mmwr.mm7024a3.

the caregivers' abilities, learning to deal with difficult situations, increased closeness with the care recipient, and satisfaction.[24]

Lalani et al. reviewed previous research and concluded that spirituality can be a means of coping with caregiving stressors while enhancing the caregivers' ability to find meaning in the caregiving role. Additionally, spirituality assists with decision-making concerning end-of-life or palliative care.[25] Meaning and satisfaction increase for caregivers who identify positive aspects of caregiving.[26]

How the Church Can Provide Support

The church can support caregivers by supporting the entire family system through meeting various needs. Support is needed for the recipient of the caregiving, the caregiver, and the caregiver's spouse and children (and potentially the grandchildren).

Recognize the Dignity and Value of the Aging

An individual's value is not based on productivity, wealth, or status. There is something we can learn from their life experiences that adds to our lives in a meaningful way.

---

[24] See Lei, Leggett, and Maust, "A National Profile of Sandwich Generation Caregivers," 801.

[25] See Nasreen Lalani, Wendy Duggleby, and Joanne Olson, "Spirituality among Family Caregivers in Palliative Care: An Integrative Literature Review," *International Journal of Palliative Nursing* 24, no. 2 (February 2, 2018): 80–91, https://doi.org/10.12968/ijpn.2018.24.2.80.

[26] See Carolina Palacio G. et al., "Resilience in Caregivers: A Systematic Review," *American Journal of Hospice and Palliative Medicine* 37, no. 8 (August 2020): 2, https://doi.org/10.1177/1049909119893977.

Care for the Spiritual Needs of the Aging and the Caregivers

Based on their research, Lalani et al. emphasize, "Family caregivers report less spiritual pain and distress and enhanced coping when they are given spiritual care and support."[27]

Visit Both the Recipient of Care and the Caregivers

Caregiving can be isolating for both the caregiver and the recipient of care. The ministry of presence can be a valuable step in combating this loneliness. Contact the individual(s) to schedule the visit ahead of time.

Have Support Teams in Place for Acute Crises

Acute crises may occur when there is a health emergency for an elderly family member. But this crisis can also occur with another family member, such as a sick child. The caregiver, who is already stretched thin, must focus his or her resources on the person in crisis. If both aging parents and a child need extensive care, the caregiver may not have the necessary time or other resources to provide appropriate care. During these emergencies, the church can provide practical assistance to the family with caregiving, driving, or meeting basic needs. At times, the caregiver may be the person in crisis. If this occurs, all generations of the family may need support.

Provide Respite Care Volunteers

Respite care can be provided by volunteers in varying amounts of time. Someone could offer an afternoon or day of respite care to allow the caregiver to attend his or her own health-care appointments, have time with a friend, attend a support group, spend time with other family members, or

---

[27] Lalani, Duggleby, and Olson, "Spirituality among Family Caregivers in Palliative Care," 90.

simply (but importantly) have some rest time. Preferably, this could be done regularly so the caregiver has rhythms of self-care for burnout prevention.

Additionally, volunteers can provide respite care for a night, weekend, or longer so the caregiver can have time away with the remainder of the family. While other family members may be utilized for this extended care, respite care volunteers can assist those family members. Many caregivers use their paid time off for caregiving responsibilities, such as doctor's appointments, so taking a vacation may not be possible. As such, small breaks, whenever possible, could help reduce their stress.

Provide a "Check-In" Person for the Caregiver

Assign an individual to text or call the caregiver weekly to check in on how the caregiver is doing and whether assistance is needed. This is an excellent volunteer opportunity for individuals with limited time or who need flexibility. Not everyone can commit to the same time weekly for volunteer work, but they may welcome this flexible opportunity. In a health crisis, it can be exhausting to communicate health status and emerging needs, so this individual can serve as a liaison for any information the family may want to convey to the church community and any requests for additional support. Another benefit is this provides a caring individual other than the ministerial staff who is in regular contact with the family.

Offer Support Groups and Referrals for Counseling

Consider providing a support group for caregivers. The support group could be either in person or via an online platform. One benefit of the online support group is the participant does not have to work through the logistics of attending in person, particularly finding childcare or respite care. If an online support group is utilized, the participants will need private spaces to join the meetings so others cannot hear what is being said in the support group. Protecting the privacy of all members is critical. Provide counseling referrals for those needing more specialized help or if a support group is unavailable.

Recognize the Exhaustion of Perpetual Loss and Anticipatory Grief

In my counseling practice, I (Karen) often work with those who are grieving a variety of losses. One of the first things I tell them is "Grief is hard work. It can be absolutely exhausting." Caregivers are often living in a state of perpetual grief due to watching the physical or cognitive decline of someone they love while anticipating the eventual death of that person. When we watch a child grow up, we celebrate the "first" milestones: first word, first step, first time saying "I love you." When observing a person in decline, caregivers experience the heartbreak of many "lasts": last word, last step, last time saying, "I love you." They cannot predict the last time for the final word, step, or proclamation of love. The fatiguing grief of these constant losses and the anticipatory grief of even greater loss need to be recognized.

Think Practically

Provide practical services such as lawn care, rides to medical appointments, cooking meals, shopping for groceries or other items, home maintenance tasks, laundry, decorating for holidays or removing holiday décor, taking care of pets or animals, helping prepare the home for a return after a hospital stay, setting up the house for a wheelchair or hospital bed, gathering medical supplies the family will need, installing wheelchair ramps or guardrails, replacing fire and carbon dioxide batteries, installing motion-sensor nightlights, or any other practical acts of service.

Provide Events for Aging Adults

Provide events for aging adults, such as offering to take them out for lunch or a special outing. In one church my husband pastored, the deacons had a wonderful ministry of providing a Valentine's banquet for the widows in the community. These events provide the aging with opportunities for social support and a sense of community.

Encourage the Caregivers to Set Boundaries

Encourage caregivers to set boundaries during this time of their lives. Setting boundaries may mean the caregiver needs to limit volunteer activities in the church or take some time off from caregiving responsibilities.

Connect Families with Information

Consider hosting experts to speak on topics related to caregiving, such as a financial planner talking about long-term planning, slip-and-fall prevention and other home-safety concerns, or strategies for coping with stress. Be familiar with community resources and events and assist the family in signing up for these services, such as meals or transportation services. Invite the entire community to these events.

Place brochures containing information about community resources in a prominent place. These resources could include recommendations for medical alert systems, identity theft protection services, meal services (such as Meals on Wheels), a local Council on Aging, senior centers, respite care, transportation services, legal aid, financial assistance, or food banks. Update these regularly.

Conclusion

In this chapter, we reviewed the types of caregiving and how it may have both benefits and stresses. We considered the impact of caregiver stress and burnout, recognizing the unique challenges facing caregivers and their families. Finally, we provided suggestions for ministering to caregivers in a way that includes the entire family system. As you work with caregivers, consider how you can provide practical help, emotional support, and spiritual encouragement.

Websites with Resources

Alzheimer's Association: https://www.alz.org
Family Caregiver Alliance: https://www.caregiver.org
USAging: https://www.usaging.org

Part 8
The Church

Chapter 23

Church Violence

On September 15, 1999, a See You at the Pole prayer rally was taking place at Wedgewood Baptist Church. A little before 7:00 p.m., a gunman entered and opened fire, killing seven and wounding another seven. The gunman fired over 100 rounds from two different handguns and exploded a homemade pipe bomb in the worship center where the youth activity was taking place. Then he took his own life.[1]

As mentioned earlier in this book, a crisis creates a turning point. When tragedy strikes a church, it can bring them closer and make them stronger, or it can destroy them. How we navigate the aftermath of church violence can heavily influence the resilience experienced by a congregation. Twenty years after the Wedgewood shooting, retired pastor Al Meredith stated, "It still hurts, but it hurts a little less each time. And the grief isn't quite so deep. And the sorrow doesn't last as long."[2]

---

[1] See "Darkness Had No Victory over the Light," https://www.wedgwoodbc.org/wedgwood-shooting.html.

[2] Christopher Connelly, "'It Still Hurts, but It Hurts a Little Less': 20 Years after a Fort Worth Church Shooting," KERA News, September 12, 2019, https://

Since the Wedgewood shooting in 1999, there have been more than twenty additional church shootings. Unfortunately, over the last several years, we have seen an increase in violence and a number of shootings occur within churches across our nation. There was a nearly two-year lull before a gunman opened fire at a church in Texas in December 2019. This shooting was followed by another two-year absence until four fatal shootings took place in 2022. Not long after, six people were killed in a shooting at a private Christian school in March 2023.[3]

Statistically, most churches will never be impacted by a church shooting, but a small amount of preparation can reap large dividends in the event the unthinkable happens. Around 80 percent of churches report having some type of security plan in place to prevent violence.[4] In addition to prevention, we will consider ways to minister to our congregations and those impacted by church violence.

Preparation

Assess Risks

Assess areas of vulnerability within the building and physical space. Which areas have a viable exit or hiding space in the event of a lockdown? Consider asking someone from outside the church, preferably with a background in law enforcement, to assess the space. They may see areas of vulnerability in the building that church leadership might miss due to familiarity with the place.

---

www.keranews.org/news/2019-09-12/it-still-hurts-but-it-hurts-a-little-less-20-years-after-a-fort-worth-church-shooting.

[3] See Aaron Earls, "How Frequently Do Church Shootings Occur?" Lifeway Research, February 12, 2020, https://research.lifeway.com/2020/02/12/how-frequently-do-church-shootings-occur.

[4] See Earls, "How Frequently Do Church Shootings Occur?"

Develop Policies and Procedures

In chapter 25, "Abuse in the Church," we will discuss the importance of child protection policies in safeguarding our children and youth. Along with these policies, we should also provide information about what should take place in the event of an active shooter. We should include policies on the emergency response protocol, along with expectations for working with children, youth, and vulnerable adults. Communicate to parents their responsibility in the event they are separated from their child (e.g., during small group Bible study). Depending on the location and circumstances, a large group of parents flocking toward the children's area could attract the attention of the gunman and make church members more susceptible to danger. It might be best for parents to shelter in place while the children and youth workers follow appropriate crisis procedures.

Depending on your position and responsibilities, familiarize yourself with your church's insurance policies. Verify coverage related to both physical and emotional injuries. Some insurance companies allow for coverage for counseling following an incident. A working knowledge of insurance coverage can help us understand what type of care and services we are able to offer those impacted.

Form a Crisis-Intervention Group

Many churches have some type of security team in place to monitor potential medical emergencies, prevent acts of violence, or accelerate response time in the event of an active shooter. Along with this security team, churches should consider adding some crisis intervention consultants to the team. These consultants could include counselors and social workers who have training and experience responding to crisis situations. We need to have a list of resources we can utilize in the event that something catastrophic happens, like the "Community Resource Guide" that was mentioned in chapter 3. If we wait until the crisis happens to find resources, our response time will be delayed.

Ministering in the Aftermath

Mobilizing the Response Team

When the crisis intervention group is already in place, mobilizing them is as simple as making a phone call. Unfortunately, there are times when we have trained people ready and willing to help, but because of poor planning and direction, their expertise and training are not stewarded well. Having a lead person in charge of the team who has experience with managing crisis situations can streamline and organize the response process. In most cases, it would be best for the crisis response leader to be someone other than the lead pastor. During a time of crisis, especially violence in the church setting, he is likely to be inundated with calls and requests from various people, including law enforcement and the media. He will be so busy addressing all of these things that he is unlikely to be able to mobilize a response team efficiently. A trained crisis response leader can alleviate the burden of ensuring that the church is being cared for during this time.

A frequent question we receive following a traumatic event is "How should we talk to our children about what happened?" We want to encourage parents, caregivers, and others who may be in a position to discuss the event with children and youth to take care of themselves first. When a collective trauma (a trauma that impacts the entire community) occurs, we are processing our own feelings and struggles while trying to care for others. Acknowledging our own feelings first can help us compose ourselves while helping others.[5]

As we approach these conversations with our children, our primary goal is to be a safe place for them as they navigate the aftermath of the event. Unfortunately, reality is that in our age of social media and online information, the ability of misinformation to spread and drown the truth is almost guaranteed. We want to make ourselves the primary source of information.

---

[5] See "Talking to Children: When Scary Things Happen," Center for Resilience and Well-Being in Schools, https://www.nctsn.org/sites/default/files/resources/fact-sheet/talking-to-children-when-scary-things-happen.pdf.

We want to consider what information our children might have already heard, correct any misinformation, and give them the opportunity to ask questions about what they already know. Before giving them any new information, we want to be mindful of what information will help them process what has happened, and we want to consider their age when determining the level of details we provide. Putting images in our children's heads that have them visualizing the traumatic event will not be helpful for them.[6]

Debriefing

Debriefing is an intervention that is used following a crisis event. The goal is to give individuals involved an opportunity to discuss what happened and prevent or reduce trauma symptoms. There are several types of debriefing: operational, psychological or stress, and critical incident stress debriefing (CISD).

Organizations may use operational debriefing as a crisis response.[7] Operational debriefing offers coworkers or peers who have encountered violence or loss the opportunity to gain closure and make meaning from the crisis. It also offers the opportunity to discuss what happened with other coworkers, which may help individuals not feel so alone in their experiences. An operational debriefing may help organizations determine whether there need to be policy changes or additional security measures in place to prevent issues in the future.

Psychological debriefing is an opportunity to discuss the stressful event and offer emotional and psychological support to prevent further symptoms of post-traumatic stress disorder (PTSD). There is little evidence that psychological debriefing is an effective mental-health intervention. Individual counseling might be best, which we will discuss shortly.[8]

---

[6] See "Talking to Children."

[7] See "PTSD: National Center for PTSD," U.S. Department of Veterans Affairs, https://www.ptsd.va.gov/professional/treat/type/debrief_after_disasters.asp.

[8] See "PTSD."

Critical incident stress debriefing (CISD) is a structured intervention intended for first responders (firefighters, paramedics, police officers, etc.) to review the experience of the crisis. CISD is not designed for the survivors of the disaster or their family members, nor is it intended to be a substitute for individual counseling.[9]

Individual Counseling

Traumatic events will impact each individual in a different manner. Individual counseling accommodates a wide range of needs and responses from those involved. Some may only need one or two sessions to process what happened and gain some additional coping skills. Others, especially those closest to the event and those with past trauma, may need counseling for an extended period of time.

A church shooting is the type of trauma that will rattle the entire community and leave even those outside the church with a shattered sense of safety and security. As expected, those within the church and those with the closest connections to the shooting will be impacted more deeply. This may include those who had been at the church in the days, weeks, and hours before the shooting occurred. Those with the deepest impact will be those who had a friend or family member in the building when the shooting occurred and those who were in the building. Previous trauma, especially if unresolved, can complicate healing and recovery from the current trauma.

Provide a list of professional and pastoral counselors who are willing and available to meet with people, and reach out to those who seem reluctant to seek help. Some might prefer speaking with their pastor first before seeing a professional, while others might prefer a counselor from outside the church.

Having counselors available before or after a church service is a great option for those who have been too overwhelmed to make an appointment to speak with someone. However, others may be reluctant to approach someone in a setting in which others can see them speaking with a counselor.

---

[9] See "PTSD: National Center for PTSD."

Increase accessibility to counseling for those who need it by providing other times during the week, if possible. A designated time in which counselors are available to speak with those who have been impacted is important, but providing a list of options for those who might want to do so in private is helpful as well.

Reestablishing Safety at Church

Following an act of church violence, church members may feel conflicted about returning to church. They may long for the sense of safety and comfort the church brought before the shooting, but are leery of returning because safety has been violated. Following the Wedgewood shooting, one girl was reluctant to return unless she could wear tennis shoes because she wanted to be prepared to run if needed.[10] As discussed earlier, people will have different responses and needs following the event. There is not a universal approach for helping all church members return in an emotionally healthy manner.

Here are a few guidelines for helping members return to church:

- Encourage a sense of togetherness. Essentially, we want to communicate to our members that coming back to church for the first time will be difficult for everyone and that we will all support each other.
- Encourage church members to come with someone who can offer them a sense of security, such as a friend, a family member, or even someone from their small group.
- Have counselors available in the event that someone wants to talk or is triggered.
- Be sensitive to the timeline of others in that it may take more time for some to return than others.

Anyone struggling to return should be encouraged to discuss this with his or her individual counselor and allow the counselor to assist the client with making the decision on when to come back.

---

[10] See "PTSD: National Center for PTSD."

For many, healing can come from taking the time to rededicate the space where the shooting occurred. This rededication can be something as simple as calling in friends and pastors from local churches to pray over the space, the church leadership, and the church members. Depending on the situation and its feasibility, the space could be renovated and possibly repurposed. These renovations could be small, such as a fresh coat of paint, new carpet, and new furniture. Or it could involve rearranging and reconstructing the space so it looks entirely different and is used in another capacity. For example, if the shooting took place near the youth space, you might consider remodeling the space and having the youth switch places with the adult rooms.

When the space looks entirely different, the church may feel a sense of restoration that can prevent them from feeling haunted by memories when they return. Of course, rededicating the space can only offer some relief to those recovering if they are doing their own healing as well.

Conclusion

We want to prepare our church for the unthinkable. A small amount of planning can allow for a more efficient and comprehensive response if an act of church violence occurs. When a catastrophe strikes the church, whether natural or man-made, we care for our church members, but we also are wise to remember the church staff. The church staff can easily become so absorbed in the crisis response that they neglect to care for themselves. We also need to provide them with opportunities to process and heal.

Chapter 24

Natural Disasters

Betsy. Camille. Katrina. Rita. These names represent just a few hurricanes that have impacted Louisiana and the Gulf Coast. For residents of south Louisiana, hurricane stories abound. Lifelong residents have a volume of experiences to share. On August 29, 2005, my (Karen's) family experienced our first hurricane as residents of South Louisiana. We were out of town on a previously scheduled trip when we discovered that Hurricane Katrina had intensified and was rapidly moving toward south Louisiana and the Mississippi Gulf Coast. The situation was grave.

I vividly recall watching the news from our hotel room while trying to shield our five-year-old daughter from the stress and concern. We began texting friends who stayed behind to see what was happening in our town. At first, we felt some relief that the impact was minimal to our area . . . loss of power . . . some wind damage . . . downed trees. We received word that nearby towns had significant tree damage. Then, we began to see the devastation to the Mississippi Gulf Coast. The situation became even more catastrophic when the levee broke, flooding the city of New Orleans. We watched the news in horror as the water rose. People were standing on their roofs, desperately awaiting rescue. Precious lives were lost.

Located at the edge of the significant damage, our church became a staging ground for disaster response teams entering New Orleans and surrounding areas. Disaster response teams from across the country began to pour into our church parking lot during the weeks after the storm. Specific images remain seared in my memory: the look of despair in the eyes of those realizing the devastation; the exhausted volunteers eating a meal in our gym after a day of physically and emotionally demanding work; a photograph of someone's large boat on the property of New Orleans Baptist Theological Seminary; videos of people standing on their roofs, desperately needing rescue; homes spray-painted with an "X," indicating the results of search and rescue; and neighborhoods utterly annihilated. To this day, Katrina's scars remain on the city's landscape and the survivors' hearts.

The United Nations Office for Disaster Risk Reduction (UNDRR) defines a disaster as follows: "A serious disruption of the functioning of a community or a society at any scale due to hazardous events interacting with conditions of exposure, vulnerability and capacity, leading to one or more of the following: human, material, economic and environmental losses and impacts."[1] Natural disasters are pervasive and costly, impacting a substantial number of people every year. In 2021, one in ten American homes (over 14.5 million) were affected by natural disasters, with almost $57 billion in property damage.[2] The emotional toll is inestimable.

Impact

Natural disasters impact both individuals and systems. Envision the impact like a stone tossed into a still lake. The closer to where the stone lands, the more

[1] "Disaster," United Nations Office for Disaster Risk Reduction," August 30, 2007, http://www.undrr.org/terminology/disaster.

[2] See Lindsey Jacobson, "Natural Disasters Hit Roughly 1 in 10 American Homes in 2021," CNBC, February 17, 2022, https://cnb.cx/3s5CupP.

significant the impact. But the ripples continue out. In addition to evaluating how a natural disaster impacts an individual, think about the physical, financial, emotional/psychological, and relational impact on each of the following:

- the family system
- the church
- the local community
- the broader region

Individuals, families, churches, and even entire communities may be temporarily or permanently displaced. Furthering the crisis for those trying to rebuild in lower-income areas, property values in these areas may drop. In contrast, property values in middle- to higher-income areas may rise after a natural disaster.[3] Additionally, as seen in New Orleans post-Katrina, properties may be abandoned and remain deserted for decades after a catastrophic natural disaster.

Consider the impact on local first responders and ministers who survived the same disaster while also working in disaster response. A community can come together to help one another after a disaster, but time and resources are limited, and the emotional toll is high. As such, help from outside the devastated area is valuable.

Phases of Disaster Response

As we review some essentials of disaster response, we will explore them through a series of seven phases: planning, weathering the event, immediate emergency response, assessment of damage and needs, realization of the losses, rebuilding and recovering, and remembering. Because of the importance of the planning stage, we will spend much of our time exploring planning considerations.

---

[3] See Aynsley H. M. Scheffert and James W. Ellor, "Addressing the Inequality of Disasters: The Role of Faith-Based Organizations in Disaster Response and Recovery," *Social Work & Christianity* 49, no. 4 (Winter 2022): 333, https://www.proquest.com/openview/c8e51f0999186abe903b734e2ba4e53d.

1. Planning: Developing a Preparedness Plan

It is important to develop a preparedness plan, particularly for natural disasters specific to your area. Think practically and with the needs of your own community in mind to effectively steward limited resources.

Develop Leadership

- Who will coordinate and lead your disaster response? Do you have a team of individuals who can plan for disasters and initiate the disaster response plan?
- Provide opportunities for additional training in disaster response for your response team and church leadership. (See the end of this chapter for some possible training options.)

Identify Needs and Available Resources

- What are the needs of your community? What are the potential immediate needs? What are the potential long-term needs? Disaster response is not "one-size-fits-all." For example, in a storm- or hurricane-prone area with many trees, a disaster response plan might include how to assist people with tree removal. Or, in an urban area where people may not own vehicles, people may need assistance with evacuation or transportation during the closure of the public transportation system.
- What resources and skills are available to meet these needs both within your congregation and in the community at large?
- What government resources are available?
- What resources are available through volunteer organizations (such as Send Relief)?

Engage in Networking

- Network with other churches to share resources and skills. Each faith community has unique skills and resources, so networking is essential in providing many options for care. Review the list below for ideas. One church will have difficulty providing all these resources, but through networking, these needs can be met:

  — food and water distribution
  — assistance with childcare
  — mental-health support
  — organization and storage for the collection and distribution of supplies
  — coordination of volunteers
  — housing volunteers
  — emergency shelter
  — cleanup crews
  — chain saw crews (for tree removal)

  In your cooperation, be sensitive to the varying theological views and faith practices that differ from yours. For example, if your partnering faith community has unique dietary needs, provide those accordingly.
- Consider joining a formal network, such as Send Relief or National Voluntary Organizations Active in Disaster (VOAD). Website information for these organizations is provided in the additional resources section at the end of this chapter.
- Network with local emergency responders and emergency management teams.
- In the case of community or widespread disasters, provide ministry to the families of first responders and others working during the crisis.
- Ensure that background checks and references are checked for volunteers.

Develop Communication Plans

- Do you have the contact information and addresses for those in your church community so you can check in with them during and after the crisis?
- How will you communicate during the crisis? Cell phones may be unreliable during and after a disaster. For example, you might establish a social media page for individuals to check for information.
- Will you provide services online if your congregation is dispersed?

Address Practical Matters

- Do you plan to use your church as an emergency shelter or to house volunteers during recovery? If so, what policies and procedures need to be in place?
- How will you care for the community's physical, emotional/psychological, relational, and spiritual needs during and after the crisis? Disaster response begins with establishing safety and attending to the physical needs of the survivors, but in the weeks and months to follow, a holistic approach is recommended.
- Encourage individuals to have a plan for their pets. For example, food and water for their pet must be added to the supply list for families who stay. For those who evacuate, people need to take their pet's immunization records and know what hotels will allow pets.
- Consider partnering with churches outside your area to provide evacuation assistance with housing or food.

Distribute the Necessary Information

Collect the following information, apply it to your setting, and distribute the information to the church members. Churches can also assist in making this available to the community at large.

- Resources and suggestions you can provide for the community to assist them in preparing for a natural disaster:
  - What to include in an evacuation "go bag." Local governments and denominational entities typically have suggestions for family preparedness and what to pack in a family evacuation bag. You can gather those resources and provide either handouts or links on your church website.
  - A suggested list of supplies for those who stay and "shelter in place."
  - Suggestions for preparing your home and church facility (if applicable). For example, storm drains and ditches should be cleaned before hurricanes and potential flooding to allow water flow.
  - Be aware of those who may be new to your area. For example, people in South Louisiana know how to prepare for a hurricane, but those new to the area are likely unfamiliar with hurricane preparation.
- Distribute a list of agencies (government, nonprofit, religious) that provide emergency goods (e.g., water, food, tarps) and services (e.g., tree cutting or removal, cleanup of homes) during the response and recovery period.

Include Vulnerable Populations in Your Plan

Identifying vulnerable populations is a vital component of natural disaster response.[4] Consider the following populations when developing a plan:

- **The elderly:** Ellor and Mayo emphasize the vulnerability of the elderly: "A review of death tolls linked to disasters documents that older adults are more likely to die as the result of a

[4] See Scheffert and Ellor.

significant disaster than are younger persons."[5] The elderly are impacted by mobility and other physical challenges, the emotional/psychological stress of the event, and challenges related to the potential need for temporary or permanent relocation.[6] Incorporate medications and medical devices into planning for the elderly. Encourage them to keep a regularly updated list of medications and doctors.

- **Individuals with physical or developmental disabilities:** Certain equipment or medications may be needed. Be sensitive to the impact of an upheaval in schedule and location on the person's sense of safety and security.
- **Children and adolescents:** Experiencing the upheaval of the unknown and the insecurity of potential displacement from their homes and schools can cause enormous stress on children and adolescents. Provide parents with resources for talking with their children about the event. Due to potential school and day care closings, assistance may be needed to provide childcare while parents seek to rebuild. Children thrive with an established routine. Experiencing a disaster disrupts their sense of safety and predictability, so parents should be prepared for potential emotional, relational, physical, and behavioral symptoms in their children.
- **Pregnant women:** The disaster may impact continuity of care because of transportation issues or loss of contact with their provider. Women may need to find a new provider in the case of temporary or permanent evacuation to another area. There is also the potential for complications or early labor during a natural disaster.
- **Individuals living alone:** Check in with those living alone. Do they need help evacuating? If they stay, do they want to shelter with

[5] James W. Ellor and Margaret Mayo, "Congregational and Social Work Responses to Older Survivors of Natural/Human Disasters," *Social Work and Christianity* 45, no. 1 (April 1, 2018): 43.

[6] See Ellor and Mayo for a discussion of these potential challenges.

another individual or family? If they are alone during the event, decide who will check in with them afterward.

- **Victims of domestic violence:** A crisis event will heighten the stress level of the home. If domestic violence is occurring in a home, there may be an increase in danger. If abuse is disclosed, follow all mandatory reporting laws. Be ready to provide referrals to your local domestic violence shelters.
- **Individuals of lower socioeconomic status:** Evacuation is common in hurricane- or flood-prone areas. But not everyone has the resources to evacuate. Lodging, gas, and food can cost hundreds of dollars for a family. During recovery, insurance companies can be slow to reimburse or provide only partial reimbursement of costs, and only after deductibles are met. Meanwhile, individuals still need a place to live, food to eat, and money to pay their rent or mortgage. In the case of complete destruction, they may only have the clothes they are wearing and whatever was packed in their "go bag" if they had time to evacuate.
- **Individuals of minority race/ethnicity and immigrants:** Assess their access to resources. Be mindful that some may distrust authorities and look to their faith leader as a more trustworthy source of information. Approach the cultural differences with sensitivity and humility. If there are language barriers, compile a list of potential interpreters who may be used in the case of an emergency.

2. Weathering the Event

During the event, some may choose to "shelter in place" while others may evacuate. Some natural disasters, such as hurricanes, provide a minimal amount of time for individuals to choose whether they will evacuate. Other disasters, such as tornadoes, do not provide enough time to evacuate other than moving from an unstable structure to something more stable. Depending on the event, people need minimal supplies, such as food and water, to weather the event and wait for emergency response (if required).

3. Immediate Emergency Response

Local responders are usually first to an emergency, but within twenty-four to forty-eight hours, first responders and volunteer disaster response teams from other areas may join them as they are cleared to enter the area. During this time, the focus is on basic needs and safety, such as providing water, food, medical assistance, and necessary cleaning supplies. At the same time, you are also trying to communicate information with those in your care and check in with them if possible. Cell phones may work inconsistently during this time.

4. Assessment of Damage and Needs

During this phase, damage is assessed. Insurance companies are contacted. In an area that has experienced widespread devastation, this can take weeks, if not months. Volunteer teams often come to the location to set up food and water stations while other volunteers assist with cleanup. For example, in the case of a flood, volunteers may help homeowners remove wet items and drywall in the home to prevent mold. Or teams may assist with clearing trees or placing tarps on the roofs of houses.

5. Realization of the Losses

Once individuals realize the extent of the losses, many are overcome with grief. They need to mourn all that was lost and how life will be impacted moving forward. Survivors may have questions such as, "Where is God in the midst of this disaster?" Some may tightly grasp their faith, while others may feel abandoned and alone. During this time, the church can respond alongside those impacted by the loss.

6. Rebuilding and Recovery

After the initial assessment of damage and the beginning of cleanup, a long-term period of rebuilding and recovery begins. Physical care can take center stage during a disaster. The first-wave response requires ongoing support, but a holistic approach should be considered in caring for the whole person.

- **Physical support:** Physical support may come in the form of goods, such as food, clothing, and temporary housing. If homes are lost, entire belongings must be replaced. Or physical support may come in the form of services, such as cleanup or transportation assistance.
- **Relational/social support:** Natural disasters can give people in a community a sense of "we are in this together," but they also can be relational stressors. According to Platt et al., social support is a protective feature for mental health. It may include the following:
  - — emotional support (e.g., empathy, companionship)
  - — informational support (e.g., information about available services or how to address disaster-related stressors)
  - — tangible support (e.g., financial loans, assistance with cooking and cleaning)[7]

  You can be flexible with what this social support may look like in a way that best fits your community. After the initial crisis has passed, you might provide support groups led by a volunteer or professional for those who would like to process their experience.
- **Emotional support:** Monitor the mental health of survivors. While more common with human-caused disasters, trauma symptoms can still occur with natural disasters and are accompanied by loss with the ensuing grief. Normalize grief as an expected response.
- **Spiritual care:** The church is uniquely positioned to provide spiritual care through a supportive community. This care includes answering difficult questions and walking with individuals as they attempt to find meaning in what happened. Teach about lament during sermons and Bible studies. Provide opportunities for

[7] Jonathan M. Platt et al., "A Longitudinal Study of the Bidirectional Relationship between Social Support and Posttraumatic Stress Following a Natural Disaster," *Journal of Traumatic Stress* 29, no. 3 (June 2016): 2, https://doi.org/10.1002/jts.22092.

individual and corporate lament as a spiritual practice to process grief and be honest before God. Offer survivors support groups that provide opportunities to process their stories and talk about the hard questions.

7. Remembering

Every year, on August 29, individuals impacted by Hurricane Katrina begin posting their memories and photographs of the damage on social media. Remembering an event and honoring those who lost their lives assists with grief. Adapt a plan for remembrance to your ministry setting, such as a time of prayer or a candlelight service. Determine what would be helpful and healing based on your congregation's unique makeup.

Conclusion

At some point in your ministry, you will likely experience a natural disaster or have the opportunity to minister to those impacted. In this chapter, we explored the impact of a natural disaster on various populations. We viewed seven phases of disaster response: planning, weathering the event, immediate emergency response, assessment of damage and needs, realization of the losses, rebuilding and recovery, and remembering. Emphasis was placed on the planning stage of disaster response with a reminder to consider the impact on vulnerable populations. Opportunities for networking and training are recommended under "Additional Resources" (listed below).

Additional Resources

Aten, Jamie D., and David Boan. *Disaster Ministry Handbook*. Downers Grove, IL: InterVarsity, 2016.

Crisis Response Care (training opportunities): https://www.crisisresponse.org.

National Child Traumatic Stress Network (training in psychological first aid and skills for psychological recovery): https://learn.nctsn.org/course/index.php?categoryid=11.

National Voluntary Organizations Active in Disaster (networking opportunity): https://www.nvoad.org.

Organizations Preparing for Emergency Needs (training opportunity): https://community.fema.gov/PreparednessCommunity/s/open-training.

Send Relief (Southern Baptist disaster relief): https://www.sendrelief.org.

Chapter 25

Abuse in the Church

Growing up, most of us were likely taught about stranger danger: "Never talk to strangers," we may have been told. Although this was sound advice, it was incomplete. Research indicates that one in ten children will be sexually abused before their eighteenth birthday. Ninety percent of children are abused by someone they know and trust, with 30 percent being abused by immediate or extended family members and 60 percent being abused by acquaintances, teachers, neighbors, or community leaders whom the family trusts. Only about 10 percent are abused by strangers. Seventy percent of children are sexually abused by a peer.[1] In addition to our stranger danger talk, perhaps we should also be talking to our children about safety as it relates to people we know. Instead of only telling our children to let us know if a stranger approaches them, we should also talk to them about letting us know if anyone makes them feel unsafe, whether a stranger, a family member, or a family friend.

---

[1] See "Child Abuse Sexual Statistics," Darkness to Light, accessed May 29, 2024, https://www.d2l.org/wp-content/uploads/2017/01/all_statistics_20150619.pdf.

The Internet poses dangers as well. With most devices, including cell phones and gaming consoles, having access to the Internet, the average age of first exposure to pornography has dropped to under ten. One in twenty-five youth experience unwanted online exposure to sexually explicit material, while one in nine youth experience online sexual exploitation.[2]

The church should be a safe place, free from abuse; however, this has not always been the case. Dating back to at least 2002, the Catholic Church has been under scrutiny for the prevalence of sexual abuse among its leadership.[3] Now, more than twenty years later, with settlements having taken place, many people with lived experiences of sexual abuse still question the transparency and accountability of the largest religious institution in the US.

In 2019, the *Houston Chronicle* posted an article related to hundreds of people who had been abused by those in positions of leadership in churches of the Southern Baptist Convention (SBC).[4] At the 2021 meeting of the SBC, messengers voted for an independent review of allegations that the SBC mishandled reports of sexual abuse.[5] Following this independent investigation, Guidepost reported that a number of those who experienced abuse in an SBC church had come forward to the executive committee of the SBC with allegations of abuse that were left unaddressed.[6]

---

[2] See Sheri Madigan et al., "The Prevalence of Unwanted Online Sexual Exposure and Solicitation among Youth: A Meta-Analysis," *Adolescent Health* 63, no. 2 (August 2018): 133–41, https://doi.org/10.1016/j.jadohealth.2018.03.012.

[3] See Michael Rezendes, "Church Allowed Abuse by Priest for Years," *Boston Globe*, January 6, 2002, https://www.bostonglobe.com/news/special-reports/2002/01/06/church-allowed-abuse-priest-for-years/cSHfGkTIrAT25qKGvBuDNM/story.html.

[4] See Robert Downen, Lise Olsen, and John Tedesco, "Abuse of Faith" (six-part series published between January and August 2019), *Houston Chronicle*, https://www.houstonchronicle.com/news/investigations/abuse-of-faith.

[5] See "Key Resolutions from the 2021 SBC Annual Meeting," ERLC.com, June 18, 2021, https://erlc.com/policy-content/key-resolutions-from-the-2021-sbc-annual-meeting.

[6] See "Report of the Independent Investigation," Guidepost Solutions, May 15, 2022, https://static1.squarespace.com/static/6108172d83d55d3c9db4dd67/t/628

People are appalled by the allegations of abuse within the church. Even worse, these allegations are mishandled or covered up. With these accusations and the mishandlings surrounding them, people have lost faith in the church and its leadership,[7] but most importantly, many are walking away from God. Those who were supposed to protect and point others back to God have abused their position of authority. They may have twisted Scripture as justification for their abuse, which further distorts a person's view of God. In the wake of these sexual abuse scandals, both the Catholic and Southern Baptist denominations have implemented a series of reforms; however, the work starts with each of us in our own congregations.

Prevention: Five Cs of Child Protection[8]

Consistency

One of the key components of effective policies is following them consistently. In the church setting, this means we follow the same policies and procedures related to the application process regardless of the people involved. Especially in ministry settings, some prospective volunteers may feel singled out when asked to complete an application with reference checks and a background check. However, if we explain this is a standard procedure for all volunteers, then it can relieve some anxiety about the process. The problem comes when we begin to make exceptions to the policies. For example, we may let the pastor's wife begin helping before she has completed her

a9326312a4216a3c0679d/1653248810253/Guidepost+Solutions+Independent+Investigation+Report.pdf.

[7] See Daniel Burke, "Catholics Are Losing Faith in Clergy and Church after Sexual Abuse Scandal, Gallup Survey Says," CNN, January 11, 2019, https://www.cnn.com/2019/01/11/us/catholic-gallup-survey.

[8] The original concept of the Five Cs of Child Protection came from *Stewards of Children® by Darkness to Light, Authorized Facilitator Manual, 2023.* See https://www.d2l.org/education/stewards-of-children.

application. Or, common to where we live, we may make the assumption that all seminary students are safe without proper vetting.

Consultation

In creating child-protection policies for your church or organization, it is important to consult with your liability insurance. Most, if not all, insurance companies are going to have certain stipulations related to screening and training volunteers and employees for coverage to be in effect. Having the input of an attorney in reviewing the policies is also beneficial.

Confidentiality

In asking prospective volunteers to disclose personal information during the application process, we must maintain confidentiality and communicate who will review the applications and where and how this information will be stored. Churches and organizations process staff and volunteer applications in different ways. In some churches, all applications are funneled through the administrative pastor's office. While in other churches, there may be a safety team that works together to review policies and applications. Whatever the process, we should communicate with prospective staff and volunteers who will review applications, and we want to maintain confidentiality regarding information in an individual's application unless it warrants reporting.

Comprehensiveness

Make sure that whatever policies you have in place are in place at all times for all events occurring on campus. When each ministry or department has its own set of policies, it is difficult to have accountability for best practices. For families to feel safe entrusting their children to our care, they need to know the same practices are being followed at all times. For example, the children's minister may follow a set of policies and procedures on Sunday mornings and Wednesday nights. Then, a mom may bring her children for childcare at a women's event and assume the same set of policies are in place. If the women's committee has been allowed to hire their own childcare workers who have not been through the application process, there could be danger ahead. Though best practices are being utilized most of the time, the gaps are still enough to leave the church vulnerable.

Communication

Communication regarding child protection policies should be ongoing. It's in our human nature to be hypervigilant following an incident or a compelling training but to lose focus several months down the road. This is why continual reminders of policies are important. We also want to clearly communicate the process for becoming a volunteer.

Sexual-Abuse Prevention Plan[9]

What Should Be Included

A comprehensive sexual-abuse prevention policy should include policies regarding the application process, background checks, one adult/one child situations, adult/child contact, supervision of employees and volunteers, training of staff and volunteers, the reporting process, and the use of facilities.

Application Process

Regarding the application process, make sure to include a deadline for completion. For example, require applications to be turned in at least two weeks before they plan on working or volunteering. This will allow time to review the application, check references, and run background checks. The deadline will help prevent workers from bringing their applications with them the

[9] *Stewards of Children® by Darkness to Light.*

first time they volunteer, which leaves no time for review. Communicate how often an application will need to be renewed. Some churches require a new application and background check every three or five years. Decide what is best for your organization and include it in the policies.

One Adult/One Child Situations

Eighty percent of abuse occurs in one adult / one child situations.[10] As a result, we need to have policies in place related to adult/child contact. Some examples could include policies related to contact outside the organization, purchasing gifts, and transportation. To break these examples down further, it's healthy for adults to pour into the lives of children and youth. Having a fan club at your basketball game can be a confidence boost. We can engage with youth outside of church and avoid one adult/one child situations. Meeting at the game or inviting other adults along can allow for you to build relationships outside of church without the risk of a one-on-one setting. Training can help youth workers identify healthy relational investments.

Adult/Child Contact

Frequently, kids and youth may need a ride to church or an event, such as a scavenger hunt. In these settings, it's best to have two unrelated adults in each vehicle. A policy related to social media interactions is important as well. Private messages and chats should not occur. If a leader would like to message the child or youth, he or she should include the parents in the interaction as well.

There may be times when a worker needs to have a private conversation with an adolescent. In this case, best practice is for the discussion to be observable and interruptible. You can have a private conversation without going into a secluded area. Although he or she may not be close enough to

[10] Darkness to Light, "Know the Statistics," Stewards of Children, accessed May 29, 2024, https://childadv.net/download/attachment/1#.

hear what is being said, make sure someone is nearby who can observe the interaction. A situation is interruptible when there is a window that allows others to see into the room and when there is a possibility of someone stopping by to check in at any moment.

Grooming is the process by which a perpetrator gains access to a child for the purpose of abuse. The perpetrator may win the trust of the parents to gain access to the child. And the perpetrator may win the child over by excessive gift-giving, telling secrets, or other things that make the child feel important. Although gifts can be given with the purest of intentions, their hidden meaning may be misconstrued, so caution should be applied.

In some cases, a person may have poor boundaries and be unaware of the risks involved with his or her behavior. We should take steps to address this behavior. In a previous version of Darkness to Light's *Stewards of Children* training, they give the following steps:[11]

1. **Describe the behavior.** For example, someone has been giving excessive gifts to a child. Singling out one child with gifts can be misconstrued and cause conflict with the other children.
2. **Set a limit.** Ask the person to refrain from purchasing gifts.
3. **Move on.** Then, we move on. If the person ceases the behavior, it's likely he was unaware he was crossing a boundary.

Now that he knows, he won't engage in this behavior in the future. If the behavior continues, we have reasonable suspicion and should address this behavior at a higher level.

Sexual Offender Policies

A church should also have a policy related to sexual offenders. Each individual situation may warrant different levels of caution. In general, currently registered sex offenders are not allowed around children, which means participation in many church and ministry settings is prohibited. Part of the

---

[11] *Stewards of Children® By Darkness to Light, Participant Manual, 2014.*

policy should include checking with the individual's probation officer about current restrictions. The church should comply with all regulations related to public and community participation, employment, and volunteer service.

Supervision of Employees and Volunteers

A written plan related to the supervision of employees and volunteers should be in place. Supervision can help us better understand the person's style and identify the best fit for ministry roles. Through periodic check-ins, supervision provides accountability that child protection policies are being followed. Also, there are times when a person may look good on paper, but there is a discrepancy between what's on paper and the reality of his or her practice. A culture of accountability is key to protecting our children.

Training

Before working, each staff member or volunteer should be required to complete sexual-abuse prevention training, along with additional training each application renewal period. Some insurance companies offer trainings, along with their policies. While not always feasible, an in-person training allows for the group to process the information they have received, along with discussing best practices for implementation. In some cases, an online training may be the only option, but offering opportunities for the information to be discussed during other meetings can be helpful as well. A few training options are mentioned at the end of this chapter.

Reporting

Every organization's policy should state clearly that mandatory reporting should take place according to state law. The policy should require that the administration be notified simultaneously but separately, and reporting is not dependent on the approval of the organization's leadership. The purpose of notifying church leadership or the clinical director of the counseling agency is not to seek permission to report. Instead, this policy is designed to engage key personnel in the event that an investigation is opened related to the report. If an investigation is opened, the investigators will likely reach out to key personnel requesting information. Having them informed in advance will help them to efficiently direct the investigators to those with relevant information about the case.

Use of Facilities

In designing or renovating a building, when possible, consider the layout from a safety perspective. Identify spaces that could isolate children and reduce accountability for adult/child interactions and peer-to-peer interactions. Windows and two-way mirrors can assist. I (Brooke) once visited a children's ministry department where there was a partial two-way mirror all the way down the hall. This allowed those walking down the hall to see into the rooms without the distraction of the children being able to see everything going on in the hallway.

In many cases, we have to work with the facilities in place. In these situations, we want to assess the risks of the space we are using and consider what areas may leave us vulnerable. If there are closets without windows, we might consider locking them to prevent access. During events such as vacation Bible school, consider how children can get from one rotation to the next without being left in an isolated situation.

Evaluate the usage of the facility before a special event with children and adolescents, such as an overnight youth retreat. We want to consider whether there are areas that should be closed off or monitored more carefully.

When Prevention Efforts Fail

Handle the Disclosure of Abuse Appropriately

When someone trusts you with a disclosure of abuse, the most important thing is to believe him or her. Be careful to ask open-ended questions, such as, "What happened next?" or "Tell me more." Leading questions may result in inaccurate or biased information, so open-ended questions are best.

Be careful not to make promises you cannot keep. When children and adolescents make a disclosure, they commonly ask a trusted adult if they can share something with them and ask them to promise not to tell anyone. Many adults have found themselves in a predicament because they promised to keep something confidential that needs to be reported. In these situations, the best response from the adult is "My ultimate responsibility is to keep you and others safe. If you share that you or someone you know is in danger, then I'll need to take steps to ensure everyone's safety." We can also assure minimal disclosure, meaning we will only disclose to those who need to know.

In the moment of disclosure, our desire is to assure the person that the perpetrator will be put away and that she will never have to worry about him again. Although that may be the desired outcome, the fate of the perpetrator and the course of the investigation is ultimately outside of our control. While we may do everything within our control to keep the child safe, we cannot control the response or actions of others in the situation.

Report Immediately

There are some misconceptions about the reporting process, with many being reluctant to report. One of the reasons people are reluctant to report abuse is that they are unsure as to whether it happened. Although the uncertainty is understandable, our job is not to substantiate the suspicion of abuse. When we make a report to local law enforcement or the Department of Children and Family Services (DCFS), we are not stating definitively that the abuse occurred. Instead, we are asking for a professional service to be performed. We are requesting those with appropriate training to investigate the claims and determine their validity. The authorities are the ones ultimately responsible for substantiating the claim of abuse.

Additionally, taking on the role of a detective and trying to investigate the matter ourselves before reporting can create further issues for the actual investigators and others involved. If we have attempted to collect additional information about the incident, it makes maintaining confidentiality difficult, which can lead to gossip. If and when law enforcement does become involved, it becomes more difficult to collect facts if people have been passing along speculations rather than factual information.

In some cases, churches have failed to report abuse. Maybe they were trying to avoid liability or protect the identities of those involved. Instead of reporting, they dismissed the staff member involved. While this may have helped the immediate situation, more damage is done in the long run when abuse goes unreported. Some churches that have reported abuse will tell you they discovered the perpetrator had a history of abusive behavior that had never been reported. When we fail to report, we are allowing the abuse to continue in another place and with another victim. Reporting and dealing with the aftermath of abuse is not easy, but the right thing is not always the easy thing.

Maintain Confidentiality

When making a report to children's services or law enforcement, we must disclose relevant information only to those who need to know. The more people we share this information with, the more people we are involving in the investigation, which can further complicate the situation. Respect the privacy of those involved.

Provide Assistance and Support to Those Involved

Following the disclosure and reporting of abuse, the church should make sure that those involved are cared for. One of the first things to do is help them find a Christian counselor who specializes in trauma. When possible, especially if the abuse occurred within the church or ministry setting, the church should pay the cost of or secure funding for counseling. Some insurance policies have allowances for counseling when an incident has occurred, so you might check with your liability insurance about its coverage.

Address the Church

The pastor or a designated representative should address the church. During a time of crisis, especially abuse in the church, the congregation needs to hear from its own leaders rather than hearing the story in the news. Use discretion to protect the identities of those who have been abused.

Be Prepared for the Long Haul

Many cases of abuse never go to trial. However, when they do, the process is typically long and difficult. As with many forms of crisis, our human nature is to show up in full force to extend care in the immediate aftermath. Our methods should include long-term follow-up and care. After abuse is disclosed, those involved may seek help and start the work of recovery. Then, after a year, two years, or maybe more, the legal system may begin moving forward with a trial.

Preparing for trial is draining, to say the least. The district attorney's office will work with those involved on testimony preparation. As it relates to sentencing, those involved may be asked to prepare a victim impact statement. A victim impact statement helps personalize the crime, allowing those impacted to describe the harm and cost to them and their families. The court may take this information into consideration when determining sentencing. For some, this may be an opportunity to confront their abuser and find closure. However, we would caution those with lived experiences to refrain from having high expectations related to closure that they may be seeking. If a person desires for his abuser to respond in a certain manner or express remorse, it could set the person up for hurt. Unfortunately, the abuser may not express any degree of remorse. He may even respond in a manner that could cause more harm.

Because this process can be stretched out over a long period of time, it is important for the church or organization to make sure there is a long-term plan in place to care for those involved. Because the process can take years, it is possible the pastor or other staff members have moved on to other churches or there have been other leadership changes. The new leaders or staff members may not be completely aware of all that has transpired or the present status of the situation. When a disclosure is made and an investigation is opened, the church should have a team of people supporting those involved. In the event that a pastor or other church leaders move to another position, a team can step in to ensure that those involved are supported throughout the duration of the process.

Conclusion

In Matthew 18, the disciples asked Jesus who was the greatest in the kingdom of heaven. Jesus responded by calling over a small child. In verses 5–6 he says, "And whoever welcomes one child like this in my name welcomes me. But whoever causes one of these little ones who believe in me to fall away—it would be better for him if a heavy millstone were hung around his neck and he were drowned in the depths of the sea." Children are in a vulnerable position and powerless to protect themselves. As adults, it is our responsibility to ensure that our churches and ministry organizations are a safe place for all children. When security breaches do occur, it is our responsibility to take measures to address the matter through reporting. The right thing is not always the easy thing, but it is our responsibility to protect.

Training Resources

Darkness to Light: https://www.d2l.org.

Darkness to Light is a nonprofit organization that offers research-based training to a wide range of organizations. You can request in-person training from an authorized facilitator or complete an online training.

Safe Hiring Solutions: https://www.safehiringsolutions.com.

Safe Hiring Solutions offers online training along with podcasts on safety and security issues. They also offer a wide range of additional services, including automated reference checks and background checks with continuous arrest monitoring.

Chapter 26

Clergy Sexual Misconduct

I don't know if I could ever trust a church leader again." "I trusted him to mentor my child." "I don't want to attend church anymore." "It makes you wonder what all is going on behind closed doors." "I guess there are no safe places on this earth." These statements, and many more, are common after learning a pastor or prominent church leader has perpetrated sexual abuse. People consider the church to be a safe haven from the chaos and depravity inherent in the rest of the world. When this safe haven is defiled, those impacted are left picking up the pieces of devastation and betrayal.

The news is full of stories related to clergy sexual misconduct. Marital infidelity and pornography use run rampant in ministry settings, along with crimes such as child sexual abuse and sex trafficking. When these stories are exposed, we are shocked and haunted by the fact that these crimes have been committed by those whom we were supposed to trust in places that were supposed to be a haven of safety. When we see these crimes committed by those at the top, we question whether power corrupts or whether the corrupt end up in power?

It reminds us of the story of King Uzziah in 2 Chronicles 26. He did what was right in the eyes of the Lord, just as his father had done. When he sought the Lord, God gave him success. God helped him defeat the Philistines, the Arabs, and the Meunites. He became successful and was granted much power. Through his success, he became arrogant. He acted unfaithfully to the Lord by going into the sanctuary to burn incense on the altar, which he was not allowed to do. The priests tried to stop him, but he persisted, and a skin disease broke out on him. He, with the help of the priests, hurried out of the sanctuary because the Lord had afflicted him. He was afflicted until his death, lived in quarantine, and was excluded from access to the Lord's temple. The Lord had given him success, but he became prideful. How will we handle the opportunities the Lord chooses to entrust to us?

Unfortunately, those in the church are just as susceptible to sin as everyone else. Some struggled with these sinful desires before entering the ministry, thinking that if they gave their lives to serving the Lord, he would take these thoughts and urges from them. Others enter ministry and struggle to cope with the pressure and stress, and the enemy seizes the opportunity. Many times in Scripture, we are told to stand firm and resist when faced with temptation. The pull of sexual sin is unrelenting, which could be the reason Scripture tells us to flee sexual temptation. In other words, we should run as fast as we can.

How Does This Happen?

The trauma left behind by clergy misconduct often centralizes around trust. If we cannot trust the church, who can we trust? Behind this is the question of how a person who was presumably called by God to bring glory to his name could defile his name and cause long-term damage to those involved.

This process never happens overnight. Whenever the truth is exposed, we are seeing the external appearance of a long road of hidden sin and inner turmoil. Small choices are made each day that cause a person to veer slowly off path until he is so far gone he does not know how to find his way back alone. In *Mere Christianity*, C. S. Lewis says, "Every time you make a choice you are turning the central part of you, the part that chooses, into something a little different than it was before. And taking your life as a whole, with all your innumerable choices, all your life long you are slowly turning this central thing into a heavenly creature or a hellish creature. . . . Each of us at each moment is progressing to the one state or the other."[1]

How Does It Begin?

As evidenced by the content of this book, ministry is stressful. When it begins to take a toll on us, we are not taking care of ourselves, our boundaries are loosened, and we are not using healthy coping skills. With a lack of self-care, our relationship with God is likely being neglected, which means sins such as pride and arrogance are likely going unconfessed. God has gifted each of us in unique ways and placed a calling on our lives. When we become so focused on our giftedness to the detriment of our calling, we are on a slow path to destruction.

Mentoring

Many pastors and church leaders long for a mentor, but it is difficult for them to find someone for whom they are also not responsible. If they are struggling, they often are unsure of where to go for help. Associational leaders are wise to consider ways to care for and support their local pastors. Pastors may be reluctant to seek counseling because they believe they should have it all together. Securing Christian counselors who understand the stress of ministry and that pastors are not immune to struggle could be an incredible resource for local pastors.

We are wise to encourage pastors to remain focused on their own spiritual development. Our ministry should come from the overflow of our personal devotional life. Many of the great leaders in Scripture served after an

---

[1] C. S. Lewis, *Mere Christianity* (New York: HarperCollins, 1952), 92.

extended time of aloneness with God. In church life, we have a tendency to focus more on a person's gifts than his character. Just because a person can articulate theological truths does not mean he has a heart that follows God.[2] When we focus more on the charisma with which a person serves than on his heart, we are missing the purity of heart God desires for his children. In the same way that Samuel was instructed not to consider external appearances when looking for Israel's next king (see 1 Samuel 16:7), we are wise to emphasize purity of heart above giftedness.

How Should We Respond?

Protect the People, Not the System

In some cases, others were aware of the illicit behavior taking place, but they did not report or address it for fear of repercussions. These repercussions may involve job loss or being ostracized for questioning an influential and powerful person. A well-respected and highly praised superintendent in a small town was forced out of a job and blacklisted after attempting to fire a coach. This coach had received multiple allegations of physical abuse and inappropriate behavior with female students. Allegations had also been made in his previous places of employment. Eventually, someone managed to capture a video of the coach physically abusing a player. To most, this would present as a simple case. Where did the problem come into play? The coach was the chairman of the deacons at the same church where the school board president attended. Church members came into the superintendent's office lodging complaints about his attempts to fire a "good man" from his job, some with threats. It also likely helped that the coach was known for his winning record.

The coach ended up resigning and accepting a position in another school system. A few years later, a female student filed a lawsuit against this

[2] See Diane Langberg, *Redeeming Power: Understanding Authority and Abuse in the Church* (Grand Rapids: Baker, 2020), 129–30.

same coach. More students had to suffer at the hands of this coach because previous school officials refused to intervene or pushed out others who had attempted to do the right thing. The school board was more interested in protecting their system and, in some cases, the relationships at their church. The right thing is not always the easy thing.

Similar stories are happening all over the ministry world. No one wants to believe a respected Christian in a position of power could be capable of such things, so they disregard it without investigating it. Some worry about creating a rift at church or at work, so they hope it goes away quietly. Although this fear may be justified, it sets more people on a path to being hurt.

Evaluate Accountability Systems

Research has indicated that the more power a person has, the less compassion he will have.[3] Accountability within organizations is difficult because of the systems of power in place. The higher you reach in a church or ministry organization, the less likely it is that anyone is holding you accountable. We should always be mindful of the amount of power we give to any one person within the church, because the more power a person has, the less insight he likely has.

When we come across people who disagree with us or question us in any way, our tendency is to push them aside because of their negativity. Our trusted group agrees with us, so we decide we do not need that kind of negativity. However, we often surround ourselves with our "fan club," the people who agree with us on everything, praise everything we do, and never question or offer an alternative. In this situation, we can be under the delusion that we have accountability when the reality is that we have yes-men who do not go against the grain when needed.

---

[3] See G. A. van Kleef et al., "Power, Distress, and Compassion: Turning a Blind Eye to the Suffering of Others," *Psychological Science* 19, no. 12 (2008): 1315–22, https://doi.org/10.1111/j.1467-9280.2008.02241.x.

How Not to Respond

Dismissing

When clergy sexual misconduct is discovered, people have a wide range of responses. In some unfortunate situations, people take a flippant or dismissive perspective of what happened. In some cases, they use faith-based clichéd phrases, such as, "Who among us is without sin?" Or they throw out something such as "God has forgiven him" or "He's a good man of God. We can't let this ruin his reputation." One's personal relationship with the accused may cloud his judgment. In other words, "I know him, and he would never do that." The truth is, yes, we are all inherently sinful, and God does forgive. However, God does not absolve us of the consequences of our actions. Also, if we are truly repentant for our sin, we should be convicted to take responsibility for our actions and make things right with those we have harmed.

Defending

For an adult to consent to something, he or she must have the capacity to choose, and it must be safe to say no. If a person, such as a pastor, has the ability to cast off someone from his or her church or community, then consent is not possible.[4] We also see victim blaming, such as "If she had not been dressed inappropriately, then she would not have been such a temptation"; "He should have come forward sooner"; or "A person his age should have the courage to stand up to his perpetrator." In chapter 10, we looked at the difference between responsibility and regret. In these examples, a person may regret how she dressed or that she did not stand up to her abuser or disclose the abuse sooner, but that does not make her responsible for the abuse. The pastor is in a position of authority, which means that consent is not possible. In some cases, we may defend because

[4] See Langberg, *Redeeming Power*, 70.

we cannot handle the alternative—that our pastor, whom we loved and trusted, has deceived us.

Other Considerations

Forgiveness and Reconciliation

Forgiveness is about letting go of anger, resentment, and vengeance. Forgiveness allows those with lived experiences to find freedom and peace. However, forgiveness does not absolve the offender of consequences. In some cases, we have equated forgiveness with sweeping sexual abuse under the rug. We tell those who have been hurt that they should forgive and let the entire thing go. This does not mean we do not hold the offender accountable for his actions. If we fail to address the issue appropriately this time, we could be creating an opportunity for the pastor to abuse again in the future.

Forgiveness is a part of reconciliation, but they are not the same thing. Reconciliation is not always recommended. For reconciliation to occur, a few things should be in place. First, the offended must be far down the path of forgiveness. Forgiveness is a process, and something such as this will likely take time, but we want to ensure that the person has made significant progress in both her healing and forgiveness. Otherwise, reconciliation could be a major setback in her recovery work. The most crucial part of this process is whether the offender has taken responsibility for his actions and expressed remorse.

Worldly Grief versus Godly Grief

Earlier we talked about how people may say the offender has been forgiven by God, so all should be well. The question is whether they have grieved their sin. Let's examine the difference between worldly grief and godly grief. Second Corinthians 7:10–11 says, "For godly grief produces a repentance that leads to salvation without regret, but worldly grief produces death. For consider how much diligence this very thing—this grieving as God wills—has produced in you: what a desire to clear yourselves, what indignation, what fear, what deep longing, what zeal, what justice! In every way you showed yourselves to be pure in this matter." When we have worldly grief, we mourn the losses of what sin has cost us. In other words, we are sorry more about being caught than we are about the harm our actions brought. Worldly grief is when we grieve the loss of our reputations and our ministry positions.

On the other hand, godly grief is when we are sorrowful for how we have sinned against God and others. We are more concerned with what we need to do to make things right with others. We take responsibility for our actions and strive to make things right with God and others. Godly grief is more others-focused, while worldly grief is self-focused. When a person is experiencing godly grief, he is more concerned with the impact of his actions on others and about making things right, rather than being self-absorbed in losing his career and status.

Accountability for the Pastor Caught in Abusive Sin

When a pastor has been caught in sexual abuse or some other type of misconduct, church leaders and friends are often conflicted. In some cases, there is a desire to help those who have been hurt by the pastor's abuse, but they are unsure what to do with the pastor. We have seen some cases where church leaders thought they were ministering to the pastor by allowing him to resign and move on because he had been forgiven, which allowed him to continue the abuse in a new place.

In other cases, church leaders hold the pastor accountable for his actions and report the abuse to the appropriate authorities, but they are conflicted about what their role or responsibility should be to the pastor after reporting. In most cases, they feel angry at the level of betrayal and devastation this person has caused. They may still be figuring out how this could have happened or how someone with whom they walked so closely could have been engaged in this level of abuse. They believe someone should walk alongside that pastor, but they are not sure they are the ones to do it.

Those who were directly impacted by the misconduct may still be processing their emotions and working through the wreckage. If they see someone within their church or community ministering to the pastor, they may struggle with thoughts that the person is defending him or condoning his actions. In situations such as this, it might be best to find someone who is removed from the situation to offer assistance. This could be a pastor from another church, a counselor who is not directly involved in this situation, or some other church leader who was not directly impacted by the abuse. This person might be in a better place to walk alongside the pastor in the consequences that are to come or the realization of the level of devastation caused. In the event that the pastor is not repentant, this person may be in a place to speak truth to his actions.

Conclusion

Looking back over instances of sexual abuse the past few decades, we have seen cover-ups in a multitude of places, including athletics and the church. I think about the people of influence who have been disgraced or forced to resign because of their part in a sexual-abuse scandal. Going back to the story of King Uzziah, how do we want to be remembered? We can be the person who protected systems over people, or we can be the person who sought purity for the church rather than the illusion of righteousness.

Whether it be vocational ministry or not, God has placed a calling on each of our lives. How will we choose to steward the gifts and responsibilities he has given us? And how will we care for those whom he entrusted to us? Perhaps Diane Langberg says it best again: "Our small, everyday choices make an eternal difference."[5]

[5] Langberg, *Redeeming Power*, 177.

Now to him who is able to protect you from stumbling
and to make you stand in the presence of his glory, without
blemish and with great joy, to the only God our Savior,
through Jesus Christ our Lord, be glory, majesty, power,
and authority before all time, now and forever. Amen.

—Jude 24–25

Chapter 27

Crisis Counseling and the Mission Field

Laura and Josh have been married for ten years and have served in East Asia for the last three. They have a seven-year-old girl and a four-year-old boy. The language spoken in the country is Urdu. Their daughter has adapted well to the language; however, her English has begun to weaken. She struggles to communicate with her grandparents when they FaceTime and is feeling disconnected from her extended family. She often switches between Urdu and English in conversation without realizing it. Her little brother was immersed in Urdu early in life and shares her struggles with English. Laura and Josh communicate well in Urdu, but they still feel disconnected when conversing in their second language with their children who have more practice in Urdu.

Their daughter attends a local school. She loves her friends and teachers but feels out of place because she looks different from them. They have different traditions and ways of celebrating holidays. Laura and Josh host a weekly English corner for local college students looking to learn or brush up on their English skills. They have built some solid relationships and shared the gospel multiple times, but no one has accepted Christ. The same goes for their daily tasks. They worry about what their mission organization will say if they continue to send in monthly reports with no converts.

On top of this, Laura recently found out she is pregnant with their third child. They are elated, but medical care in East Asia is not the same as it is in America. She is also unable to find some of the vitamins and medications recommended by her doctor. Her last delivery resulted in an emergency C-section when her son's heart rate dropped suddenly, which makes her anxious about the upcoming delivery. She wishes her parents could come and help out for a few weeks, but they have jobs in the States and have a difficult time being able to break away to visit overseas.

Political tensions are mounting, with many of the nationals threatening to overthrow the government. This unrest brings anxiety to Laura and Josh. They try to focus on their work, but their minds are concerned with the safety of their children. They wonder if it's time to take leave and how they will know if and when they need to leave. They think of the preparations that need to be in place in the event they need to make a quick evacuation.

Though the location and circumstances may vary, any missionary could face an issue or combination of issues similar to the example just given. A deeper understanding of the daily struggles missionaries face on the mission field can help us understand how to better pray for, support, and offer assistance during times of crisis.

Struggles Missionaries Face

Loneliness

Being separated from your friends and family in an unfamiliar culture with a new language is isolating. Missionaries often long for the familiar: a local restaurant, familiar face, or worship service in their native language. Those who are single often long for companionship. Families may struggle to juggle all their responsibilities with their children and wish they had extended family or friends nearby to help.

Work-Life Balance

Those of us raised in America have become accustomed to a typical work-week. Either we are working a set number of hours per week, or we are assigned a project that we work on until completion. In most cases, the mission field does not work quite like this. Some missionaries may engage in leisure activities or spend time at a local coffee shop, hoping for the opportunity to build relationships. It may take time to determine the most effective options for relationship building. Then, there is the question of how success is measured. Is it about the number of times the gospel is shared or the number of converts?

As it relates to the gospel, the Holy Spirit is responsible for convicting; however, our American society tends to place an emphasis on numbers. As a result, many missionaries may feel a sense of shame for not producing the big, dramatic numbers they feel are expected by those back home. Others may struggle with feeling as though they are not doing enough and default to overworking. This can be especially true in medical missions. Medical care overseas is often not as readily available or as advanced as what we have in the US. In other countries, people may wait long periods of time for simple medical care and procedures. These needs can overwhelm medical missionaries to the extent that they are fearful of taking a day off because they know it is unlikely the people they serve would receive adequate medical care without them. Being able to balance an alternative work schedule with self-care is an important component for weathering any crises that may come.

Teaming

Some of us have worked in environments that we felt were healthy and life-giving. We loved our coworkers, were able to steward our gifts well, and felt a sense of affirmation in the work we were doing. We may have also worked in places that were unhealthy with high levels of conflict and a lack of cohesion among the group. We may have struggled with loving the work we did while being miserable with the work environment. Unfortunately, this may also be true for missionaries.

Because we are all inherently sinful and flawed, disagreements and difficulties may arise while attempting to work together in a productive manner. We also have different personalities and styles of communication. Serving overseas—away from your family, friends, and what is familiar—can amplify any work-related conflict. Sometimes we survive rough seasons at work because of our support system. But when your support system is miles away and you are unsure where to turn for help, the longing for home can be nearly unbearable.

Further, just as sexual harassment and sexual abuse can occur in the workplace, they can unfortunately also take place on the mission field. As with other issues pertaining to life overseas, the reporting process can be complicated by distance. Supervisors may struggle to address concerns taking place on another continent, and those serving overseas may find it difficult to present their case to those who are unable to observe the interaction firsthand.

Trauma

Traumatic events can occur anywhere, but we typically feel safer in our homes, surrounded by loved ones. Being in another country away from everything and everyone that is familiar makes it more difficult to handle traumatic events when they arise. Even the things we take for granted, such as being able to speak face-to-face with another person in our native language about what has happened, are likely gone.

In addition to the traumatic events that we all might experience from time to time, there is also the stress of working as a missionary in some countries where there is no freedom of religion. Being restrictive with communication and taking extra precautions before engaging in worship or other church-related activities can feel cumbersome at times. In some cases, missionaries have been forced to relocate because there were concerns about their safety or they noticed that people were following them.

Third-Culture Kids

Third-culture kids (TCKs) grow up in a culture other than their parents' or their own culture or nationality. A significant portion of their formative years are spent in a different environment. Depending on their developmental stage and the circumstances in the culture in which they are living, they may experience certain degrees of struggle, such as loss of identity and belonging. When children are doing well and thriving, a load is taken off parents. Let's consider some of the struggles TCKs face so we can prepare them and their parents for the journey abroad.

Loss

TCKs may feel a sense of loss of family, friends, or the familiarity of what has been left behind. These losses may occur when relocating to another culture or even when returning to the culture of their nationality. When struggling to learn a new language and trying to find their feet in an unfamiliar culture, TCKs long for something that feels like home.

Identity and Belonging

TCKs may struggle to find themselves in the midst of an environment that seems unfamiliar. They have learned different ways of being and relating. As a result, they struggle with how much to retain from their other culture and how much to embrace of their new culture. When they travel back and forth between the two, they may have difficulty identifying with either.

Trauma

Around 20 percent of TCKs have reported four or more adverse childhood experiences (ACEs),[1] which is higher than the general population. This number of ACEs places them at high-risk of negative outcomes later in life. Research has indicated that TCKs report higher levels of emotional abuse and neglect and are more likely to have a family member within their home suffering from mental illness than the rest of the general population.[2]

Protective Factors

Having the opportunity to live abroad can be an enriching opportunity. TCKs see how God works through different people in various places and cultures. Although we would love to shield our children from hardships and suffering, we are unable to do so whether we live in the US or abroad. We want to consider ways to build protective factors that will enable our children to withstand the storms of life, including living abroad.

The struggle with supporting TCKs is that many of the research-supported protective factors center around community involvement and social support,[3] which can be difficult to find overseas. However, the protective factors related to the family environment can be utilized regardless of location. These include being able to talk to their families about their feelings, feeling that their families stand by them during difficult times, and feeling safe and protected by an adult in their family.[4] In the next section of this chapter, we will discuss ways to prepare mentally and emotionally for the

---

[1] See chapter 11 for more information about adverse childhood experiences.

[2] See Tanya Crossman, Elizabeth Vahey Smith, and Lauren Wells, "TCKs at Risk: Risk Factors and Mitigation for Globally Mobile Families," TCK Training, December 2022, https://www.tcktraining.com/tcks-at-risk-white-paper.

[3] See Christina Bethell, Jennifer Jones, and Narangerel Gombojav, "Positive Childhood Experiences and Adult Mental and Relational Health in a Statewide Sample: Associations across Adverse Childhood Experiences Levels," *JAMA Pediatrics* 173, no. 11, http://doi.org/10.1001/jamapediatrics.2019.3007.

[4] See Bethell et al.

mission field. As with parenting in any circumstance, we want to make sure we take care of ourselves first so we are equipped to take care of our children.

Other protective factors that may be more difficult to secure for TCKs include participating in community activities, a sense of belonging in high school, feeling supported by friends, and at least two nonparent adults taking an interest in them.[5] Being able to participate in the community and find a sense of belonging at school and among friends can take time when you move overseas. We want to encourage our kids to continue working toward these goals.

Upon arrival in another country, TCKs might not immediately have local access to a group of friends or nonparent adults who are investing in them. Their home church might consider creating a weekly or bimonthly schedule for both adults and the TCKs' friends to sign up to pray for them and find a way to send encouragement. This encouragement could be a gift from home or something they are unable to obtain in their current location. They could also arrange for FaceTime and Zoom meetings, where they are able to talk in real time and pray together. They could reach out via email on their assigned week to ask for specific ways to pray for the child and his or her family. Although these gestures may not take away the grief and loneliness that may be present, they can significantly ease the transition and offer a healthy manner in which to process the changes.

A Wholesome Experience on the Mission Field

Preparation

Before sending a missionary overseas or into a difficult part of the United States, attempt to ensure as much stability as possible. This includes addressing and resolving any health-related issues, along with financial issues. Health care overseas is not always optimal, and minimizing major health concerns on the field can significantly reduce stress. Managing stress on the field can

[5] See Bethell et al.

be significantly improved when finances are in order. Having a significant amount of debt weighing on you can distract from the work at hand.

Being proactive and managing mental-health concerns can set a person up for success on the mission field. Discussing past grief and trauma can be uncomfortable, but past issues left unresolved may surface during our deepest moments of despair and isolation. The stress of ministry and missions may trigger unresolved issues from the past. Understanding how our past has impacted us will equip us to manage any triggers that may arise later on.

The loneliness many experience on the mission field can bring temptations such as pornography or other unhealthy sexual behavior. We should encourage missionaries or those aspiring to serve in this capacity to consider their areas of vulnerability. For example, what type of sexual sin are they likely to struggle with, and what safeguards need to be put into place? For some, a safety plan or personal code of ethics may be helpful. Having a plan in place for how they will manage temptations and vulnerabilities can reduce the likelihood of being caught off guard. They can process these struggles with a peer or mentor and then work together to formulate an accountability plan.

Emotional Health and Interpersonal Relationship Skills

In his various books related to emotionally healthy spirituality, Peter Scazzero discusses a number of things that can impact our emotional and spiritual health. Family of origin (the family a person grows up in) is one of the things he mentions. Most of us learned things, whether explicitly or implicitly, from our families of origin that may still be with us and are unhealthy in our current families or ministries.[6]

Because we live in a fallen world, all of our families are broken to some degree. Going back and exploring past experiences and hurts can increase our awareness of how we perform under another person's authority, how we

[6] Peter Scazzero, *Emotionally Healthy Spirituality: Unleash the Power of Authentic Life in Christ* (Nashville: Thomas Nelson, 2006), 106–10.

manage conflict and resolve differences, and what we believe about relationships and gender roles, among other things. We may also discover how we have come to handle brokenness and vulnerability. Are we willing to allow others into our vulnerabilities and weaknesses? Or do we cover them at all costs and refrain from seeking help when needed?[7] With the stress of ministry and living overseas, we need to move past our struggles by asking for help when needed. Likewise, our mission organizations need to be intentional about creating a climate of safety for those seeking help.

To address these issues, you might refer back to the exercise in chapter 12 under "Reflecting on Our Past." We want to find healing from our early experiences and extend forgiveness as needed. Moving forward without the excess baggage can promote a healthier family and ministry. Anything that has not been dealt with will most assuredly come out in a stressful season of ministry. Addressing as many of these past issues as possible before going on the mission field can minimize triggers in a stressful season. It can also help us become more aware of our vulnerabilities so we know how to better care for ourselves.

In any spiritual walk, we encourage believers to prioritize being with God above doing for God. At home, missionaries may have several layers of built-in accountability, including their church, small groups, mentors, families, and friends, but these people are often missing on the mission field. Although it is true that virtual gatherings are more common and readily available than in the past, it's not the same as being able to see how a person is doing each day. When we are not with them physically, we are only hearing their perspective. We may not even be aware they are struggling or beginning to slip.

Ongoing Support

Stateside family members, friends, and churches should consider ways to offer ongoing support for the missionary. A few practical ways this could

---

[7] Peter Scazzero, *Emotionally Healthy Discipleship: Moving from Shallow Christianity to Deep Transformation* (Grand Rapids: Zondervan, 2021), 190–93.

take place would be a church setting aside time during their worship services or prayer meetings to pray specifically for a missionary. This could serve as a reminder to check in with the person in advance for specific prayer requests he or she might have. Otherwise, it's easy to get busy and not pray with intentionality. Reaching out to those serving overseas and asking for specific ways to pray for them, then reporting back to them, can be a source of encouragement that they have not been forgotten.

Being overseas when friends or family members are struggling with health or personal issues is difficult. They know they are called to the work they are doing, but they also long to be physically present with their family members and friends. In cases in which they cannot return home or the trip may be delayed for a while, we want to step in and help where we can. We may be able to help when they are unable, provide them with updates, or check on things as needed. Depending on their situation, they may not always be able to return home for funerals or other special occasions; we want to make sure they are supported as they grieve losses or experiences they are missing.

Conclusion

When we think about missionaries, we may often think of terrible living conditions, no running water, and endless suffering. In some cases, this could be true, but we need to give attention to the emotional struggles that take place on the mission field. We want to take measures to assure that missionaries receive preparation before serving overseas along with appropriate support while on the field.

Additional Resources

TCK Training, https://www.tcktraining.com.

This website offers training and research to equip those who care for TCKs.

Part 9

Care for the Helpers

Chapter 28

Vicarious Traumatization and Compassion Fatigue

Being present with others during some of the darkest moments of their lives is a privilege. The opportunity to have a front-row seat at watching God work in the midst of pain and brokenness can be a sacred moment, but it is also a heavy responsibility.

Many of us avoid people in pain. In some cases, we feel at a loss for words and inadequate in our ability to help. Other times, we try to avoid the emotions that pain elicits. We may be physically present but emotionally checked out. At first, this may appear to be the more emotionally safe response; however, we miss out on connection. The only way we can connect with others is to enter their emotional space.

Being fully present with others in pain is a courageous decision. When we choose to sit with others in their pain, we are transformed. It may be heavy, but it is worth it. The impact of carrying the traumatic stories of others has been described as an occupational hazard.

The terms *vicarious traumatization* and *compassion fatigue* are often used interchangeably in the world of helping professionals. Although these terms are similar in nature, there are a few differences. Both result from working with those who have experienced or are experiencing trauma. Vicarious trauma focuses on the inner experience of the helper, dealing with his or her worldview and core beliefs.[1] On the other hand, compassion fatigue occurs when the helper becomes numb toward the person he or she is helping. Empathy becomes a struggle. The helper may find himself becoming irritated or impatient with those he is helping.[2]

Consider the following examples:

Susan works at a ministry center for women who have been trafficked or experienced domestic violence. For the past three years, she has listened to the stories of these women. Some of them were abused by their spouses serving in key leadership positions in a church, while others were trafficked by a pastor or community leader they should have been able to trust. After hearing some of the unimaginable trauma experienced by these women, Susan has struggled with understanding how a good God could allow such suffering in the world. She begins to doubt her faith, and her relationship with God grows distant.

Jennifer works as a counselor for women who have experienced complex trauma. When helping her clients process their trauma histories, she has noticed herself feeling numb while her clients express intense emotions related to their past experiences. During her counseling sessions, she finds herself becoming more frustrated with her clients and the decisions they are

---

[1] Connie Jones and Susan Branco, "Trauma-Informed Supervision: Clinical Supervision of Substance Use Disorder Counselors," *Journal of Addictions and Offender Counseling* 41, no. 1 (April 2020): 2–17, https://doi.org/10.1002/jaoc.12072.

[2] See Carolyn Knight, "Indirect Trauma: Implications for Self-Care, Supervision, the Organization, and the Academic Institution," *The Clinical Supervisor* 32, no. 2 (November 2013): 224–43, https://doi.org/10.1080/07325223.2013.850139.

Professionals vary widely on the definition of these terms. We have cited the articles that informed our definition of these terms, although we acknowledge that others may define them otherwise.

making. Previously, she had been patient and willing to meet them where they were. Now, she struggles to empathize with her clients. She feels a sense of shame because of her difficulty connecting with her clients.

Susan is questioning her worldview, which is common with vicarious traumatization. Jennifer is exhibiting signs of compassion fatigue. In Jennifer, you see a sense of apathy and lack of connection. Working with those in crisis increases the likelihood that we will experience one or both of these, so let's consider how to navigate them.

Dealing with Vicarious Traumatization

Know Your Own Story

The more aware we are of how our past may impact our present, the better able we are to recognize how the stories of others are impacting us. If we notice that we are having strong reactions to a story we hear or that we are triggered by an experience of someone we are trying to help, it may indicate that there is something we need to process further with a colleague or counselor. Being able to discuss and journal about these things can help us heal from our past along with creating a greater awareness of how our previous experiences may be impacting our present. "Only when we know our own darkness can we sit in the darkness of others."[3]

Be Aware of Hidden Motivations for Helping

When asked why we minister to those in crisis, most of us would say that we are called by God or that the love of God compels us to serve. Both of these things may be true, but we need to be mindful of any hidden motives for service. Some of us may derive a sense of self-worth from helping. While serving others may naturally bring a sense of joy to us, we should be cautious

[3] Pema Chödron, *The Places That Scare You: A Guide to Fearlessness in Difficult Times* (Boulder, CO: Shambhala, 2001), 50.

when we get to a place of basing our self-worth or identity on how much we are able to help.

Codependency may be present in helping. It stems from the intense need to be needed. Codependent people will help others to the detriment of their own well-being. They feel responsible for other people and may experience shame when their helping efforts are not effective.

Codependency can also result in having a savior complex. As the name implies, a savior complex is when we feel the need to save someone. In attempting to save the other person, we may absolve the person of the consequences of his actions. We may attempt to do most of the work for him, which makes it unlikely that he will learn to take responsibility for his own actions. It may also communicate that we believe this person is incapable of accomplishing the necessary tasks, which can diminish his confidence.

Know the Meanings Attached to Giving and Receiving Support

Attaching our self-worth to our ability to help others also makes it difficult for us to receive help in our time of need. In *Rising Strong*, Brené Brown tells us, "When you judge yourself for needing help, you judge those you are helping. When you attach value to giving help, you attach value to needing help. The danger of tying your self-worth to being a helper is feeling shame when you have to ask for help. Offering help is courageous and compassionate, but so is asking for help."[4] If we attach judgment to receiving help, we are more likely to push ourselves to the point of burnout rather than seeking help when needed. "Until we receive with an open heart, we are never really giving with an open heart."[5]

The first time I (Brooke) read this, my immediate response was "That's not true." The more I thought about it, the more I realized there's more truth to this statement than I would like to admit. When we pause to evaluate our

---

[4] Brené Brown, *Rising Strong: How the Ability to Reset Transforms the Way We Live, Love, Parent, and Lead* (New York: Random House, 2017), 180.

[5] Brené Brown, *The Gifts of Imperfection* (Center City, MN: Hazelden, 2020), 31.

reasons for not seeking help in times of need, what do we find? In ministry and counseling, are we concerned that our vulnerability means we are less than perfect? Does the fear that others might discover this cripple us?

Several years ago, I had lunch with a friend. While catching up, I shared with her about some things going on in my life that I was struggling with. Her response was "I can't believe this. You're a real person." Not knowing where she was going with this, I asked her what she had previously thought I was. She told me that since I was a counselor, she thought I had everything together in my life. Although I was sorry to disappoint her, I questioned whether we were living in the same world. No one leaves this earth unscathed, and we will all experience trials and a wide range of crisis situations while we're here. In his human form, Jesus himself was vulnerable and asked for help (Mark 14:32–34). Recognizing our humanity means that today I may be the helper, while tomorrow I might be the one needing help.

When we judge our needs as weaknesses, we may open the door to codependent behavior. Denying our own needs while we see the needs of others as valid shifts our motivation in helping. Instead of offering assistance to a fellow person in our shared humanity, we are finding our worth in our ability to help others.[6] We are now sitting above them rather than walking through life with them.

In her research, Brené Brown discovered that people with the healthiest boundaries exercise compassion most effectively. Compassionate people are not afraid to ask for what they need and are comfortable declining. When they say yes, they mean it. Their boundaries keep them out of resentment. When we agree to serve a specific person or in some capacity because we genuinely want to, we are usually not as concerned with the responses of those involved. However, if we agree to something because we were guilted or pressured, we are likely to have higher expectations for the responses of others.[7] In other words, when we end up helping in situations that we did

---

[6] See Bethany Dearborn Hiser, *From Burned Out to Beloved: Soul Care for Wounded Healers* (Downers Grove, IL: InterVarsity, 2020), 69.

[7] See Brown, *Rising Strong*, 114–15.

not desire to be a part of in the first place, we feel entitled to a certain degree of appreciation and acknowledgment. When these demands are not met, we grow resentful.

For example, there is a single mom in your neighborhood who has three elementary-aged children. She has a steady job, but it requires her to be at work during the morning carpool time at her children's school. She needs someone to pick up her children and take them to school as she is making her way out the door to head to work. The first neighbor she asks, Abby, is happy to help, but she is only able to help two days a week. She wishes she could help more, but she knows she would run the risk of being late to work the other three days of the week and does not want to add unnecessary stress to her life. The second neighbor she asks, Sarah, can really only commit to two days but feels guilty and agrees to the other three days.

Getting kids ready for school, especially when they may not always want to go, is no easy feat. Often, one of the neighbors arrives as the mom is scurrying out the door with one kid crying and another one not dressed. The first neighbor, Abby, who only committed to two days a week, believes the mom is doing the best she can, so she helps one child finish getting dressed and consoles the child who is upset. Similar scenarios present on the other three days when the second neighbor, Sarah, arrives. The first week, she does not mind helping. She knows the kids are on a new schedule, and it may take some time to adjust. However, over time, she grows resentful toward the single mom for not having her kids ready when she arrives.

The few extra minutes it takes Sarah to help the children get ready end up making her late for work. She never addresses this with the mom because it makes her uncomfortable. Instead, Sarah grows increasingly frustrated and is often impatient with the children. One day she arrives, and yet again, the children are not ready and are complaining about not wanting to go to school. Sarah ends up making snide remarks to the children about how their mom is incapable of getting them ready for school and criticizes them for not being ready and whining about school.

The oldest child mentions this exchange to the mom that afternoon, and the mom is stunned. She had no idea her children were causing so much frustration for Sarah or that she was late to work because of her kids not being ready. In the mom's experience, the kids may delay in getting dressed for school, but they are quick to do so once they realize it's time to go. She was under the assumption that the kids were getting ready as she was leaving and that they were almost ready when the neighbor arrived. She also did not realize her children had been getting so upset in the morning. They complained about school a little before she left, but the mom assumed they had moved past all this when the neighbor arrived. The mom feels terrible because she hated to ask Sarah for help in the first place. She never wanted to cause extra stress for her, and she assumed Sarah would have declined to help or let her know if there was a problem.

In this example, we see that Abby was willing to set boundaries and be realistic about how she could help. She was compassionate and generous in her assumptions about the mother. She did not plan to help kids get dressed or to console the ones who were upset, but she knew the mother was working hard and doing her best. So she was happy to step up. Sarah avoided the discomfort of telling the mom she could not help out three days a week and also did not discuss the problems with the kids getting dressed or being upset about school. Instead, she allowed resentment to fester and took out her frustration on the kids and caused the mom to feel terrible for having asked her. Setting appropriate boundaries and being realistic about how we can help allows us to serve others from a place of compassion.

How to Mitigate the Effects of Vicarious Traumatization

Take Time to Process What You Have Heard

When we take in the suffering of others, we need a safe place to process these experiences. Sometimes, we need someone to help us as we come to terms with the depravity of humans and find ourselves wrestling with the evil in this world. We need someone to help us as we struggle to find God at work in the midst of suffering or when we're plagued with our own doubts about our faith. We want to be intentional about finding safe places and people with whom we can share. Being able to talk through these things can be cathartic, which can alleviate the burdens we shoulder.

We also need to create work environments in which people feel safe sharing how they are being impacted by the stories they are hearing. When we are not encouraging our colleagues to share their struggles with work, they may feel alone, which can perpetuate the belief that they are having a difficult time because they are internally flawed. Believing we are defective because we are negatively impacted by a client's story can worsen the emotional strain already in place. Vicarious traumatization is a workplace hazard to which we are all susceptible, and we need to support each other.

Pastoral ministry can feel isolating, which makes it difficult to find support. Some pastors serve in small churches, where they have no other staff members to confide in. Others may find it difficult to reach out to their pastor, who is also their supervisor. An event that has impacted the entire church staff and congregation may call for debriefing with someone outside of the situation. In our seminary classes, we encourage students to build relationships with those sitting next to them. Following graduation, they are likely to disperse across the country and overseas to serve in different places. Maintaining these friendships allows them the opportunity to discuss struggles they are facing in their churches with someone in a different place. It offers safety for them and anonymity for those involved.

When moving to a new area, consider reaching out to local pastors and arranging a time to meet. Local pastors can help you better understand the area in which you are serving. Also, with different backgrounds and experiences represented, you can learn from one another and support one another in your work. Having a group of pastors united to serve the city reaps benefits for the local community.

Look for Post-Traumatic Growth

In chapter 9, we discussed post-traumatic growth as a shift that takes place in a person's worldview following a traumatic event. In the same way those with lived experiences encounter post-traumatic growth, those in helping professions can experience it as well. As we are processing through the stories we hear, we want to reflect on the following questions:

- How has working with this person changed me?
- What have I learned from this person's experience?
- How has my perspective on life been altered?
- How have I seen God at work?

As we reflect on these questions, we want to look for ways in which we have grown through the process of helping others. If we notice negative changes or a more cynical outlook on life, then we may want to work through these things with a colleague or with a counselor.

When to Refer

Referring a client is not a reflection of inadequacy on the part of the minister or counselor. Referrals acknowledge that we all have different strengths and areas of expertise. As a result, we are trying to ensure that the person has what he or she needs to navigate a crisis. In many cases, those in crisis will seek the help of a pastor or church member before they reach out to a mental-health professional.

When meeting with a person in crisis, ministry professionals should discern whether this is a person who needs a little extra support during a time of crisis or a person who needs the help of a professional. In making this determination, a few things to consider might be the number of sessions required, the intensity of the crisis, and the level of clinical expertise required.

Although there are exceptions, in general, if a person's crisis cannot be resolved in four sessions or less, it's highly likely they will need a professional counselor. It's important to communicate this at the beginning. I know of several ministers and lay leaders who began meeting with a person in crisis. They didn't want the person to feel abandoned, so they continued meeting with the client while the crisis continued to escalate beyond their level of expertise. In many cases, this can lead to burnout; in some cases, it can even cause harm to the person.

In addition to communicating the expectation for the number of sessions up front, another way to connect people with the appropriate help without them feeling abandoned is to continue providing support and following up throughout the process. This could mean checking in with them occasionally to ask how the sessions with the new counselor are going. You can also continue meeting for coffee to offer support in addition to counseling.

The level of clinical expertise required is likely correlated with the intensity of the crisis. Some of the most complex crisis situations require in-depth training. Situations involving past trauma, marital infidelity, and complex grief are likely to require long-term counseling and should be referred to someone with expertise in these areas.

In some cases, referral may be related to areas of expertise, while other times it may be related to time. There are seasons of life in which, as much as we would like to help, we may not have the capacity to help in a way that would serve the other person and ourselves well.

Five Dimensions of Self-Care

Self-care should not be a one-time event that occurs when we are on the verge of burnout. Rather, we should seek a lifestyle of self-care that prevents us from reaching our breaking points. The practice of self-care and boundaries is not intended to proceed in a linear fashion. Instead, it is likely a winding road in which we sometimes deviate too far to one extreme or the other. By practicing self-care, we increase our awareness of our personal limits so that when we get off track, we can get back on.

The primary goal of boundaries is to promote safe and healthy relationships. Boundaries are intended to be parameters put in place for our overall well-being.

Physical

We are all human, and as a result, our bodies have physical limitations. With our bodies being temples of the Holy Spirit (1 Corinthians 6:19–20), we need to make sure we are caring for ourselves physically. Consider the following:

- What makes you feel stressed?
- How does being stressed make you feel?
- How do you usually act and react when you're stressed and overwhelmed?
- What are your biggest priorities?

A solid understanding of our stress triggers and how stress tends to manifest itself in our lives can help us take appropriate precautions to avoid burnout.

We tend to think we can take on more work and responsibilities as long as we love what we're doing. However, our bodies still have physical limitations. Although our passion for our work may fuel our motivation, there will come a time when our bodies suffer the consequences if we are not taking care of ourselves physically.

Emotional

It's easy to get caught up in the savior complex, thinking that we are the only ones who can help or that if we do not help, no one else will. While he was on earth, even Jesus did not do everything, go everywhere, or heal everyone. To serve longer and more effectively, we need to put boundaries in place to protect ourselves and our time with our spouses and children.

For us, one of the points of consideration is how many nights of the week we are gone. It does us no good to have counseling appointments scheduled in the evenings the majority of the nights of the week, helping others with their marriages and families while ours are falling apart because we're not home with them. For many of us, this is a continual shift in balancing our work and home lives. Early in our practice, we both had schedules that had us working late a few nights a week. When we began having children, we shifted away from these appointments out of the best interests of our families for this season of life.

Earlier, we discussed that the most compassionate people have the most clearly defined boundaries. So we should continually ask ourselves, "What boundaries do I need to put in place so I can work from a place of integrity and extend the most generous interpretations of the intentions, work, and actions of others?"[8] Though it is uncomfortable to decline serving opportunities, we're doing a disservice to both ourselves and others when we make commitments out of guilt or people-pleasing because we could end up resenting those we are trying to help. When we are presented with a request, we can best serve ourselves and others when we "choose discomfort over resentment."[9]

Relational

We need to take care of our marriages and children along with nurturing friendships with other adults. When we maintain mutually nurturing friendships outside of counseling, we are much more likely to serve our clients without falling into codependency or other unhealthy dynamics in the counseling relationship. A solid support system includes having people in our lives who engage in accountability with us and are comfortable challenging us when they are concerned about our well-being. They also give us a safe space to process our current struggles.

---

[8] Brown, *Rising Strong*, 123.

[9] Brené Brown, *Rising Strong as a Spiritual Practice* (Sounds True Audio Recording: 2017).

Personal

We need to remember that our identities are based on who we are in Christ, not on our performance. At the end of the day, it does not matter what we accomplished or what is left undone. Our worth is found in what Christ did for us on the cross. We need to set aside time for ourselves to make sure we recharge and refresh in a way that is beneficial for us.

Philippians 2:4 says, "Everyone should look not to his own interests, but rather to the interests of others." We often use this verse as a reason to focus on others to the detriment of ourselves. However, this verse is not saying we should neglect ourselves to care for others. Instead, it is telling us to be concerned about others in addition to ourselves.

Spiritual

We cannot model what we do not have. If we want a growing, loving relationship with God, we have to pursue it. Matthew 11:28 says the presence of God restores. According to Acts 3:19–20, repentance leads to refreshing. What specific action could you take to go to him? Spiritual maturity develops when we emphasize "being with God before doing for God."[10]

Conclusion

We have to take care of ourselves before we can care well for others. Knowing our own stories and how they impact us, while being aware of our personal limitations, can help us to serve both ourselves and those we are helping. We want to maintain a solid identity of who we are in Christ, which means our primary motivation in serving others is from the overflow of what we have.

---

[10] Peter Scazzero, *Emotionally Healthy Discipleship: Moving from Shallow Christianity to Deep Transformation* (Grand Rapids: Zondervan, 2021), 37.

Additional Resources

Hiser, Bethan. *From Burned Out to Beloved: Soul Care for Wounded Healers.* Downers Grove, IL: InterVarsity Press, 2020.

Scazzero, Peter. *The Emotionally Healthy Leader: How Transforming Your Inner Life Will Deeply Transform Your Church, Team, and the World.* Grand Rapids: Zondervan, 2015.

Chapter 29

When Crisis Hits Home

July 5, 2019. My husband, son, and I (Karen) were going to see the latest summer action movie. But first, we dropped by an eye specialist for a quick appointment because of an unusual change in my vision. We never made it to the movie. Instead, we were dealing with a crisis.

The news was scary. Complex retinal detachment. Retinal tears and holes. Surgery. Both eyes. It was all a blur of words, thoughts, and emotions. Although I am typically private about my health information, I immediately asked my husband to request people to pray for me. He quickly typed out a group text to friends and family.

Within what felt like only minutes, a deacon at our church walked into the office. He lived over an hour away, so I was shocked by how quickly he had arrived. By God's mercy, he was in town for work and dropped everything to rush over and be with us. I remember nothing he said, only that he sat with us and prayed with us. He was a comforting presence amid a crisis and also available to take care of my family's practical and physical needs as they waited.

That afternoon, I was wheeled into surgery for both of my eyes with the hopes of preserving as much sight as possible. I will never forget the nurse in the hall who whispered (a little too loudly), "Stop. Let's bring in her son so she can see him." If I hadn't realized the gravity of the situation before she hastily spoke those words, I certainly did at that moment. As I drifted off under the anesthesia and my body trembled with the unknown, I focused on the comfort of everyone who was praying for me at that moment and the tremendous amount of support I knew we would have if the outcome were life-altering.

The crisis impacted my family for several months due to additional surgeries and recovery limitations, such as not being able to lift or drive as I recovered from each subsequent surgery. As a counselor, my time away from work affected me too. Not only was this a health crisis, but it also impacted our finances.

This event has not been our only crisis in our thirty years of ministerial life; we are not alone in our experience. All of you reading have either experienced a crisis or will experience one in the future because crises are a part of life. Ministers and counselors can experience any of the crises mentioned in this book. And as you have previously read, both groups can experience compassion fatigue and vicarious traumatization, which can also become crisis points in their lives. In this chapter, we speak primarily to ministers, but the suggestions also apply to counselors. Occasionally, we will talk directly to counselors.

The Plight of Pastors

Pastors and other staff ministers are uniquely impacted by church-related stressors and the overall stress of caring for a church. Following an account of the many crises and threats to his life that he faced in ministry, the apostle Paul wrote, "Not to mention other things, there is the daily pressure on me: my concern for all the churches" (2 Corinthians 11:28). Ministry itself can present chronic stress, which can lead to the crisis of burnout.

In a 2021 Barna poll, 38 percent of pastors in the United States reported that they had "given real, serious consideration to quitting being in full-time ministry" during the previous year.[1] Another study conducted by Lifeway Research on evangelical and Black Protestant pastors revealed the following statistics, which I categorized into areas of stress:[2]

Time Stress

- 71% of pastors report feeling they must be "on call" twenty-four hours per day.

Emotional Stress

- 63% report their role is "frequently overwhelming."

Stress of Feeling Isolated

- 38% feel isolated.

Stress of Demands and Expectations

- 50% report the "demands of ministry are often greater than they can handle."
- 23% report facing "unrealistic expectations" from their church.

---

[1] "38% of U.S. Pastors Have Thought about Quitting Full-Time Ministry in the Past Year," Barna Group, November 16, 2021, https://www.barna.com/research/pastors-well-being.

[2] See "Pastor Attrition Study 2021," Lifeway Research, https://research.lifeway.com/wp-content/uploads/2022/01/Pastor-Attrition-Research-Report-2021.pdf.

Family Stress

- 31% report "the demands of ministry" prevented them from spending time with their family.

Interpersonal Conflict Stress

- 28% report their church experienced "significant conflict" during the previous year.
- 39% experienced a "significant personal attack."

Financial Stress

- 41% report they are "often concerned about their family's financial security."

Pastors may also struggle with physical and mental illness. In one study, 26 percent of pastors reported "struggling with mental illness;" with 17 percent of all respondents reporting a formal diagnosis of mental illness.[3]

Often, a church crisis impacts the personal life of a minister. For example, a natural disaster that impacts a church and community also impacts the ministers living in that community. Or consider the potential financial crisis the church might encounter after the disaster. A church financial crisis may eventually impact a minister's salary, thus leading to a personal financial crisis for the minister. COVID-19 impacted many ministers and their churches as they sought to make church services accessible online or through other methods, all while mourning the death of beloved church members and community members who did not survive the effects of the virus.

[3] Aaron Earls, "Pastors Have Congregational and, for Some, Personal Experience with Mental Illness," Lifeway Research, August 2, 2022, https://research.lifeway.com/2022/08/02/pastors-have-congregational-and-for-some-personal-experience-with-mental-illness.

In addition to ministry-related stress, personal crises impact ministers. Ministers must navigate deaths in their families, chronic and acute illness, children who develop substance abuse disorders, marital issues, loss of a child, caregiving for their parents, natural disasters, and other crises creating profound impacts on ministers and their families. The impact of experiencing multiple crises, particularly in a short amount of time, is cumulative.

Responding to Personal Crises

How can the minister or counselor respond to personal crises? Let's consider a few areas of emphasis.

Accept Support

When a crisis hits you as the helper, accept help and support from others. Sometimes, receiving help is difficult for the helper. If this is true for you, try answering the following questions to explore why:

- When was the last time you *asked* for help? What was that experience like for you?
- When was the last time you *accepted* help? What was that experience like for you?
- What are your concerns about asking for help?
- Can you identify one or two people whom you can call when you are in crisis? Depending on the crisis, this might be in your current church or outside your church membership. Ideally, there will be people in both.
- In the Lifeway Research study cited previously, 84 percent of pastors felt they needed to "protect their image as a pastor."[4] Do you believe this describes you? If so, what aspects of "image" are you striving to protect?

[4] Earls.

- Who are the encouragers in your life?

Allow the individuals you identified to support you in times of crisis. It is good for them to have an opportunity to minister and good for you to receive ministry.

Recognize Your Limits

Humans have limits. God created us this way, and it serves as a reminder that we are not God. Peter Scazzero refers to this concept as the "gift" of limits.[5] We have limits in what we can accomplish in a given day with our physical bodies, gifts and abilities, and much more. We are especially aware of our limits during times of crisis when we often feel stretched like a rubber band on the verge of breaking.

Another component of accepting our limits includes ministering when we are too close to the situation to help. At times, it is best practice to bring in outside help. Sometimes, we are too close to a situation or individual to minister effectively. For example, if you have relatives in the church who are in crisis, another minister or leader in the church or outside the church may need to step in.

Rest

In the Lifeway Research study, 86 percent of pastors reported that they "unplug" at least once per week for a day of rest. Consider whether you are getting a day of rest. If so, ask yourself if the day actually feels restful. If not, consider what would improve the restfulness. Do you need a break from social media or your phone? Do you enjoy something creative, such as cooking, art, or woodwork? Is there a hobby you once enjoyed that you

[5] Peter Scazzero, *Emotionally Healthy Spirituality: It's Impossible to Be Spiritually Mature While Remaining Emotionally Immature* (Grand Rapids: Zondervan, 2017), 147–49.

might revisit? If you sit at a desk all day, do you want to spend the day hiking outdoors or participating in something that actively moves your body? Do you need solitude, or do you need to be with people who encourage and energize you? Think carefully about how you are spending your time of rest.

Experiencing a crisis is hard work and affects your emotional and physical well-being. Your mind and body need sleep, yet sometimes sleep is difficult during a crisis. If sleeping is an issue, consider the following sleep-hygiene tips:

- Establish a routine for bedtime. Most of us parents realize the importance of a bedtime routine for our children. Adults benefit from a bedtime routine as well. A sample bedtime routine might be having a warm cup of herbal tea, taking a shower or bath, washing your face, brushing your teeth, and briefly reading something that is not too engaging. (Avoid books you might be tempted to stay up all night reading.)
- Make your bedroom a comfortable environment: a cool temperature; comfortable, freshly laundered bedding; and minimal bright lights or noise. Avoid playing the television in the background or placing a bright clock near you. Many individuals find a noise machine helpful in reducing awareness of unwanted background noise.
- Avoid caffeine for several hours before bed.
- Avoid using electronics, such as your phone, for two hours before bed.
- Use your bedroom only for sleep and intimacy with your spouse. Avoid watching television, working, answering emails, and scrolling social media in bed.
- Go to bed at approximately the same time each evening, ideally when you experience a natural wave of sleepiness. And wake at approximately the same time each morning.
- If you cannot fall asleep within twenty minutes, or if you awaken during the night and cannot fall back asleep, get out of bed and

read something unlikely to hold your interest until you are sleepy again.

- Exercise is helpful for overall stress reduction and sleep, but avoid exercise for approximately three to four hours before bedtime.
- Eat balanced, healthy meals during the day, but avoid heavy meals close to bedtime.
- When you wake in the morning, step outside into the sunlight before picking up your phone or another screen.

If you struggle with sleep after trying these tips, speak with your doctor.

In addition to sleep, we need rest in quietness and solitude. By this, we do not mean to isolate yourself from others but to allow some time for quiet reflection by yourself. During this time, you can pray, read Scripture, meditate, and sit silently. As a counselor, I (Karen) have noticed many individuals are uncomfortable with rest in the form of silence and time alone for reflection. There are many possible reasons for this. Some might feel guilty for not being "productive." When alone and quiet, others may become aware of uncomfortable feelings they are experiencing, which may not be as noticeable when busy. If you are struggling with rest, explore what might be happening beneath the surface.

In some cases, you may need to take some time away. If finances allow, you might consider renting a place to stay for a few days. If finances are also in crisis, consider going to a retreat center, camp, or ministry that provides reduced or free rates for ministers.

Reinforce Boundaries

You may need to temporarily increase boundaries during a personal crisis. If you do not have healthy boundaries, begin clarifying and implementing them in your life today. For example, you may need to set boundaries on your time and availability. A boundary might include turning off your phone at designated times because 24/7 availability is an ingredient for burnout, particularly if you are already in crisis. You may need to develop a rotating "on call" system of leaders for your place of ministry so you are not constantly aware (and potentially on edge) that your phone could ring with an emergency at any time, day or night. Even emergency-response workers and medical professionals take time off from being on call.

Process Grief

With crisis typically comes some form of loss. Give yourself permission and space to grieve. Allow yourself time for journaling, praying, and reflecting. You might consider writing a prayer of lament. Or you might process your journey with a friend, mentor, or counselor. Taking the time to read a book about your particular type of loss can also be helpful. So much of a minister's or counselor's time is spent reading books that help him or her minister well to others. But, at times, we must focus on words that help us through our journeys. Identify and consider joining a support group during a crisis.

Consider Counseling

You may find that personal or family counseling helps you work through your crisis. Counseling has helped me (Karen) work through crises in my life, including my eye surgeries. If you are struggling with feeling overwhelmed, being constantly on edge, experiencing anxiety, having difficulty thinking or concentrating, or feeling like a dark cloud of sadness is following you around, consult a professional counselor.

Ministers may hesitate to engage in personal, marriage, or family counseling. This reluctance may stem from a variety of reasons. One practical issue is the difficulty of finding a counselor with whom you do not have a dual relationship. If you cannot find someone in your town, consider a nearby city or the use of telehealth.

Another reason for the hesitation to seek counseling as a minister may be the desire to appear as though we "have it all together" or the notion that if we are spiritually mature enough, we will not need counseling services.

Instead, consider modeling for your congregation the wisdom to seek support when needed and the recognition that emotional health and spiritual health are interconnected.

Planning for the Future

Because crises happen to all of us, planning ahead is recommended. Consider the suggestions below and ask yourself other ways you might prepare.

Build a Community of Support

Proactively develop a support system for yourself. Include other ministers or counselors in this support system. For ministers, you might find it helpful to befriend a retired minister. Consider setting up regular times to meet with other ministers or counselors, even if not everyone can attend each meeting. Both ministry and counseling can be isolating professions, so building a supportive community is critical. In a crisis, you have a support team in place.

Add Crises into Your Budget

Prepare financially for emergencies. Even if this means only saving a small amount per week, build an emergency fund for financial crises and crises that may impact your earnings. Consider speaking with a financial professional for advice about saving. Additionally, you might consider purchasing insurance plans for situations such as disability or cancer if your church does not provide those or if you are a self-employed counselor.

Have a Plan for Emergency Time Off

For ministers, establish a written plan with your church leadership about what will take place should you need some unexpected time off. For counselors, particularly those in private practice, taking time off requires planning both from a financial standpoint and for the welfare of your clients. It is wise to have at least two other counselors you trust willing to take referrals from you if you cannot counsel for a short time.

Conclusion

Reflecting on the crisis I (Karen) experienced with my eyesight, I am thankful for those who ministered to us. Though it is difficult for me to ask for help, the journey through that crisis would have been exponentially more difficult to endure without everyone's support. I will leave you with one final note. When you experience a personal crisis as a minister, please remind yourself of the following:

It is okay to need help.
It is okay to ask for help.
It is okay to accept help.

Allow others to minister to you.

Additional Resources

Scazzero, Peter. *Emotionally Healthy Leader: How Transforming Your Inner Life Will Deeply Transform Your Church, Team, and the World.* Grand Rapids: Zondervan, 2015.

———. *Emotionally Healthy Spirituality: It's Impossible to Be Spiritually Mature While Remaining Emotionally Immature.* Grand Rapids: Zondervan, 2017.

CONCLUDING THOUGHTS

We are grateful to have you on this journey with us. Our world is filled with plenty of hardships and never-ceasing crises. In a broken and lost world, we need to meet people where they are and point them to the God who loves them and will never forsake them.

As we part ways, we hope you remember that connecting with the emotional experience of another requires courage, but it is worth it. Without hope, change cannot occur, so our desire is always for others to see the hope of Christ.

Crisis situations can also evolve. In this book, we discussed the role of social media in crisis situations, which is something we have all learned to navigate over the last few decades. We have all lived through a global pandemic, which is not something we ever thought we would see during our lifetimes. We encourage you to keep learning and growing in your crisis counseling and management skills. There is always more to learn and none of us ever fully arrives.

Above all, we care for ourselves so we can continue serving the Lord as long as he allows. Those in the helping professions often experience a higher turnover rate. We want to keep our focus on God so we can finish the race well and be good stewards of the people and opportunities to which he has entrusted us.

Closing Prayer

Lord, give us eyes to see the needs around us, the provision to meet these needs, and the strength to persevere in the midst of suffering. Help us to remember that you are sovereign and our Redeemer. Your Spirit goes before us and is within us. Thank you for allowing us to be a part of your work in a broken world that is desperate for the hope of the gospel.

APPENDIX

Community Resource Guide

Here is a list of resources that might be helpful to include in a community resource guide:

- Pregnancy counseling centers / young mothers' needs
- Programs for children and adults with developmental disabilities, including therapeutic services, schools, Early Steps, and autism resources
- Domestic violence services
- Housing/utility assistance
- Local food banks
- Legal assistance
- Substance abuse/addiction, including rehab centers, outpatient programs, and support groups
- Mental-health professionals / suicide intervention
- Hospitals
- Assisted living / funeral assistance
- Reentry resources for the formerly incarcerated

Having this guide in place can allow for a more efficient response during a time of crisis. Taking the time to build relationships with some of the key people involved with these organizations can streamline the assistance process.

Questions and Considerations When Looking for a Prospective Counselor

1. What is your approach to understanding people's problems and helping them grow and change through counseling? Please describe this process.
2. What are some books or other resources that you recommend on a regular basis or that have influenced your approach to counseling?
3. Are you a Christian? How does your faith affect your view and practice of counseling?
4. Do you bring Christian truth into your counseling practice? How? What role does Scripture play?
5. Do you go to church? If so, where and how long have you been a member?
6. What is your educational and professional background? What role does it play?

Sample Suicide Safety Contract

Name: ______________________________ Date: ____________________

Today, I have said some things about death or about hurting myself that have made others concerned about my safety. Others have told me how valuable my life is, but they want to make sure that I know how valuable my life is. I will complete this contract with another caring person so both of us will feel comfortable that I value my life and that I know what to do if I start feeling like I could harm myself again.

Behaviors that signal the need to use this plan (thoughts, images, thinking processes, moods, and/or behaviors):

1.

2.

3.

Things I can do or tell myself to make myself feel better (coping methods, relaxation techniques, problem-solving approaches):

1.

2.

3.

People who care about me whom I can call when I feel overwhelmed:

Name	Relationship	Number
1.		
2.		
3.		

Places to go to help take my mind off my problems for a little while:

1.

2.

3.

Hotline numbers I can call:
Include numbers of both local and national hotlines. Try to include some with 24/7 access, for example, Suicide and Crisis Hotline: Call 988.

**You can always call 911 for help. Tell the operator that you are in suicidal danger.*

1.

2.

3.

Symptoms of Mental Illness in Adolescents

The purpose of this symptom list is not to offer a diagnosis of a mental illness for an adolescent. That should only come from a trained medical or mental-health professional. This list is to offer some guidance on when to refer adolescents for mental-health services or an evaluation.

Depression

Five or more of the following symptoms lasting at least two weeks can indicate that an adolescent may be struggling with depression:

- Consistent feelings of anxiousness or emptiness
- Loss of interest in activities, including ones they enjoyed previously
- Withdrawing from friends
- Appetite and weight changes (in either direction)
- Changes in sleep patterns (both sleeping too much or significantly less than normal). We typically stereotype adolescents as sleeping all the time. The key consideration here is whether there is a significant change in sleep patterns.
- Slower pace of physical activity, thinking, or speech
- Reduced energy, feeling "run down" almost every day
- Persistent feelings of worthlessness or excessive guilt
- Difficulty concentrating or making decisions, which may result in failing grades
- Persistent thoughts of death or suicide or attempting suicide

If you notice an adolescent struggling with five or more of these symptoms for at least two weeks, you may want to consult a medical or mental-health professional, such as a counselor or a pediatrician.

Anxiety

- Persistent fears and worries about everyday life
- Irritability
- Difficulty concentrating
- Extreme self-consciousness
- Withdrawal from social activities
- Avoidance of new or difficult situations
- Chronic complaints of stomachaches or headaches
- Refusal to do schoolwork, resistant to attend school, drop in grades
- Repeated reassurance-seeking
- Difficulty sleeping
- Possible substance abuse as a coping mechanism for anxiety

If you notice any of these symptoms lasting for four to six months, you may want to refer the adolescent to a medical or mental-health professional.

Attention-Deficit/Hyperactivity Disorder (ADHD)

ADHD can involve any or all of the following:

- Inattention
  - — Not paying close attention to details, making careless errors
  - — Struggling to follow multistep directions
  - — Being easily distracted, which makes it difficult to follow through on tasks until completion
  - — Avoiding tasks that are difficult or require sustained attention
  - — Losing one's belongings or other items
  - — Having difficulty remembering appointments and activities
- Hyperactivity
  - — Finding it difficult to stay seated
  - — Fidgeting

- — Talking excessively
- — Constantly in motion
- Impulsivity
  - — Having difficulty waiting one's turn
  - — Interrupting others
  - — Answering questions before they are fully asked

If you notice symptoms in one or all areas of inattention, hyperactivity, or impulsivity, you may want to consult your medical provider.

GENERAL INDEX